Social Researching

The Editors

Colin Bell is Professor of Sociology at the University of Aston.
He has also taught at the Universities of Essex, New South
Wales and Wisconsin-Madison. His previous books include
Middle Class Families (Routledge & Kegan Paul, 1968) (as co-
editor) *Doing Sociological Research* (Allen & Unwin, 1977) and
(as co-author) *Fathers, Childbirth and Work* (EOC, 1983).

Helen Roberts is a feminist and sociologist who works as Senior
Researcher at Bradford and Ilkley Community College. She
edited *Women, Health and Reproduction)* (Routledge & Kegan
Paul, 1981) and *Doing Feminist Research* (Routledge & Kegan
Paul, 1981) and is co-author, with Ann Oakley and Ann
McPherson, of *Miscarriage* (Fontana, 1984) and author of
Women, the Patient Patients (Pandora Press, 1984).

By the same editors

Colin Bell
Middle Class Families
Power, Persistence and Change (with Margaret Stacey)

Helen Roberts
Women, Health and Reproduction
Doing Feminist Research

Social Researching

Politics, Problems, Practice

Edited by
Colin Bell
and
Helen Roberts

Routledge & Kegan Paul

London, Boston, Melbourne and Henley

First published in 1984
by Routledge & Kegan Paul plc
39 Store Street, London WC1E 7DD, England
9 Park Street, Boston, Mass. 02108, USA
464 St Kilda Road, Melbourne,
Victoria 3004, Australia and
Broadway House, Newtown Road,
Henley-on-Thames, Oxon RG9 1EN, England
Set in Baskerville 11/12 pt
by Columns, Reading, Berkshire
and printed in Great Britain
by
The Thetford Press Limited, Thetford, Norfolk

Library of Congress Cataloging in Publication Data

Social researching.
Bibliography: p.
Includes index.
Contents: The SSRC, restructured and defended/Colin
Bell — Negotiating the problem: the DHSS and research
on violence in marriage/Jalna Hanmer and Diana Leonard
—Researching spoonbending/H.M. Collins — [etc.]
1. Sociology—Research—Addresses, essays, lectures.
2. Sociology—Great Britain—Addresses, essays, lectures.
3. Women social scientists—Great Britain—Addresses,
essays, lectures. I. Bell, Colin. II. Roberts, Helen.
HM48.S568   1984   301'.072   83-24801

British Library CIP available

ISBN 0-7100-9884-7

Contents

Notes on contributors

Colin Bell has edited two previous collections of social research essays (*Doing Sociological Research,* 1977, with Howard Newby and *Inside the Whale,* 1978, with Sol Encel) but remains unrepentant. He is currently researching aspects of unemployment and renewing his acquaintance with community studies. He previously taught at Essex and New South Wales and has been Professor of Sociology at Aston since 1980. Restructuring consequent upon the financial assault on the university in 1981 led to his becoming Head of the new Social & Technology Policy Group in the renamed Faculty of Management and Policy Sciences.

Harry Collins has researched and published extensively in the sociology of scientific knowledge using areas of modern physics and of parapsychology as case studies. In 1981 he edited a special issue of *Social Studies of Science* entitled *Knowledge and Controversy: Studies of Modern Natural Science* (vol. 11, no. 1) and in 1982, with Trevor Pinch, he published *Frames of Meaning: The Social Construction of Extraordinary Science* (Routledge & Kegan Paul). He is Senior Lecturer in Sociology and Director of the Science Studies Centre at the University of Bath. He has two children, aged six and three.

Janet Finch is a sociologist who currently works in a department of social policy and her research interests span both areas. She has conducted empirical research projects on wives of the clergy and on pre-school playgroups, and has undertaken social policy research in the fields of community care and education. She has worked as a school teacher and in teacher training, and has been a lecturer in social administration at Lancaster University since 1976. She is active in the British Sociological Association and its women's caucus and is Chairperson of the Association 1983-4.

Ronald Frankenberg was born in 1929 and has taught sociology and social anthropology at Keele since 1969. Since his postgraduate days at Manchester his general intellectual concern has been to invite others to test against their own experience his view that small-scale social process illuminates and gives meaning to large-scale social change rather than the reverse. He has pursued this theme through studies of the community, wartime bombing policies, medical anthropology, creative literature, violence against women and in Wales, Zambia, United States, India and currently central Italy. He believes that his interpretation in this light of Durkheim, Marx, Mao and Gramsci is the most useful not only to sociology, social medicine and social policy but also to politics. He has benefited and suffered from the difficulty posed for colleagues on the right and comrades on the left in accepting its legitimacy as a subversive position. He has been justly criticised on occasion for being male, white, middle class and frivolous.

Hilary Graham is a lecturer in social policy at the University of Bradford. She is currently an honorary research fellow at the Open University where she is carrying out a study of the organisation of healthcare within the home.

Jalna Hanmer studied sociology at the University of California in Berkeley and began her employed life as a community worker in the East End of London. Later, when teaching community work at the London School of Economics, she became active in Women's Aid. Moving north, where she lives in a collective household with her son, she now co-ordinates the Diploma/M.A. in Women's Studies (Applied) at the University of Bradford. She researches and writes on violence to women and reproductive technology and is part of a group producing a new radical feminist magazine, *Trouble and Strife.*

Nicky James trained as a nurse at the Middlesex Hospital, London. She worked in a coronary care unit in Tunbridge Wells before doing a sociology degree at Stirling and Aberdeen universities. A three-year SSRC grant was received for full-time research into death and dying. She is now completing her PhD and co-ordinating a homeless alcoholics recovery project.

Richard Jenkins is a social anthropologist who studied at Queen's University, Belfast and took his doctorate at Cambridge. At present he works at the SSRC Research Unit on Ethnic Relations, the University of Aston in Birmingham, doing research into the West Midlands labour market. He is the author of *Hightown Rules* (National Youth Bureau, 1982) and *Lads, Citizens and Ordinary Kids* (Routledge & Kegan Paul, 1983), and co-editor of a forthcoming book about ethnicity and business activity. He has worked in the past as a pop musician, a welder, a drawing office clerk and a youth worker.

Diana Leonard started her employed life as a teacher and then switched to do a research degree in anthropology while living in Wales and with small children. This resulted in *Sex and Generation: A Study of Courtship and Weddings* (1980). She now teaches sociology at the University of London Institute of Education and has just completed three years' secondment to the Open University to chair the team producing a course on the *Changing Experience of Women.* Diana Leonard has been active in the Women's Movement. She helped to found the Women's Research and Resources Centre and remains active in the publication group it founded (Explorations in Feminism). She is now part of a collective producing a new radical feminist magazine, *Trouble and Strife.*

Jennifer Platt is Reader in Sociology at the University of

Sussex, where she has taught since 1964. She is joint author of J.H. Goldthorpe et al. *The Affluent Worker* (3 vols) and sole author of *Social Research in Bethnal Green* and *Realities of Social Research*. Her current research is on the history and sociology of sociological research methods.

Helen Roberts is a feminist, a sociologist and a mother. She is Senior Researcher at Bradford and Ilkley Community College and edited *Women, Health and Reproduction* and *Doing Feminist Research* (both Routledge & Kegan Paul, 1981) and author of *Women, the Patient Patients* (Pandora, forthcoming).

Sue Scott is currently employed as a Research Officer for Nottinghamshire County Council, working in the area of community health. She was previously a research officer for the Health Education Council, and Research Associate and Honorary Research Fellow in the Department of Sociology at the University of Lancaster. She is a member of the Executive of the British Sociological Association and of the BSA Committee for the Equality of the Sexes.

Introduction

Colin Bell and *Helen Roberts*

This collection of essays is a reflection on the dramatically changed circumstances under which social science is being carried out in this country. Since the July 1981 University Grants Committee letter to all universities, cuts have fallen disproportionately on social science's university base and in the maintained sector research is being similarly eroded. These bases and their associated postgraduate activity have been the essential material means, along with SSRC, by which social research has been done. They are currently under grave threat. The essays that follow reflect that. Indeed far more than was the case in our previous collections we recognise the financial and political context in which we go about social researching. Hence the opening chapters do confront the realities of funding — the internal workings of the SSRC and the policies of the DHSS. The future policies toward that rapidly dwindling species — the full-time, fully funded British postgraduate student in sociology — are at the time of writing far from clear. Sue Scott's contribution is a unique account of researching both their situation, and that of their part-time colleagues. This is important as so much of British sociology's research edifice has its origins in postgraduate work. We know far too little about how such work is done — so disparate as they are, Richard Jenkins's piece on Belfast and Nicky James's on hospices are much more valuable than all the public concern about so-called 'completion rates'.

The organisation of this book falls easily into three parts.

Bell, Leonard and Hanmer start with the funding agencies. That social science is under increasing political pressure is evidenced virtually every day. We must therefore take funders seriously.

The second and largest section of this book is on actual research — much of it still ongoing. This gives an immediacy to some of the pieces (e.g. Frankenberg's, James's and Scott's) that was lacking in some of those we have previously produced. They were produced shortly after the events they describe, and so noticeably lack that air of *post facto* justification so rightly criticised in earlier pieces. Indeed Frankenberg is writing about work which is still continuing, and Scott and James about work which is in the process of being written up. So whereas the previous collections, and in particular *Doing Sociological Research*, tended towards accounts which reflected on research published, these three reverse the process. We have accounts of some of the problems of pieces of research where the full story has yet to be told.

There is an illuminating comparison that can be made between some aspects of the research roles played by Harry Collins, Richard Jenkins and Nicky James. All three could be said to have used participant observation and yet this label is not very indicative of both the constraints and opportunities they faced. All had .to develop 'native competence' — Collins's terms for a sociologist becoming a scientist doing 'real science' on parascientific phenomena. He had to learn how to 'do science' whilst being a sociologist. Jenkins *was* familiar with life on Belfast council estates — he had previously been a youth worker and though not exactly an insider was not an outsider to Ulster culture. There were, though, clear limits and constraints to his participation — he could not push his luck. Collins could create and construct his data settings, whereas to a far greater extent Jenkins had to take what was given and go with the flow in a very 'unstructured' setting — at least in comparison with Collins's labs. James, though, was a nurse and had been additionally trained to work in hospices. Her data setting was structured but 'natural' — like Jenkins's but unlike Collins's, in that she did not create it. To a far greater extent than Collins, she had 'native competence', but must at times have been more 'participant' than steadfastly pushing forward participant comprehension. Her opportunities for observation and understanding came from her having a 'real' role (we find it difficult to express it any other way) that was of immediate significance in the research setting. She, unlike Collins and Jenkins, will have no alternative but to write herself into the report of the research. Jenkins is in the William F. Whyte *Street Corner Society* tradition (though less of an outsider than he was), making occasional appearances in the monograph but with an obligatory reflection on the fieldwork — that appears as his chapter here. Collins does not have to appear at all in his account — this is perhaps a weakness of the 'strong programme' in the new sociology of science. James, without losing any of the other two accounts' reliability and validity, has to put herself into her account. Could this difference between her and the other two be gender-related? What we are now calling the 'strong programme' of feminist sociology would see some of these differences in the way that research is organised, carried out and written up as being based on the gender of the researcher. James herself suggests that she had, by the time she began to reflect on her fieldwork, 'begun to explore the explanatory value of gender relations'.

Such a reflection is developed in different ways in the chapters by Finch, Graham and Frankenberg. Each recognises the sterility and impossibility of attempts to launder any research totally of 'bias', and that the research process should take on board both the larger political and more day-to-day realities of gender relations.

And the third section confronts publication. Platt shows just what happens to 'classics'. When was the last time, those of us who teach should ask ourselves, we actually read *The Affluent Worker* studies before teaching them to unsuspecting students many of whom were born *after* this study was carried out? And one of us (Helen Roberts) shows the way in which research enters the public domain in a manner that the original researchers nearly always find difficult to control. Yet one of the reasons social science has had so few defenders lately is perhaps a lack of care and attention to detail we have all shown in addressing our varieties of audiences.

We had originally hoped that it might be possible to produce something that might have been called a 'Sociological Research Yearbook'. As the editors of three collections of essays on social research, *Doing Sociological Research*, 1977 (edited with Howard Newby), *Inside the Whale* 1978 (edited with Sol Encel) and *Doing Feminist Research*, 1981, we were convinced of their value as more than just teaching material — though these books are used extensively on undergraduate social science courses and even by 'A' level students. They are an important part of reflecting critically on research methodology and we believe that they have contributed to a more realistic and usually more accurate understanding of social science. The accounts are, we know, also a source of comfort to other social researchers. We thought that they should be regularly updated.

There is certainly no shortage of material. Both of us have had the experience that once the books were out, others (previously known *and* unknown to us) contacted us with further offers to write in similar vein about their own experiences. We thought that as monographs and texts were published we would ask their authors to reflect on them and in some cases this would give them the opportunity in the interests of a dialogue to respond to their reviews. We had also thought that we could commission 'state of the art' pieces on current fields and techniques. All this we still think is a very good idea — such a yearbook could be the focus of methodological debate and would allow the monitoring and up-dating of trends — in funding as well as in approaches. Publishers, however, thought otherwise and all those we approached doubted that it was a commercial proposition. It was suggested that we 'internationalise' this yearbook — obviously with an eye on the North American and Antipodean market. We rejected this. While we saw their financial and intellectual points, we thought that we wanted to concentrate on sociology in one country. National sociologies are startlingly divergent — we sometimes wonder whether there is anybody left in Britain who regularly reads the *American Sociological Review* let alone the *Australian and New Zealand Journal of Sociology* (that is if they have the opportunity to, and their libraries still subscribe to both,

in the current financial situation faced by all further education institutions in Britain). We wanted the yearbook to be a
focus of debate here, with the peculiarities of the British
social situation fully taken into account. There are, for
instance, virtually no similarities between the experience of
being a postgraduate in Britain and that of being one in the
USA. Indeed Americans are surprised that we pay so much
attention to it in this book and in earlier collections. After
three years of unsuccessfully trying to persuade British
publishers to take on such a project we were finally delighted
by our current publisher's willingness to add to the *genre* at
all. And we must admit that now we have renewed our
acquaintance with the rigours of editing we are far from sure
that we would have actually welcomed the labour and
responsibility involved in producing such a yearbook.

Not only have the times changed politically and economically for social science since *Doing Sociological Research* —
they have changed intellectually. The introduction to *Doing
Sociological Research* reflects upon the break-up of what is
referred to as the hegemony of positivistic epistemology. This
break-up was attributed to 'external' events, '1968 and all
that', as well as from 'within' structuralist marxism on the
one hand and phenomenologically influenced ethnometho-
dology on the other (in addition, the confidence-sapping
efforts to 'reform' or 'repair' positivism were noted). So
instead of one, and only one, good and true way of doing
sociological research, there were now many — and *Doing
Sociological Research* was dedicated to what was called a
'decent methodological pluralism' that fell short of the
wilder shores of anarchy. The unity of 'positivistic' sociology
was clearly exaggerated, but there was an additional fundamental flaw in the argument in that Introduction that needs
to be corrected. That Introduction confuses the methodologies of individual sociologists with the structure of sociology
as a whole. Individual sociologists — no matter how tolerant,
catholic and eclectic — are very unlikely actually to be
methodological pluralists. To get research done they do
adopt a methodological position (usually some careful
sceptical reformist positivism). It is the structure of sociology
that became pluralist not sociologists themselves. The

difficulties that this poses for the funders of social research
(e.g. the SSRC) are remarked upon in Colin Bell's first
chapter that follows this Introduction.

The most revealing omission from the sweeping generalisa-
tions that are made in the Introduction to *Doing Sociological
Research* is any mention of feminism. Not only are there no
female contributors to the book, but the challenge to and
critique of orthodox social science that all varieties of
feminism presents were *nowhere* mentioned. Clearly *Doing
Feminist Research* was designed in part to put that to rights,
as is this book.

We think that the differences over 'the feminist position'
(in itself a gross oversimplification) within the social sciences
can be put like this. There seems to be a 'weak' and a 'strong'
programme in the feminist critique. We are deliberately
drawing on a distinction currently made within the sociology
of science. The weak programme would take gender seriously.
We could then no longer tolerate (nor fund?) studies that
purport to be about social mobility in Britain, or the social
position of 'white-collar workers' that ignore and exclude
women. Studies that don't take into account half the population would be recognised for what they are — partial and
limited. We would have thought most practising social
scientists would have little difficulty in accepting the weak
programme. And steps could be taken immediately to put it
into effect. (The fact that such steps have not been taken
may indicate that we are over-optimistic in thinking that
most social scientists would, in fact, accept the weak programme.)

The strong programme is, however, different and would in
some versions be even more deeply threatening to existing
social science as it is practised. This would suggest that
feminist research not only redresses the balance where
women have been omitted but can provide a basis for a
'better' sociology than one which is shot through with
masculinist assumptions, practices and research programmes.
At best that masculinist sociology is silly and mistaken, at
worst it is a powerful mystifying ideology that, whilst mas-
querading as 'science', obscures the real interests of (mainly)
male social science, defends the sexist status quo and

endorses the subordination of women (as well as female social scientists). Further, the 'strong programme' maintains that women not only could and should do a different kind of social science but that they can do 'better' social science. On the simple level of visibility, there can be no doubt that social science would be much improved if it looked at the whole world rather than only part of it. But more than that, the 'special skills' which women have as social scientists are recognised by feminists and non-feminists alike. Dingwall (1980) has written of the worth of 'personable young women' as interviewers, while Finch argues cogently in this volume for the particular rapport which women have with other women in talking about their lives. But there is more to the strong programme than that. As one reviewer of *Doing Feminist Research* pointed out (Stanley, 1982), there is more to doing feminist research than women aware of women's unequal status doing research on other women's unequal status. She asks, 'What about those of us who are women, feminists, who see women not only as oppressed but also as powerful and free — or those of us whose work focuses exclusively on men as oppressors and thus as (to say the least) important in producing women's oppression' (p. 118).

None of our contributors adopt in their chapters the strong programme in its strongest version, but most of the women, at least, and some of the men have moved well beyond the modest (but to some in power, unacceptably bold) proposals of what we call the weak programme. The feminist 'strong programme' cannot be merely dismissed as an 'ideology of the oppressed'. It is as strong a competitor for the epistemological space occupied by the social scientists as is marxism.

Without arguing that feminist research is in some mystical and undefinable way 'better' than other sorts of research, several of our contributors point out that a female inter-viewer and her female respondents are in a shared structural situation — and this shared situation is important. As Sartre (1963, quoted in Morgan, 1972) points out: 'Research is a living relationship between men' (sic) . . . 'Indeed, the sociologist and his "object" form a couple, each one of which is to be interpreted by the other; the relationship between them must be itself integrated as a moment of history' (p. 72). While it would be adopting too crude a position to suggest that some shared disadvantage with those we research is vital, it does encourage the development of certain insights, as, for instance, feminist sociologists' work on childbirth has shown.

Absences should be remarked upon. One piece that was written for *Doing Sociological Research* was completely lost — a prominent social scientist threatened a writ when an account was produced by a sorely abused researcher of that person's attempts to censor and control his research. The difficulties of getting Roy Wallis's piece on researching the scientologists published are obvious from *Doing Sociological Research* — we had to publish a 'reply' by them which in no way answered some of the more damaging accounts of their behaviour. We lost from Robert Moore's piece on Sparkbrook a revealing, but potentially libellous remark attributed to a local MP — revealing, we and Moore thought, of some cynicism towards racial issues. Stan Cohen and Laurie Taylor circumnavigated the Official Secrets Act to talk about doing — or rather not doing — research on and in prisons. Colin Bell's reflections on the Banbury restudy gained a certain mild notoriety — because of its exposed position after the loss of the piece just mentioned and the self-censorship of others with a view to avoiding writs. And, it must be said, because of the willingness of the other Banbury researchers to allow the piece to see the light of day. A great deal was lost in all cases.

We have lost one piece from this book that we bitterly regret. It reflected with acute sensitivity the experience of the (female) research staff on a major and greatly respected (and oft-cited) project. It revealed a great deal about the relationships between them and the (male) director which in turn exposed grave flaws in the basis of the research findings. Their powerlessness and the nature of, in this case, male power in the research setting ironically mirrored that of the women whom they were studying. Their experience was, we believe, a common one. And yet because of these research assistants' exposed and dependant position in the ever-growing reserve army of lumpen-intellectuals (exposed because it is virtually impossible to disguise the project on which they worked) the piece was withdrawn. Indeed we were rather opposed to any attempt to disguise the project as we thought that the social processes involved in producing this study were at least as important as the famous accounts of the project's methodology written by the director. Furthermore, their personal experience of the research labour process at the very least called into question and could have been seen to undermine the glossy finished product. But of course these research assistants, denied advancement in a shrinking research labour market, were also very dependant on that project director for their next jobs — how on earth could they not name him as a referee? And would other researchers have them if they were known to have an inclination to produce accounts of the backstage work? We of course believe that the project director could only grow in stature by allowing the account to be published — and of course he could dispute and answer it through the normal academic channels to which he has ample access. We are pretty fed up with research monographs that are carefully 'on-stage'. Theatrical productions, though, are designed to deceive and we all welcome the opportunity to suspend disbelief for a couple of hours or so. We thought that social science was something completely different. It is those who most subscribe to what is usually thought of as a more positivistic research methodology who most object to these kinds of accounts precisely because they have the most to lose.

If sociology is to be more than a skilfully *constructed* device then the research process should be less opaque and more open to scrutiny. In any case, we have lost a remarkably fine piece that exemplified that position — and its loss reinforces what we know about the position of research assistants, who in this case happened to be female, in today's labour market. (And do they simply 'happen' to be women?) There is a very real fear of the blacklist (redlist was perhaps a more accurate name — now it may well become a lavender-list with known feminists replacing 'marxists' as the hierarchy's bogeypeople). We were reminded of something we were surprised to find in Max Weber's *Economy and Society*.

> In the field of scientific research and instruction the bureaucratization of the inevitable research institutes of the universities is also a function of the increasing demand for material means of operation. Liebigs' laboratory at Giessen University was the first example of big enterprise in this field. Through the concentration of such means in the hands of the privileged head of the institute the mass of researchers and instructors are separated from their 'means of production' in the same way as the workers are separated from theirs by the capitalist enterprises (p. 983).

This is just as true of 'big sociology' as it is of 'big science'. There are other absences that should be remarked upon. In *Doing Sociological Research* there are no female contributors — and none were solicited. There are no excuses but some partial explanations. *Doing Sociological Research* wanted 'owning up' accounts of British studies that already occupied a secure place on the undergraduate curriculum. So, for instance, it was natural to go after one of the authors of *Race, Community and Conflict*. One of the authors of *The Affluent Worker* study was approached (not Jennifer Platt) who after some 'humming and haaing' eventually refused. As an editor, Colin Bell was disinclined to approach one of the very few women who had produced such a study — Margaret Stacey's *Tradition and Change* — as he himself wanted to write up *his* own experiences of being a research assistant on the Banbury restudy. Given the original conception, there are not many candidates — but the vision was blinkered.

Just as importantly, *Doing Sociological Research* only included (other than the scientologist David Gaiman who had to be included in order to get Roy Wallis's piece published) people all of whom were men, who were well known personally to the editors. It was if not an 'invisible college' then a friendship network that is one aspect of male hierarchical power in sociology. Hegemony works in many ways and, internal to many parts of the academic profession, it works through particularistic personal social relationships. In ways that needed to be reflected upon *Doing Sociological Research* really did mirror masculinist power in sociology. (All but one contributor now occupy chairs in Britain or abroad. They did not then, but none of them would attribute their success to their contribution to *Doing Sociological Research*.) The usual objection to that position is that those men had something to say, had done something; but then so had the contributors to *Doing Feminist Research* (none of whom have since become professors). The fact remains that *Doing Sociological Research* reinforced and continues to exaggerate male ascendancy in British sociology.

This was further exemplified in the recent special issue of *Sociology* devoted to research methodology, that had only one female contributor (out of 14). *Inside the Whale* is different. Again the contributors were expected to have interesting tales to tell and were all personally known to the editors. But because it was produced slightly later — and from the School of Sociology at the University of New South Wales which has a relatively good record in appointing women, there are many more female contributors (12 from 18), but only 4 contributions out of 10 are by females, as more of their pieces are multi-authored in a much more collective way than the pieces by men. That last point did not strike us as significant at the time yet clearly indicated a somewhat different approach to sociological production than that exemplified by the male authors.

Helen Roberts had some revealing experiences when she originally tried to get *Doing Feminist Research* off the ground. Teaching a postgraduate methods course at Bradford, she had found *Doing Sociological Research* useful, but as a feminist attempting to incorporate feminism into her work, found the gaps in the book referred to above unacceptable. She wrote to the publisher's editor, suggesting that the lack of work by feminist researchers was a serious problem in the book, and not just a superficial omission, given that by 1978 when *Doing Sociological Research* was published feminism was already having an important influence on work in sociology. She proposed to him a book in which women researchers might describe their projects, past and present, and discuss the influence of feminism on the research at every stage from the formulation of the problem to the writing up of the data. His reply was as instructive as it was patronising. He wrote:

> At the time *Doing Sociological Research* was planned, we were mainly looking for major research projects from which important and seminal (sic) accounts had been published in book form . . . I do not think that the necessity or otherwise of a feminist methodological contribution ever really occurred to us. We were not intending the book to be comprehensive or to cover all styles or modes of research. So I would not accept what you say about the significance of an absence of female research in the Bell and Newby book . . . All that being said, and with the omission (if not the admission of it) made, then we are left with a rather small and specifically feminist market for the kind of book you have in mind . . . This might more appropriately be a book for the (rather mixed) Tavistock Series.

In fact, the book which became *Doing Feminist Research*, was taken on by a feminist editor at Routledge. Like *Doing Sociological Research*, it sold well, though we have no way of knowing whether these sales are only to the 'small and specifically feminist market'.

Once it did appear, the fact that there was only one male contributor (David Morgan) raised a good many more sociological eyebrows than the fact that *Doing Sociological Research* had included no women at all. Interestingly, Morgan's was the only chapter referred to in the special issue of *Sociology* on methodology (vol. 15, no. 4, 1981), an illumination perhaps of the points Morgan himself had made about homosociability. Although the idea for *Doing Feminist Research* certainly came from *Doing Sociological Research*, the two collections were slightly different in conception. *Doing Feminist Research* was less concerned with the 'true story' behind the big project, and more concerned with the practical day-to-day problems of doing feminist work than with broader epistemological issues.

Perhaps partly for this reason, no pieces were lost through libel and, as Bell rightly pointed out in a review (in *New Society*), the lack of gossip and stories 'spilling the beans' might be seen to reverse sexist expectations.

What is true of both the previous collections, and we trust, this one, is that stories about real research and its problems are not only a good deal more instructive, on the whole, than conventional methods textbooks, they are also a good deal more readable.

1
The SSRC:
restructured and defended
Colin Bell

This opening chapter reflects on changes within one of the key funders of social science research in Britain — the Social Science Research Council (SSRC). It makes apparent the changing context of research funding in the last few years. The dangers of this kind of instant history are very apparent — will we still have a SSRC when this book appears? And yet, such is the speed with which some changes have occurred it is necessary, at the very least, to record some of the events along the way. Sociologists are going to have to take much more seriously than they have hitherto the political and economic context of their research activity. Science policy is an established, if ill-determined and at times rather incoherent, field of academic study — social science policy, with the partial exception of eduction studies, hardly exists. This chapter's intent is to set the ideological scene — along with Hanmer and Leonard's piece on the DHSS that follows it, and makes a contribution to the background of social science policy.

It is to be regretted that this chapter is not more revealing than it actually is. Members of the SSRC sign the Official Secrets Act when they join, and it has not proved possible within that constraint and those of the British libel laws to reproduce all the stories that might have been expected in this chapter. Confidences have been kept and the price is a blander account than we would have hoped.

The early 1980s were the worst time for British universities, since . . . well, for a very long time. There are no easy historical comparisons (indeed the word of these years might well be 'unprecedented') — and our feelings of affront are magnified because most of us have known nothing but expansion. Robbins has become Nibborism — Robbins in reverse. If we are not suffering an Henrician dissolution, then at least Sir Keith Joseph is regarded by many in higher education as some latter-day Thomas Cromwell. And social science has borne the brunt of the assault — by directive of the UGC which, in its infamous July 1981 letter with no discrimination and little discernment, suggested a substantial reduction in the number of undergraduates reading social science. Given the discipline's differential institutional strength within universities, it was to be expected that sociology would suffer disproportionately in comparison with, say, psychology and economics, let alone marketing, accountancy and something called business administration. We have been cursed to live in interesting times.

And if this was not enough, the much-maligned SSRC was first assaulted, then (partly in defence) restructured itself in the face of considerable hostility from social scientists. Then, unprecedentedly — that word again — got itself reviewed by no less a figure than Lord Rothschild and quite unexpectedly was given a virtual clean bill of health (aside, that is, from the odd disfiguring wart — a small matter when most of us expected the wise Lord to diagnose terminal cancer). Sir Keith Joseph appeared to accept Rothschild's review almost completely. The SSRC was saved. This chapter will focus on these extraordinary events and will draw, in part at least, on my experiences of being a member of the Sociology and Social Administration Committee of the SSRC during them.[1] I was appointed to that Committee in September 1979 and was, in effect, sacked (expelled from the family as the Chairman of the SSRC might put it) in the summer of 1982. I, like most but not all of my colleagues on that Committee, was not invited to join the new committee structure.

At a time when there was less epistemological anomie about than for over a decade, when for example erstwhile Althusserians renewed their interest both in the Labour Party

and empirical research, some phenomenologists and ethno-
methodologists moved beyond programmatics and produced
substantive findings and everywhere feminists were revita-
lising research programmes so just when sociology was
recovering its empirical nerve there was a sustained and,
many suspected, politically motivated assault on the institutional base of sociology in universities and higher education
generally and on one of its key funding agencies, the SSRC.
In order to defend itself, I shall argue, it restructured to
reflect the key spending ministries and appeared to shape up
to be ready to take on the research and development work of
the emerging corporate state. We shall see, though, that it is
not quite like that.

Divergent views of the SSRC

There are now a number of substantial pieces on the SSRC
from disgruntled sociologists. Two of the most famous are
both from Aberdeen — Robert Moore's (1978) 'Sociologists
not at Work' and the chapter by Geoff Payne (1980) in the
book *Sociology and Social Research* that he wrote with
Robert Dingwall, Judy Payne and Mick Carter. I shall,
however, concentrate on two other pieces by way of introducing a discussion on the restructuring of the SSRC.
    The secretary of the SSRC during this interesting period
was Cyril Smith, and he has made some remarks which bear
on the SSRC and sociology in his unpublished paper, 'The
Changing Social Organization of the Social Sciences in
Britain and its Implications for Intellectual Orthodoxy'.[2] It
is especially valuable because of the position acquired by the
author at the top of the SSRC's bureaucracy. Equally
interesting though, is the view from the 'outside' of Jason
Ditton and Robin Williams in their 'The Fundable vs the
Doable: Sweet Gripes, Sour Grapes and the SSRC'. Not
unexpectedly, the vision of the SSRC and its workings that
emerges from these two papers is far from coincident.
    Smith tells us — and he is surely correct — that 'changes in
the social organisation of the social sciences have *inevitably*
affected the content of the discipline' (p. 2). It is necessary

then to pay even greater attention than he does to these changes. He is concerned to examine three 'orthodoxies' — the one that concerns us most here is what he calls 'the almost defunct tradition of Systematic Empiricism within British Sociology' (p. 2). He concludes that (in comparison with both the Cambridge Keynesians and the Experimental Psychologists — the other two orthodoxies that he considers) 'the LSE sociologists (of the immediate post-war period) were a failure — their students developed more unity of purpose and thought than their teachers' (p. 8). Smith sees this tradition as having come under fire in the 1960s from 'those who wished to reinstate the actors' meanings back into sociological interpretation . . . and . . . secondly from those of a more radical persuasion (p. 9). And, he notes, with the 'existence of so many schools in sociology', it is difficult to 'agree on common criteria of intellectual significance' (p. 33). This might be expected to make the work of funding bodies such as the SSRC very problematic. This is notwithstanding the fact that the creator of the SSRC could be considered to be Michael Young who, as Smith points out, 'was never able as Chairman of the SSRC to offset the strong theoretical undercurrents running in sociology and other social sciences with his own preferences for applied and relevant research' (p. 21). The sociology committee of his period and all of those since were left 'to follow their own line of academic and non-dirigisme and theoretical eclecticism' (p. 21). If that was true in the late 1960s, it was also true in my experience of that committee from 1980 to 1982. That it was restructuring was, in part, designed to cure. Smith concludes of British sociologists as a whole that 'there is one thing they seem to share in common and that is a distaste for empiricism' (p. 31). The problem as he would see it was how to get them to apply for support for fundable and doable research. That, too, is the focus of Ditton and Williams's paper, though at times it is difficult to believe that they are talking about the same British sociology.

Any serious student of the SSRC is indebted to the investigative work of Ditton and Williams (1981) — though their paper is really so much about sociology, which as we shall see is a small and diminishing part of the Council's activities, that whilst it is directly relevant to this chapter it will have irritated other social scientists, let alone SSRC 'bureaucrats' who are a somewhat undifferentiated target in their critique. Ditton and Williams's problematic is not like Smith's — how to get people to do empirical work — but the opposite, how do those who want to do empirical work get funded. Or as they frequently wonder, 'how on earth did they get the money?' They ask that question of fieldwork-based research which they claim is doable but unfundable — as opposed to research that is fundable but not doable (p. 5).

They see the SSRC as a key force behind the bureaucratisation of reason — as a methodocracy (their neologisms deserve wider currency) founded on the triple alliance of bureaucracy, conservatism and positivism (which infects its judgment with rigidity, timidity and neophobia) (p. 12). This implies, in the Mertonian language that they adopt, a preference for ritualism and a denial of innovation. In good knockabout style they say that 'the effect of this, in more practical terms, is a preference for large positivistic surveys conducted by old people using traditional methods' (i.e. just what the secretary of the SSRC says they *don't* get) 'over small, nonpositivistic pieces of non-survey based research carried out by young people using new techniques' (p. 31). Yet, as they themselves recognise, the only alternative to what they see as the inept and incompetent bureaucratic operation of assessment is most likely idiosyncratic — stitched together by corruptness and patronage. And they are not very keen on that either.

Their central accusation is that something they refer to as 'the SSRC bureaucracy' is wresting control over the nature and type of publicly funded social science research from those who carry it out. They may well be gifted visionaries, but they spoke too soon. The Chairman, Mr Michael Posner, may well have done this through the 'restructuring' that I will discuss below, but that had not happened before — remember the remarks of Cyril Smith about 'academic non-dirigisme', 'theoretical eclecticism' and 'a distaste for empiricism'? When Ditton and Williams were writing the academics were, as far as the bureaucracy was concerned, all too much in control. This 'wresting' did take place — but after they wrote.[3] And not a moment too soon.

I write that as an original opponent of restructuring, but the central thesis of this chapter is that, without that restructuring, the SSRC would not have come through the Rothschild review and hence survived Sir Keith's fierce gaze.[4] Restructuring was a life-and-death matter for the SSRC — Rothschild could have recommended closure. All the evidence is that the Secretary of State would have both welcomed and accepted such a recommendation. We need therefore to examine what led to restructuring and then the proposals themselves.

Restructuring

In 1965 the SSRC had seven subject committees (Economics, Economics and Social Statistics, Political Science, Psychology, Social Anthropology, Sociology, Management and Industrial Relations) and three 'panels and other bodies' (the Committee for the next 30 years, Educational Research Board and the Automation Panel). The ratio of subject committees to 'panels and other bodies' is a fair indicator of the ratio of the 'responsive' mode to the 'dirigiste' — of work done in response to academic applications as opposed to policy-orientated initiatives launched from the centre.[5] Five years on, there were thirteen subject committees (additions included Geography, Planning, Economic and Social History, and the Educational Research Board had become a 'subject') and only one new panel — on Mass Communications. Three research units had been established: Industrial Relations, Race Relations and the ill-fated Survey Unit (what price survey-based positivism, Ditton and Williams?). By 1975 there was a Research Initiative Board *and* Research Grants Board *between* the panels and subject committees and the Council. There were still thirteen subject committees, but now six panels (Area Studies, Linguistics, Pollution, Social Responsibility and Industry, Transmitted Deprivation — an earlier indication of Sir Keith's impact on the SSRC, and North Sea Oil) as well as five research units, including the

Cambridge Population Group and the Socio-Legal Centre.
By 1980 there was a dramatic change — there were now
seventeen subject committees organised into four groups and
including additionally Area Studies, Computing, Transport,
and Social Sciences and the Law. With the demise of the
survey unit there were now only four research units, but five
'designated research centres' and *thirty-eight* panels and other
bodies.[6] This is surely a complexity quite out of keeping with
its budget and led to accusations of over-administration and
time-wasting. In 1968 the percentage of funds invested in
responsive research was 36.7 — by 1980 this had dropped to
25.9. Or, as Philip Abrams has put it, because the SSRC has
been haunted by the idea of being useful 'resources have
been shifted progressively away from the self-doubting,
methodologically inhibited basic academic disciplines towards
those fields in which practical applications and serviceable
personnel directly responsive to the demands of high level
policy are more confidently offered' (Abrams, 1981, p. 533).
And, as he notes in addition, in 1975 more than 70 per cent
of the money assigned to new research programmes went to
support work orientated to the purposes of economic planning and administration. In 1976 all but £57,000, out of
£625,000 spent on new research programmes, went to support work on economic forecasting, organisational decision-
making and management, management and performance in
education and the analysis of public-sector policy.

    Sociology's percentage of the research grants 'committed'
was highest in 1971-2 when it reached 19 per cent (behind
the usual leaders, economics, with 23 per cent) and was down
to 10 per cent by 1979-80. Of funds actually spent, sociology
and social administration in 1979-80 was down to 6.8 per
cent (compared to economics, 20.2 per cent). To summarise:
the SSRC was spending a declining proportion of its declining
budget (down by 20 per cent in real terms since 1978 — even
before Sir Keith lopped off another 8 per cent in October
1982) on responsive research and within that declining figure
sociology and social administration was getting a steadily
smaller share. The distribution of postgraduate awards shows
a very similar pattern.

    When restructuring was proposed, it did not seem to us

SSRC watchers that its intention was to rectify this situation as far as sociology was concerned. Indeed it seemed designed to administer the *coup de grâce* to the subject committees and to sever the intimate link between them and what had hitherto been seen as their true constituencies — the disciplinary-based university departments.

Committee members were told (in a letter from the Chairman) in July 1981 that

> the central feature of the new system will be a small set of multi-disciplinary committees, supported by a toughened machinery for referencing. The grouping of research projects will thus be changed — they will be grouped more by topics to be studied than by disciplines employed. We believe that this new system will make it a more effective instrument for helping the social sciences: and I would say, a more potent instrument for helping the social sciences help society. Any change in the pattern of the research we support will be gradual, as committees develop a balanced programme and Council itself is *enabled to exercise some explicit choice*.[7] But the 'balance' and 'choice' will be between claims on scarce funds for competing problems or areas of investigation, not between disciplines — the disciplinary skills to be employed will emerge from the process of decision making and will not be imposed *a priori*. Our ability to encourage multi-disciplinary work will increase.

The Chairman assured us that fundamental work would not be neglected as 'In the social as in the natural sciences, research often takes years to mature and years more often pass before practical conclusions can be drawn.' He adds interestingly that 'no one wants us to become the instrument of governments or even of Government, and "problem solving" is not the only approach to scientific work of significance and quality. Our new structure will not tempt us to forget these truths.' That is a significant enough document to be quoted at some length. It was in the hands of committee members well before the publication of the SSRC's 'A Change in Structure for Changing Circumstances' which, despite the invitations to 'constructive criticism' that the Chairman's letter also contained, showed that the die was cast. What was outlined in the July 1981 letter was what we got – it was a *fait accompli*. The bureaucracy, or rather the Chairman, had indeed wrested control.

It was decided by the July 1981 Council that there were to be (and now are) six committees: Social Affairs, Economics, Environment and Planning, Education and Human Development, Government and Law, and Industry and Employment. In September 1981, 10,000 copies of the famed 'beige paper' on restructuring were distributed (Posner refers to it as a 'white paper with green edges'). In effect we were told (paras 33-9) what the issues for discussion were – and the wrath of the Chairman fell on anyone who had the temerity to question the assumptions enunciated elsewhere (let alone the unstated ones). Those issues were: the membership and composition of the new committees (I analyse this below); the necessary changes in the referencing system (as there would be fewer disciplinary experts on the committees themselves, they would in effect have to rubber stamp referees' decisions on the more arcane academic frontiers); what to do about postgraduate *training* (my emphasis – as opposed to education, as most of us thought about it) now that the disciplinary-based committees has disappeared; and how to protect fundamental research.

The Sociology and Social Administration Committee discussed it (in the dark, then by candlelight in the library of the fused National Liberal Club on the evening of Sunday 1 November 1981, in an atmosphere so redolently symbolic that it almost seemed that any further comments, like us, were redundant). Our overall judgment was that the proposals were inadequate. Indeed we said in our formal reaction that we found the restructuring document 'naive' in that it 'seemed to attribute the failure of policy implementation to researchers or research sponsors and not to the diversity of interests among policy makers'. The new committees mirrored so closely government departmental responsibilities that they could be seen to be in competition with them. We believed that this would undermine the case for the separate existence of the SSRC in the longer term. We noted that these new committees could not really have much of an interest in subject maintenance and therefore in longer-term research — and *only* the SSRC had such an interest in the past. There are, we stated, well ahead of Rothschild, no alternative funders for such research. We noted the need for a wide and pluralistic panel of referees and urged the appointment of sociologists to *all* the committees. Of special note (*pace* Ditton and Williams above) is that we wrote that

> As far as the Research Resources and Methods Committee was concerned [we] wished to draw attention to the value of people experienced in qualitative research including ethnographic field workers and researchers using audio and video techniques for observational purposes. Sociologists should be called upon in addition to statisticians and computing experts, so that a diversity of worthwhile research methodologies could be protected.

We were amazed, we said, 'about the scant attention given to postgraduate training'. We recognised that 'the SSRC was the largest single sponsor of full-time U.K. post-graduate students' and so urged (to no avail) that procedures be evolved to safeguard the links with universities which are, we stressed, unlike the new SSRC Committees, organised along disciplinary lines. We wanted reconstituted postgraduate sub-committees on a disciplinary basis to guide the new committees in the allocation of resources.

The atmosphere was well captured by Stuart Weir in his 26.11.81 article in *New Society*, 'The SSRC and its family'. We no longer doubted that the restructuring represented a decisive shift in policy away from disciplinary-based research to a more active policy-oriented research — 'from universities (at a time when the U.G.C. was implementing unprecedented — that word again, cuts in their budgets) towards Whitehall, Westminster and industry,' (p. 365). That there was no proper consultation had created widespread anger, anxiety and resentment — much directed towards the SSRC's strong-willed 'paterfamilias'. Certainly those of us who dared to question the assumptions of the restructuring documents got short-shift from him — indeed some of us got plain, simple, old-fashioned abuse.

One consequence of the restructuring of the SSRC that we can immediately assess is the composition of the new committees. The universities that have been left out in the cold are so startlingly similar to the UGC's hit list as to provoke all sorts of, probably unwise, thoughts about conspiracies. There is nobody from Aston, Brunel, Salford, Bradford, Herriot-Watt, Strathclyde, Dundee, Loughborough or Surrey — the ex-CATs, or Technological Universities as they think of themselves, that suffer so disproportionately under current UGC policy. The only new universities *un*-represented are Stirling and Keele. There is no one from the University of Wales (Cardiff, Swansea, Aber and Bangor) — other than UWIST, none from Ulster, or Exeter. With the curious exceptions of Durham and Newcastle, the membership of the new SSRC committee structure is drawn from those universities upon which UGC's sun shines. This is likely to have dire consequences for the equitable distribution of scarce research funds and postgraduate awards.

Two further observations can be made about the composition of the new committees — firstly, what about the much discussed representation of 'the wider world'? This turns out to be the civil service, 'quangos', local government and only very slight (6 out of 105 committee members) representation from industry and banking. It is not truly 'corporate' though — no representatives of trade unions, 'consumers' or 'citizens'. And my second observation is that only 13 of the 105 are female, which suggests that, in the rather unedifying correspondence during the late summer of 1982 in the THES between Margaret Stacey and John Goldthorpe, she had a point. So not so much an emerging arm of the corporate state but a bunch of sensible establishment chaps — 25 per cent from Oxbridge and London, concentrated in the older, bigger universities. No doubt no conspiracy, but that is just how most of us would have predicted things would turn out if the SSRC restructured.

And along came Lord Rothschild

When the full history of science and social science policy in the twentieth century comes to be written Lord Rothschild will undoubtedly get a whole chapter to himself — but his relationship to the SSRC perhaps little more than a footnote. It will be a curious footnote and will refer to a series of events that were fairly incomprehensible at the time and are likely to be totally baffling in the future — obscured as they are by political overaction in the first place and eventual political inaction. Just as the SSRC was undertaking the major restructuring just described, the Secretary of State initiated a review of its activities by Lord Rothschild with the following terms of reference:

1. Which areas, if any, of the SSRC's work should be done at the expense of the ultimate customer rather than the Exchequer?
2. Which areas, rightly supported by the Exchequer, could be done at least as well and as economically by other bodies, who would receive payment from the public purse either on a once and for all or recurrent basis? The bodies concerned should be identified; and
3. Which areas, if any, at present supported by the Exchequer through other bodies could better be covered by the SSRC?

This inquiry was initiated — at the end of 1981 just as the Secretary of State (yet again) reduced the SSRC's budget — for the 1982 financial year, from the expected level of about £22.0m to £20.9m which represents a further 5 per cent cut over and above the 20 per cent cut suffered since 1979. It was difficult to believe that Sir Keith was neutral in his attitude towards the SSRC — especially in the light of press leaks which suggested that both he and the Chancellor of the Exchequer would welcome the opportunity to wind up the SSRC. It really did look as if Lord Rothschild was expected to provide that opportunity. In the event he didn't and the whole exercise actually produced very little.

Given those terms of reference, few social scientists were confident that they could be weighed on the balance of the famed 'customer-contractor' principle and not lose. Lord Rothschild, against many people's expectations (but not the

Chairman of the SSRC who remained confident throughout),
'spared the axe' — as the people said at the time.

What though should be understood by the 'customer-
contractor' principle? And how did its author largely ignore
it in relationship to the social sciences? Lord Rothschild himself put it like this (in a letter dated 24.2.82 to British university vice-chancellors):

> I was, of course, referring to cases of the following
> sort:
> (i) The Ministry of Agriculture, Fisheries and Food is in
> the best position to know what the country's agri-
> culture priorities are. It is therefore in a position to
> say (purely for example) to the Agricultural Research
> Council 'we would like a greater effort to increase
> the yield of baking wheat in the U.K. and are pre-
> pared to pay for the associated R & D'.
> (ii) An analogous case involving the D.H.S.S. and the
> Medical Research Council might concern absentee-
> ism due to 'backache'.

However, he went on to tell the vice-chancellors that 'it is
not particularly useful to discuss the ultimate customer in
these cases' — and he pointed out that there are great difficulties in identifying the 'ultimate customer'. Do, he wondered, government departments represent the customer or is
it the citizen who eats bread and prefers it cheap — or in the
second case is it the sufferer from backache as Lord Rothschild suggests, or 'the citizen who suffers tax-wise from the
lack of productivity caused by backache'? Quite correctly,
he points out that even greater difficulties arise with the
social sciences. Indeed it could hardly be otherwise and he
comes close to recognising the difficulty of specifying 'in
whose interest' 'x' or 'y' really is.[8] And as he told the vice-
chancellors, 'Everyone, I think, recognizes that social science
has not turned up great generalizations, with the associated
predictions, that occur in the natural sciences; and the prob-
able explanations of this *lacuna* is well known even if some
dispute their justifications'.[9]

It is of course impossible to know just what advice Lord

Rothschild received — who he talked to and to whom he listened. (Several people have pointed out to me that Lord Rothschild's domicile is in Cambridge, not the City of London, Chingford or the Surrey Woods. Far be it from me to doubt his objectivity but no doubt he at least discussed his task with his distinguished neighbours.) Yet the evidence is that most who chose to respond to him also chose to defend the SSRC — and doubt his terms of reference. Many pointed out that there are no 'ultimate customers' for social science research — except, as Chelly Halsey has said, that they are our grandchildren. Attempts to identify them are doomed to failure and it was generally felt that there was little scope for passing costs onto the private sector. At best the first term of reference is based on a misunderstanding — the 'customer-contractor' principle was never meant to be applied to the research councils — the SRC (SERC) and the SSRC whose primary purpose is the support of fundamental research (as opposed to the ARC, MRC and the NERC) (Halsey, 1982a, p. 336). The second term of reference was generally understood to mean: could somebody or organisation, like a government department, the UGC or the British Academy take over all or some of the SSRC's work? Few felt that there was any evidence that these bodies could undertake the work of the SSRC better or more economically — indeed it is the general opinion that no suitable alternative funding agency exists — other than perhaps the UGC. Some have suggested that there could be a case for transferring some of its national allocation for research to the Research Councils. This would lead, however, especially given the composition of the new SSRC committees, to there being those universities that were allowed to do research and those that weren't. Rothschild rejected dismemberment and, by page 4 of his report, seems to have rejected his terms of reference too.[10]

Sir Keith Joseph in the end (October 1982) satisfied himself with cutting a further 8 per cent from the proposed share of the science vote that would have gone to the SSRC.[11] More misery but much better than many had feared. This represents £6m from the £73.3m provisionally allocated to the SSRC over the next three years. This was, of course, against the advice of both Lord Rothschild and the Advisory Board for the Research Councils. It may be that this is more public relations to fill out — in the words of the THES editorial writer (22/10/82) 'what would have been otherwise a shamefully insubstantial response to the Rothschild review'. Quite why so much effort should have been expended on a body which accounts for a mere 4.4 per cent of a £464m total science budget must lie in the other outcome of Sir Keith's ruminations on Lord Rothschild's report — his obsession with the title Social *Science* Research Council. His last defence was to complain about the word 'science'. There must be something very odd about British politics when the last refuge is epistemology. It does seem as if Lord Rothschild managed to defend the SSRC, and my analysis is that he could do so in part by ignoring his terms of reference and then because the SSRC, pushed, poked and bullied by its chairman (against widespread opposition from within the SSRC and throughout the academic community) had already started to restructure itself. By October 1982 Lord Rothschild's Report, out since May, was being seen as a forthright vindication and so all could agree that to destroy the SSRC would be 'an act of intellectual vandalism'.

It is no exaggeration to say that because of political interference precisely nothing has been achieved in reforming the SSRC. The restructuring takes us no further over vital matters such as postgraduate education — let alone the identification of research areas. Indeed a lot of time and effort that could have gone into these areas went into writing memos to Lord Rothschild — and earlier to the Chairman of the SSRC on restructuring by fiat. More solidarity was expressed and shown to the SSRC than was good for it as the Secretary of State for Education grasped for something/ anything to axe. In the words of that same THES editorial, 'Sir Keith Joseph revealed himself to everyone's sad satisfaction as an inexpert and passionate individual.' It is, though, less likely now that any minister in the near future will take on the social science establishment — for good or ill the SSRC is now here to stay. 1982 saw — against all expectations — the SSRC *established*, but established 'restructured', de-disciplined, dirigiste and firmly in the control of good chaps in the academic centre. Indeed, like the rest of the social science profession, the SSRC is likely to become increasingly sclerotic. The price of victory (really, of survival) is likely to be caution and policy application. Sir Keith's inept assault may actually have results which will not displease him — should he ever calmly review the results of his actions.

Notes

1   To declare a further interest: I have applied twice to the SSRC for funds — in 1973 with Howard Newby for a project that was called 'Capitalist Farmer in the Class Structure' (the key publication that resulted is *Property, Patronage and Power: class and control in rural England* (Newby et al. 1978) though there are a dozen or so chapters in other books and papers that have also been published by myself, Newby and the two research officers, Peter Saunders and David Rose) and whilst I was a member of the S & SA Committee, I applied in 1980 with Lorna McKee for a project called 'Family Organization in times of male unemployment'. I was successful both times.
2   An unpublished paper which we have been given permission to quote. The views expressed in the paper are personal to the author and not necessarily those of the SSRC.
3   Their paper is dated August 1981 and presumably was written at least slightly before then. The July 1981 meeting of Council was the first place privileged to hear of the Chairman's plan for re-structuring and we on the committees received more details of it, from Committee chairmen, in September (though we had had a vague letter from the Chairman of the SSRC dated July, 81). The 'beige paper' on restructuring was not published until October, 1981 and was called 'A Changing Structure for Changing Cir-cumstances'.
4   I am well aware that Lord Rothschild claims not to have con-sidered 'restructuring'. That though is not likely — it would have been an obsessive interest of most of the social scientists with whom he consulted. It is hard to believe that a complex organisation such as the SSRC could have a major external review whilst proposing to work in a different manner with a different philosophy without those proposals being considered in that review.
5   Of course the subject committees could and did take initiatives — though that could result in a new panel to which academics could 'respond' i.e. apply to a panel. Nevertheless, even before we look at the monies involved, most SSRC-watchers would concede my point.

6 They deserve to be recorded in full.
Working Party on Support for Research Methodology
Crowd Behaviour Panel
Distributed Array Processor Steering Committee
Research Grant Panel
Survey Active Committee
Population Centre Steering Committee
U.K. Statistical Sources Steering Committee
Young People in Society Working Groups
Accountability in Education Panel
Addiction Panel
Children in Care Panel
Corporatism and Accountability Panel
Health and Health Policy Research Panel
International Activities Sub-Committee
International Exchange Scheme Steering Committee
Pre-school Education Working Group
Transmitted Deprivation
Central and Local Government Relations Panel
Election Studies Advisory Committee
Government and Industry Working Party
Inner City in Context Panel
Monitoring of Labour Legislation Panel
Economics Computing Centre Steering Committee
Economics of Industry and Public Enterprise Panel
Joint SSRC/EOC Equal Opportunities Panel
Energy Research Panel
Macro-Economic Research Committee
Mass Media Panel
Open Door Scheme Steering Committee
Work Organization Panel
Information Sub-Committee
Manpower Information Panel
Research Training Initiatives Panel

7 My emphasis: After restructuring academics were a minority on the Council.

8 Those of us who understand society as having *irreducible* conflicting interests in the short, medium and ultimate term recognise that this problem is not 'solvable' except by political fiat. This is argued at length in my chapter 'Studying the locally powerful' in Bell and Encel (1978).

9 In those weeks while we were 'waiting for Rothschild', *The Times* diary challenged social scientists to give examples of the practical uses of the social sciences. A contributor to this book, I am delighted to be able to report, won herself a bottle of *Veuve Clicquot* with the following examples:

Jennifer Platt wrote:

> Michael Young and Peter Willmott's finding that the form
> of the extended family was still alive and well in Bethnal
> Green in the 1950s, with much mutual aid between norm-
> ally separate households. They related this to housing
> policy and it has had considerable influence on the whole
> approach to the planning of rehousing.
>
> Joan Woodward and her team's discovery that there is not
> just one most appropriate management structure for indus-
> trial firms, but that the most successful companies have a
> management structure that is adapted to their technology.
> This has radically changed thinking about management.
>
> George Brown and Tirril Harris finding in a model of
> meticulously careful research of the social causes of depres-
> sion among women. They show that there are vulner-
> ability factors, that where these are present provoking
> factors initiate depression; and then there are symptom
> formation factors which affect the form that the depression
> takes. They demonstrate that these factors combine to
> produce particularly high rates of depression among work-
> ing class women with children at home.

This was under an article by Robert Jones, director of Journalistic
Studies at City University that was entitled 'Why Lord Rothschild should not swing the axe'.

10 See 'An Enquiry into the Social Science Research Council' by
Lord Rothschild, May 1982, Cmnd 8554.

11 That represents the £6m allocated to the so-called 'new blood'
lectureships — 300 a year for three years, 200 of which are to be
in 'Science', 70 in 'information technology' and only 30 in
'arts' — divided into 15 each in arts and the social sciences. Their
location is to be largely decided by the Research Councils and so
the SSRC can only claw back 5 per cent of this cut for all the
social sciences. What better indicator of current government
policy?

2

Negotiating the problem: the DHSS and research on violence in marriage

Jalna Hanmer and *Diana Leonard*

In their chapter, Jalna Hanmer and Diana Leonard describe the results of their long-term watching brief on developments in the research funding by the DHSS on marital violence. Renewed consciousness of marital violence arose from the activities of Women's Aid and the Women's Movement culminating in a Parliamentary Select Committee reporting in 1975. The DHSS, required to do something, agreed to fund academic research, and the academic response was, according to the authors, 'a characteristic hands up, eyes down'. As well as reviewing the history of the DHSS research funding and detailing the systematic exclusion of the practitioners – Women's Aid – from DHSS-funded research, Hanmer and Leonard explore the territory between research and policy, and the possibilities which exist for funding agencies to define – and thus circumscribe – a problem.

This chapter is concerned to explore some of the politics of research. It looks at what was defined as 'real research' in one instance and at who was enabled to undertake it, viz: the processes by which a state institution (the DHSS) attempted to delineate and restrict the questions to be explored in a particular area (marital violence). Having observed developments in this field over the last decade from the standpoint of both activists in the Women's Liberation Movement (including Women's Aid) and sociologists working within university departments, we became convinced that good research questions (i.e. those which extend the analysis and our understanding and which suggest fruitful changes in policy) come only from working with those involved in trying to improve their situations, and with continuing study of a particular area over an extended period of time.

In the field of violence to women, the efforts of women to help each other began with the discovery that many women were abused in the home, which widened to a concern about public sexual violence and the representation of sexual violence in pornography, then to the sexual abuse of children, particularly girls, by men in positions of trust and authority in relation to them, and sexual harassment at work. Each stage enlarged the definition of the problem. The role played by the state in patterning individual behaviour, and the ways it critically affects the problems women face (by, e.g., granting violent men access to children, or the particular horrific situation it creates for immigrant women) and the way its agents restructure the problem of male violence as one of women's mental health only slowly became apparent. This widening of the problem and clarification of the role of the state came not from academic studies, but from practice in refuges for battered women, rape crisis centres, and local women's groups. By following the twists and turns in understanding and developments at grassroots level, and witnessing the occasions of outright confrontation between a social movement and its opponents, we have been able to see the formulation, and reformulation, of central issues as possible research questions. And by reflecting on and constantly reappraising such long-term patterns as we describe here, we have seen and tried to understand how a dominant ideology (that of the happy nuclear family as the best basis for a stable society) is maintained under changing conditions and against substantial criticism.

In this paper we shall trace the origins of the call for research on violence in the home by looking first at the growth of Women's Aid and how this led to the setting up of a Select Committee on Marital Violence. We will examine how the DHSS became involved and why they suggested research (1971-1976). We then look at the first projects they considered funding and the response of Women's Aid to the information they were able to obtain. We also look at how Women's Aid were shut out of research formulation and the history of their relationship with DHSS research initiatives from 1976 to 1982. We end by describing the major research questions that have arisen out of the experience of Women's Aid and we have added a postscript on what we think the DHSS and other state agencies will do next.

We shall argue that, from the start, the DHSS did not want to know the extent of the problem and sought ways to respond which would have minimal impact on existing policies and procedures. In 1976 its response was to commission particular types of research. However, the research produced exactly the conclusions which those who knew about the area (i.e. the National Women's Aid Federation, NWAF)[1] had initially put forward and which the DHSS did not like. This is rare. The literature would have led us to expect that funded research would reproduce broadly the values of the funders. This makes the example particularly interesting in relation to the study of the role of the state in reproducing, or maintaining, dominant ideology and practice and resistance to it, for it shows the (moderately successful) use of evasive tactics by a subject group, and emphasises that researchers are distinct from, and can at times be in opposition to, the state agency itself. However, the example does not reflect particularly well on academic researchers, as far as we are concerned, for they accepted large sums of money which might (and we know it is only 'might') have been otherwise spent. And, of course, the DHSS is not beaten. It still hopes the problem will go away (i.e. fade from public consciousness). If it does not, we anticipate the Department will simply try a new tack.

The origins of research on 'domestic violence'

In the late 1960s small groups of women began to meet to

discuss their personal lives in order to raise their consciousness about the social situations in which they found themselves. These groups discerned many areas of oppression common to the women within them, some of which were very painful and embarrassing to reveal, including violence from the men with whom the women lived. As more groups came into existence they began to work together and went on to develop local women's centres. The incidence and savagery of violence in the home did not become fully evident until there were women's centres, probably because until then no effective action could be taken. But women soon began to ask to be allowed to stay in the centres in order to escape from their husband's abuse.

The first women's centre to respond to this request was in Chiswick, London, in 1971, even though the centre's lease from the Council specifically forbade the use of the premises for residential purposes, given their inadequacy (Sutton, 1978 and Rose, 1978). The Women's Liberation Movement realised that a major area of women's oppression was being uncovered, and within six months the second house (or 'refuge') opened in Lambeth. Groups to set up refuges formed rapidly and by 1975 there were thirty-five around England, Scotland and Wales, some with and some in the process of obtaining houses. Many of the early premises were acquired by squatting, because hostility from local authorities to this form of aid to women was widespread. Every refuge that opened was quickly filled to overflowing, a pattern that continues to this day.

The refuges, particularly the one that developed from the women's centre in Chiswick, received wide publicity. Erin Pizzey, originally one of a number of women active in the centre, became the sole organiser of Chiswick Women's Aid when she was able to negotiate a house from the property company, Bovis. Through her husband, Jack Pizzey, a producer on the BBC programme *Man Alive*, she had contacts with the media which she was able to exploit with panache. This enabled many women in need to find out where they and their children could go for safety, and helped enormously to publicise the issue. As public concern grew the government responded by establishing a Parliamentary Select

Committee in 1974.

By 1974, Erin Pizzey was in receipt of a small DHSS grant for national work and after the first national conference for those involved in Women's Aid, she appointed a worker to contact other groups. In 1975, at the second national conference, representatives from the different refuges decided to form a national organisation, the National Women's Aid Federation (NWAF). Pizzey's refusal to join with almost all the other groups became known within Women's Aid as 'the split' and decisively influenced NWAF's relationship with central government over the next few years. 'The split' intensified efforts to influence the Select Committee on Marital Violence and it also affected subsequent relations with the DHSS and researchers.

Bringing oppression to light and putting it on the political agenda is a difficult task — and the purpose of a political movement. It took four years, from 1971 to 1975, to bring violence to women out of the shadows and turn it from a private sorrow into a public issue. With the establishment of a Select Committee to investigate the issue and to make recommendations for Government action, the first stage of the struggle could be said to have been won (Parliamentary Select Committee, 1975).

The NWAF submission to the Select Committee stressed the need for solid financial support for the refuges which existed, and for more refuges. From the start all the Women's Aid groups had been desperately short of money, since providing a refuge requires at least the maintenance of a house and the provision of material help for women and children who often leave home with nothing but the clothes on their backs. By 1974 most refuges were surviving primarily on rent payments to individual women made by the Supplementary Benefits Commission, an always quite inadequate sum. Despite these difficulties, the Federation wanted to keep refuge provision in the voluntary sector. They did not believe local authority social service departments, with their history of unhelpful social work attitudes and practices towards women assaulted by men in the family, were capable of making an adequate response.

On the recommendation of NWAF, the Select Committee

visited several local authority areas to see the appalling conditions in which refuges were working because of a lack of funds and governmental co-operation. The Committee also asked for evidence from relevant central Government departments who were required to respond. The DHSS in its submissions made it clear that it was not interested in extending the work of local authority social service departments to encompass provision for battered women, even though social work with families is a prime responsibility of the personal social services. The DHSS had to offer to do something, however, given the amount of public and parliamentary attention focusing on this issue. Their suggestion was to undertake research.

The Select Committee accepted the recommendations of both the DHSS and NWAF by concluding that the DHSS should undertake research and that aid to women should remain in the voluntary sector. It suggested funding for the latter should come from local authority discretionary grants to refuges, and that the DHSS should finance a national co-ordinating network.

The government accepted the views of the Select Committee, and £75,000 was allocated for research through the DHSS. After some negotiation, £15,000 was given to the Federation to organise the national network rather than to Erin Pizzey who was competing for funds. In accepting the central grant, NWAF won the battle for recognition but in effect agreed that funding for local groups would remain discretionary. This has proved to be a major stumbling block, as even today many refuges receive no local authority grants, and even those that do get a substantially lower rate than comparable local authority hostel accommodation.

The DHSS and research on marital violence; and WA's response

The DHSS then circulated a letter to a number of heads of university departments asking for research proposals, and its Research Liaison Group on Homelessness and Addictions was given the task of sifting through the replies. The DHSS have subsequently claimed that they canvassed widely for research suggestions and that this step was 'relatively unusual' (DHSS, 1978). Some circulars doubtless went no further than the head of department's wastepaper basket, while others were replied to or handed on. We know that in a number of cases the heads of departments themselves responded with research proposals, while in others the circular was passed to a member of staff who had already done work in a (seen to be) related area (though not to his research assistants who had done the fieldwork and much of the analysis).

So far as we know, no head of department told the DHSS that they should go to the people who knew about battered women, nor did many, if any, professors look around for unemployed women sociologists with experience of Women's Aid. The old response of eyes down, palms up, carried the day and those most advantageously placed lined up with their projects (Nicolaus, 1972).

The first news that the Federation had that money was now available from the DHSS came through individual members of women's aid groups employed in universities. But we ourselves, who were known to be interested in violence to women and the family, and were employed in universities, didn't hear for some time, and never saw a circular. At this time NWAF was negotiating for funds to set up its central office and it had already applied for, and been refused, money for an information officer. At the next meeting with the DHSS, headed by Michael Meacher, Under-Secretary of State, members of the finance group were very angry at what they interpreted as a betrayal of their organisation by the DHSS, since NWAF in its submission to the Select Committee on Violence in Marriage had asked to be kept informed of research funding. NWAF knew that their member groups were the major source of information about battered women and their children. The DHSS failure to consult was interpreted as a deliberate bypassing of them. It was feared that the DHSS would sponsor research antithetical to the interests of women; that the abuse of women within their own homes would again be marginalised by being reduced to a personal problem, and by placing the blame upon the women themselves ('they ask for it').

Women's Aid's view was that women are victimised because

men are permitted by society to maltreat them. It is the position of women in society that is central to understanding why women are battered. Men and women have differential power in the family and society generally, and no understanding of male violence to women in the home can proceed without a recognition of this basic fact that informs all social structures and processes. In relation to women, men occupy superordinate social and familial positions regardless of their social class.

In 1976 women in the WA were primarily concerned to confront violence to women by direct action, not theoretical exposition. They sought to make the issue public and to provide refuges as an escape route from marriage or a breathing space so women could reassess their lives. There was considerable hostility to the idea of research being done in the area. This hostility often came from group members who had been through higher education in the late 1960s and whose understandings came from this experience. They saw research as an alienating process whereby accounts were extracted from events or experience and divided into understandings derived from the social location and politics of the researcher. Research methodology, with its emphasis on so-called objectivity, was seen as inevitably leading both to a denial of reality and to the confirmation of the dominant ideology.

None the less, a research group was among the first subgroups to be set up by the newly formed Federation, since sufficient member groups were aware that the distribution of funds for research was tied to the issue of defining (or redefining) 'the problem', and that the previous 'do nothing' approach of the personal social services could and would change if the status quo was threatened and/or if public understandings of wife abuse changed. They therefore anticipated that the struggle for 'the explanation' of wife battering would be metaphorically bloody.

Members of the research group thought it important to monitor any DHSS — or otherwise funded — research that might take place. They were convinced that those sections of the state whose role it would be to manage this 'social problem' would, of necessity, seek to realign understanding of its nature in ways that did not question prevailing cultural interests — in this instance the maintenance of male social and familial domination. In addition, while far from clear on how it was to be done, the research group wanted to find ways of making accessible the information about battering contained within the experiences of individual Women's Aid groups.

At the NWAF conference in 1976, the research group presented a paper entitled 'Research Grants or What Do the Poor Have but Their Information?', in which they made these points and put forward the strategies the DHSS might adopt given its commitment to research (NWAF, 1976a):

(1) it could fund the Federation or individual members to undertake information-gathering and processing;
(2) it could negotiate with the Federation for access to the information already gathered;
(3) it could fund its own people to enter refuges one by one to gather information; or
(4) it could try to bypass NWAF in some way.

The DHSS seemed already to have ruled out (1) and (2); so the question was, how should NWAF respond to (3) and (4)? It was decided to:

(i)   firm up the initial statement to the DHSS that its researchers could not presume access to member refuges, by saying they would *not* get access;
(ii) put pressure on individuals seeking grants not to proceed, but to tell the DHSS to approach NWAF instead; and
(iii) to set up alternative research and ways of doing research.

The first strategy was not wholly successful. Not all groups were affiliated to the Federation and one particular group which *was* affiliated supported a researcher who was seeking funds to study their refuge. NWAF agreed because of this support and because she was a woman and her DHSS grant proposal asked for a very small sum of money.

The second strategy — to use the British Sociological Association network to tell men not to 'colonise' the area —

worked with some but not with others (there being always the argument 'If *I* don't take it, someone worse will').

The third strategy produced a number of pieces of alternative research.

(a) A pamphlet was swiftly published criticising existing research, (NWAF, 1976b). This focused largely on the victim blaming perspective, which assumes that women have control over their relationships, and could stop the violence or the relationship if they wanted to. If they did not, it was because they had personality defects.

(b) The Federation's finance group reviewed its efforts to get money to employ an information officer. She would enable groups systematically to monitor and write up information in the three areas already seen to be of key significance: income maintenance, housing, and law enforcement, and would disseminate the knowledge and expertise gained by the groups to relevant others. The three areas selected were chosen not only because they were the ones which constantly recurred as problems in the day-to-day running of refuges, but also so as to
  . focus on *state* services which *prevented* women from escaping violent men. This, it was hoped, would challenge the dominant ideology that women were responsible for what happened because they chose to stay with (or to return to) violent husbands or cohabitees.

The Minister agreed to reconsider this proposal and, in 1976, funds were made available. But this appointment was never considered to be 'proper' research by the DHSS. The Minister seemed to be responding to a political situation and the sum involved, £5,000 per annum, was minuscule. On the Federation's part, the post was deliberately called an information officer because member groups did not want the term research to be used, and 'officer' was seen as sufficient concession to the DHSS.

(c) The April 1976 NWAF conference also considered a preliminary draft of a research project on the housing needs of battered women. This project was brought to the meeting by a member of a refuge group who had been negotiating with the Department of the Environment but who had decided not to continue with an individual application. The aims of the research, the areas to be investigated and the questions to be asked were carefully scrutinised and, after considerable debate, a research design emerged. A survey of women living in refuges at a given moment in time was to be followed by personal interviews with a smaller sample focused solely on housing. This was accepted by member groups as in no way likely to produce information which could be used to discredit battered women, and an acceptable form of state subsidy. The proposal was accepted and funded by the DOE (Binney, Harkell and Nixon, 1981). Possibly the relationship with this government department developed in a different way because the DOE, unlike the DHSS, does not have as a primary task the regulation of family life and the maintenance of an idealised conception of the family. It was also recognised at the time as a new and lively Department.

Time has shown the 1976 NWAF research group analysis to have been substantially correct. The DHSS did seek an unchanged definition of the problem, and it did try to work around/ignore the NWAF and to penetrate refuges using its own men (and women). Over the following six years a gulf has existed between the aims and practices of this section of the state and the aims of the WLM and Women's Aid, with occasional points of open conflict between it and the DHSS research bureaucracy, and between the DHSS and individual research projects. Before looking at these points of conflict, we will first outline the sort of research the DHSS was interested in.

Projects the DHSS was considering in 1976

NWAF was unable to obtain information on the full range of applicants for the DHSS money and of course the reason why some research projects were accepted and others rejected is confidential. They did know, however, of the three which were finally funded and of two which were seriously considered; and also of two submitted by women lecturers and one by a woman professor which were rejected (though the last was not markedly different from one which was ultimately accepted).

The two considered but not funded (one because it was withdrawn) came from senior men who proposed to compare in depth a small number of couples where marital disharmony involved violence, with those where it did not, and/or who had other kinds of problem. Although these projects did not survive, the DHSS did not lose interest in this approach. The Homelessness and Addictions Research Liaison Group's document on funding of February 1978 (DHSS, 1978) included a wish to see research into factors that distinguish violent and non-violent couples. Behind this continuing interest lay a belief that violence from men to women in the family is deviant behaviour and qualitatively different from other means of resolving conflicts in interpersonal relations.

The other three proposals under discussion in 1976, which were funded were:

1 Mervyn Merch, University of Bristol, who intended to investigate views on the problems of wife abuse and show how they are being met by relevant professionals, such as solicitors, doctors and police, by interviewing these professionals as well as women who have been in refuges. The sums initially under consideration were £5,000 per annum (total £15,000). The report of this project is now with the DHSS.

2 Professor Ronald Frankenberg, Keele University, who was understood to be seeking £5,000-6,000 per annum (total £15,000-18,000). His original intention was to employ a social worker for three years who, during the first eighteen months, would look at what services, if any, existed in the Keele area. Professor Frankenberg had contacts with Trent Trust, a women's aid house in Keele (not affiliated to the Federation) in which he hoped the social worker could have a room for the second eighteen months so that a twenty-four-hour advisory service could be set up and monitored. This latter idea was dropped before the grant was made. His application also suggested a study of the family networks of

battered women in order to determine if social isolation was a significant factor in marital violence. This was rejected by the DHSS. Ultimately, his research concentrated on interviews with agencies and battered women on the definition of the problem and the evaluation of services, including the police. The report of this project is now with the DHSS.
3 Jan Pahl, University of Kent, who was given £1,500 to study the Canterbury refuge (NWAF affiliated). Her report was published by the DHSS (1978) and a further substantial grant was given to her to follow up women who had left the refuge. The report of this project is now with the DHSS.

The DHSS organised report-back in 1978

The first invitation to NWAF to state its views on research needs to the DHSS did not occur until two years later, in 1978, when the Homelessness and Addictions Research Liaison Group called a meeting for researchers into marital violence. But, even then, this was apparently something of a mistake and occurred only because one of the national workers happened to be in the right place at the right time to overhear mention of the meeting. She requested an invitation for NWAF representatives to give a paper.

This paper politely welcomed the inclusion of WA in DHSS discussions on research around domestic violence, and again asserted that the causes of violence from men to women in the family are linked directly to the position of women in society. It called on the DHSS to recognise in its research effort the power dimension exposed by a rhetorical question from Willie Hamilton MP (when Chairman of the Select Committee on Violence in Marriage three years before). He had asked: 'Why should it be the wife and children who have to leave and not the husband?... Why should we not create hostels for battering husbands?' (Parliamentary Select Committee, 1975, p. 190). In practice *and* in law men do *not* have to leave home and turn to hostels; the proposal is nonsensical. The paper again gave housing, law enforcement and income maintenance as priority areas for research. These, it argued, are the social arrangements that currently impede but could assist a woman in altering her situation. It also said that social work intervention is largely useless and suggested that research emphasis on it diverts attention from more meaningful areas.

The DHSS paper to this meeting, however, said that their research effort was going to remain restricted to two areas; the setting up and role of a woman's refuge, and the attitudes and responses of helping agencies to the problems of the battered women.

A major project ongoing at this time and represented at this meeting was that of Rebecca and Russell Dobash. This was sponsored by the Scottish Home and Health Department (Dobash and Dobash, 1979). They had applied to the DHSS Cycle of Deprivation Committee for funds to extend their research from Scotland into England in 1976, but were refused; possibly in part, they think, because of their commitment to an analysis of battering that recognises the social position of women as the major contributory cause of their position in marriage. The Dobashes were nevertheless invited to the DHSS meeting for researchers into marital violence and they were unwittingly responsible for an interesting and revealing exchange between the representatives from the DHSS and the DOE about the relation between research and state policy.

Towards the end of the meeting, the DOE representative asked the Dobashes to give their views on the policy implications of their research. The DHSS spokesman objected, saying that the question was inappropriate. After an exchange in which the DOE representative maintained that research was only undertaken in her department to aid policy decisions and that the views of researchers were always of interest even if not always followed, while the DHSS replied that policy was not the concern of researchers, a compromise was reached and all DHSS-funded researchers were asked to give their views. The researchers appeared to be somewhat disconcerted by this exchange. Only the Dobashes were prepared to specify the basic knowledge needed to inform policy decisions. Whether politic or truthful responses, this was a telling moment for those who believe that DHSS research is so much flannel, designed to cover and hide rather than to expose and confront.

The restriction of the DHSS research effort to refuge provision and the attitudes and responses of helping agencies
does not allow engagement with major issues, but rather
hangs on to the outworn ideology that the interpersonal
explains all — even if this ideology is not recognised and
acknowledged by specific projects. A belief in the explanatory
power of the interpersonal leads inexorably to a belief that
there is an opposite but equal issue regarding battered husbands, and this was raised at the 1978 meeting by a woman
social work teacher and researcher. This game was played out
in full in the US in 1978 when data collected by Murray
Straus, Richard Gelles and Susan Steinmetz was used to support a report of widespread husband assault in an article for
Victimology (Steinmetz, 1978). Their research methodology
was contested by Elizabeth and Joseph Pleck, Marilyn Grossman, and Pauline Bart (1978) and the debate raged among
those with knowledge of wife abuse. The British intellectual
struggle never reached this point, perhaps because research
money was not so lavishly dispensed, but the same attitudes
are readily available to anyone working with and for battered
women and, without doubt, lurk just under the surface
among many researchers in this country (for example, see
Freeman, 1979, and Bates, 1981).

Report-back in 1979

A second DHSS-sponsored seminar for researchers was organised in September 1979 by Mervyn Merch at the University
of Bristol. Membership was again restricted and Women's Aid
did not learn of the meeting in advance and was not invited.

By this time several new projects had received small
funding:

(i)   a survey of the statutory and voluntary response to
      domestic violence in Wales (Dr Sara Delamont, Univer-
      sity of Cardiff);
(ii) a study of the experience of marital violence and the
      social work response (Professor Peter Leonard and

Eileen Macleod, University of Warwick);
(iii) an examination of the problem and evaluation of the present provision for battered women (Anne Elsey, Cranfield Institute of Technology);
(iv) an assessment of a 24-hour crisis centre which covered marital violence among other problems (Mr S. Kew, Institute of Family and Environmental Research).

The areas identified for further research appear to have been expanded as a result of this meeting to include the nature and causes of domestic violence, but no research projects were funded in these areas (DHSS, 1980). Their emphasis on social work provision and on predictive factors, the escalation of violence, and ways in which conflicts between partners can be resolved or managed so as to prevent violence, would seem, however, to present the same limitations on understanding as before.

Report-back 1981: the Kent conference

The next point of conflict between WA and the DHSS came at a large meeting financed by the Homelessness and Addictions subgroup in 1981 at the University of Kent at Canterbury. This included representatives from many social work agencies, the criminal justice system, housing, and research institutions such as the SSRC. The English Federation's representation (NWAF had become WAFE)[1] at the conference was set at five, but this increased by some women obtaining entry from the organiser, Jan Pahl, as *bona fide* researchers, and by some WA members finding places through other organisations. The final delegation stood at thirteen. The programme was to consist of reports on the projects funded by the DHSS, a WAFE researcher on the DOE project, and Rebecca and Russell Dobash. WAFE negotiated for three months to be allowed to deliver a document prepared by its research group as a plenary paper but without success. This detailed (over 10 pages) work which the DHSS *ought* to have commissioned — or which it should fund in future.
As they were mandated by the English Federation to put

its position to the conference, its representatives prepared a
statement asking for a democratic vote from the conference
floor on WAFE's right to present its paper. After being
threatened with expulsion if they did not sit down and be
quiet, the organisers eventually agreed to allow the Federation's representatives to go ahead.

WAFE suggested research topics ranging through the limits
women set on their own behaviour for fear of reprisals (as
opposed to 'what women do to precipitate violence'); suggestions on the usefulness of the literature on torture and
enforced dependency in looking at the long-term effects of
violence in the home; the need for information on the
general health of battered women and their treatment by
doctors, casualty departments and mental hospitals; their
drug usage and attempts at suicide; the crying need for a
national incidence study — including more on murder and
molestation *after* divorce; assessment of the gap between the
abstract rights and the actual remedies available to women;
surveying the attention given currently to domestic assault,
and possible improvement programmes in police, social work,
health visitor and lawyers' training; the hidden poverty in
violent homes; the magnifying effects of immigration and
nationality problems; the history of men's violence to women;
the relationship of violence in the home to violence in public
places; the differences between men's and women's violence;
and the links between wife battering and the abuse (including
sexual abuse) of children.

WA representatives saw the main aim of the Kent conference to be a self-congratulatory public relations exercise by
the DHSS. This backfired in the sense that all the research
reached two conclusions — that Women's Aid is the only
agency providing substantial help to women who leave home
because of violence and that professional help offered by
statutory DHSS agencies, i.e. local authority social service
departments, is inadequate or worse. The research could only
conclude that Women's Aid should be better funded so that
the extent of the problem could be met. The final summing
up by Lady Plowden, however, did not mention the financial
need of refuges, nor the recommendations from discussion
groups, many of which made the same point. She opened and

closed the seminar with the same message — whatever the evidence, there would be no more resources and no serious redistribution from social services departments to Women's Aid. These views were confirmed by DHSS officials at the meeting.

As a result of WAFE's intervention at the Kent conference, two representatives of Women's Aid were invited to the DHSS Liaison group on Homelessness and Addictions for the first time in December 1981 to present the views of WAFE on research. The representatives took WAFE's requests to the meeting, to be told that the three issues now seen to be in greatest need of investigation were either not the responsibility of the DHSS (i.e. the incidence of violence to women and the problems of immigrant women), or not possible to pursue because of a decision by the DHSS no longer to fund research in this area for the foreseeable future (i.e. research into funding of refuges).

From WA's point of view, something in the region of a quarter of a million pounds has been largely wasted by the DHSS on research. Faced with a problem they did not want but were required to do something about, the DHSS chose a way out which would least rock the boat. They did not want to provide direct help to battered women, and they did not want a feminist knowledge to penetrate their understanding of family and married life. They chose research projects which focused on interpersonal causes and helping agency responses. These restrictions were inherently reactionary as they ignored larger social processes and interconnections between social phenomena. They inhibited understanding of the subjective experience of women themselves, even where this actually was sought. We do not regard research in the areas which interested the DHSS as unnecessary, but we believe it must go hand-in-hand with studies of the incidence of male violence to women, the effects of male violence on women and girls, the ways in which social institutions and organisations promote or challenge male violence to women, and the history of violence to women. To eradicate long-standing, entrenched social behaviour involves much more than a study of the immediate behaviour itself.

In WA it was argued that good research could only be

rted from the perspective of those experiencing, or helping
ose experiencing, violence,[2] but the DHSS would not en-
age on this level. When they gave NWAF money it was for
other reasons and, with the exception of a small grant for
research on children in refuges, it was never given by the
DHSS research apparatus.[3] The DHSS never acknowledged
that WA had a research role to play, which, while giving a
certain freedom, had the effect of boxing the Federation in
and excluding it from the world where the symbolic (or the
written understanding of reality or theory) is produced. In
an important sense WA was trivialised, seen merely as a victim support group, which made more difficult the work of
developing its interpretation of male violence to women.

We still feel, however, that NWAF's response to research
into violence to women by men in the family came as close
to breaking the mediating role of women, by refusing to
provide men with what they wanted, as was possible at that
point in the herstory of the struggle against male intellectual
hegemony. The Federation would not allow women to 'be
observed' by social scientists; and they were very clear that
they did not want 'that rubbish' – the sophisticated (male)
concepts of the world, the required way in which women
must think of their world – to invade the area. But the problem remained; if 'their' way was to be rejected, how were we
to reflect and write? The solution at the time was largely to
just struggle; to resort to unintellectualised action as that
was all that felt safe. The Federation may have been right –
to have moved an inch away from concrete reality might
have meant that 'their' thoughts, learned at university and
by participation in the social world, might have become
overwhelming. At the time, radicalism was high and anti-
intellectualism and anti-male sentiments prevailed. People
do not get as angry now about social research.

What now appears as a new theory of knowledge – viz:
that to understand the phenomena you must start with the
perspective of those who are subordinated – came from
consciousness-raising in the Women's Liberation Movement
and gained much from other social welfare movements such
as claimants unions and squatters (even if we didn't realise
this clearly at the time). In the mid-1970s feminists certainly

didn't see their approach as an epistemology – or even a methodology. It was just political action. It was not 'research'. Only when feminists were excluded from 'real' research and had to struggle anew against imposed definitions and answers to the wrong questions from 'neutral' researchers, 'value-free' civil servants or 'experts', did the relationship become apparent.

We are now much clearer that knowledge is not conceived abstractly but is a dynamic process in which theory develops from practice and that changed understandings help produce changes in material circumstances. The symbiotic relationship of theory and practice forms the basis for the work of WA. It both creates and tests its theory in its daily work, which gives it the authority to direct future research. Women's Aid is not made up of the foot soldiers who are to be informed by the DHSS generals what to think about the experience of pain, humiliation and degradation faced by countless women all over Britain.

What of the part played by the researchers who were not part of Women's Aid? They were all humanistically sympathetic to battered women and supporters of the Federation and its refuges. They reported the appalling or uncomprehending attitudes of certain 'neutral' professionals (police, doctors and social workers) and substantiated that lawyers (who are supposed to be partisan) were of most help to the victims of abuse. They confirmed with systematic data much that Women's Aid knew from experience. They often tried (even if not in the 1979 meeting!) to be honest brokers with the DHSS on behalf of women. But they didn't (with the exception of the Dobashes) get down to *generating* new questions; and they didn't seem to feel they needed to be more than nice and distantly supportive to Women's Aid.

At this stage, then, we feel that DHSS has not been able to obtain either the acquiescence of Women's Aid, or the support of researchers, sufficiently to *secure* the dominance of its 'new' ideology of domestic violence (i.e. a slightly more permissive and kindly attitude towards battered women) while maintaining support for the patriarchal family in more or less its present form. We therefore suspect it will change tack somewhat. If we may indulge in a little crystal-ball gazing, we believe that it will seek to divide Women's Aid, and probably not in terms of a challenge to or an undermining of its ideology, but in terms of its practice. We think the DHSS will put pressure along the only-too familiar line of WA being for women-only and its strong pro-woman stance. The only major resource put into Women's Aid centrally is the grant for the national office and network, and this has been, and will continue to be, the way by which the DHSS will try to gain political leverage with WA. The exclusion of men from support groups may also be attacked by local authorities; and disagreements among women about the exclusion of men from refuges may be exacerbated and used to split the Federation. Or an alternative challenge to Women's Aid practice may be to hand the package over to the sterner rule of the Home Office, as a 'victim support scheme'. As to the researchers, now well versed in the area, and with lots of important new questions to answer — there looks likely to be no further funding. Some have already moved their wagons on. WA, if it can systematise and publish its knowledge, may have the initiative at last, for the worst of reasons.

Notes

1   Women's Aid is a generic term describing the work of groups providing refuges for women who have experienced physical, sexual and mental abuse, and their children. These groups belong to national federations in England, Wales, Scotland and Northern Ireland. Initially the National Women's Aid Federation included Wales and Northern Ireland as well as England. Scotland was always separate and set up the same year as NWAF. When Wales and Northern Ireland established their own Federations the National Women's Aid Federation (NWAF), became the Women's Aid Federation England (WAFE).

2   The WAFE proposals for future research will be published in full in Hanmer and Saunders (Hutchinson, 1984). Learning that the conference papers were to be published, and not being approached by the editor, WAFE asked that its paper be included (Pahl, forthcoming). As this was refused, alternative sources for telling this story among sociologists, feminists and the public at large had to be found.

3   At the meeting for researchers in 1978 it was made clear that the DHSS were interested in funding projects on children in refuges.

In 1979, NWAF accepted a small grant to collect information on children in refuges. This project never had the full support of NWAF groups who feared that the DHSS would use research on children as a way of attacking women, by blaming them for any disturbances their children might be suffering from either a result of leaving home or from having lived in a home with more violence than is the social norm. This project went through several transformations and ultimately concentrated on what should be done for children in refuges and the resources that would be needed to do this work.

3

Researching spoonbending:
concepts and practice of participatory fieldwork

H.M. Collins

In this chapter Harry Collins reflects upon and generalises from his experiences of working with 'spoonbenders'. Empirical studies in the new sociology of science — the so-called 'strong programme' — face, more acutely than most, problems of reliability and validity, objectivity and replicability. When the focus is 'spoonbending' the problems of what is happening — or whether anything is happening and how to report it, are massive. In addition 'observer effects' must always be suspected and allowed for. Collins cuts through many of these problems and introduces us to the useful distinction between 'unobtrusive observation' and 'participant comprehension'. In the latter Collins tells us that 'we sociologists became scientists in our own right and can comment on the experience of doing this type of experimentation from our own experience, as well as from the experience of others with whom we shared a small segment of our lives.' He had to acquire 'native competence'. In this Collins is unlike the central figure of Alison Lurie's novel Imaginary Friends — *which could have been loosely based on Festinger's study* When Prophecy Fails, *that is also discussed in this chapter. That fictional sociologist, it will be remembered, became so 'participant', so native to the cult he was studying that he was incarcerated in a mental hospital. But as he remarks with reference to that classic study* Asylums, *'Goffman only did it from the outside.' The great virtue of Collins's models is that it makes more visible 'the nature of the compromises involved in most (fieldwork) research decisions'.*

Introduction

Setting out to do some participatory research on scientists investigating 'spoonbending' (Collins and Pinch, 1982) I started to worry about how much my own participation was 'disturbing the situation'. This chapter is intended to offer a practical guide on matters like this.

A standard approach to participant observation treats the options available to the researcher as lying on a continuum between complete participation — with associated difficulties of observation — and total concentration on observation with hardly any participation. For example, Marion Pearsall, in her article 'Participant Observation As Role and Method in Behavioural Research' (1970), divides her treatment of the topic into four sections labelled: 'complete observer', 'observer-as-participant', 'participant-as-observer', and 'complete participant'. She points to the lack of opportunities and risks of ethnocentrism and 'egocentricism' as the major disadvantages of the first of these. 'Going native' is seen as the major disadvantage of the last, along with the difficulties of keeping full records of what is going on, while remaining unexposed. Pearsall recommends one of the middle courses, remarking that it is possible for the participant-as-observer 'to collect minutely detailed data on a wide range of topics and verify them by careful cross-checking from multiple sources'. Other authors (e.g. Bell, 1969) have categorised participant observation in terms of the nature of the social system to be entered, and the constraints this imposes on the participant regarding choice of overt or covert role.

No doubt *the practice* of participant observation has taken many forms and, doubtless, the range of *practices* can be ranged on a scale from participation to observation and overt to covert, but the most fruitful way of looking at this range of practices is, I suggest, as a range of compromises where the ideal solutions are not open to the fieldworker. The ideal solutions lie at either end of the continuum. What is more, the continuum turns out not to be a continuum at all, for the ideals aim at quite different sorts of results and they grow out of two quite different philosophical and methodological traditions.[1] In practice the researcher who is aiming for one ideal, while forced to compromise on fieldwork role, should be worried about one sort of deficiency, while a researcher, in the *same* fieldwork role, who aims at the other ideal should be worried about quite another sort of deficiency. The choice of method and technique available to the participant observer is not then wholly constrained by expediency — that is, the possibility of successful accomplishment of one role or another; it depends upon the philosophical and methodological presuppositions of the research in hand. The thinking fieldworker finds that the available literature does not solve certain philosophically based, but very practical, problems. What I will try to do in this paper is to sketch the field implications of idealised researches and then illustrate these ideals with studies which seem to come reasonably close to the ideal type. I will carry out this exercise under two headings which label the two traditions as they work themselves out within participant observation. Thus I divide participant observation into 'unobtrusive observation' (which includes much more as well) and 'participant comprehension'.[2]

Unobtrusive observation

An archetypal study that made use of unobtrusive observation was Festinger et al., *When Prophecy Fails* (1956). The essence of the method is that the investigators want to observe the actions of others while disturbing those actions as little as possible. The investigator wants to disturb the situation as little as possible because he believes (as a good positivist)[3] that it is his (read 'his or her') job to discover 'what is really going on out there' and, hence, that 'observer effects' are bound to be distorting. In 'unobtrusive observation' the necessity of participation presents essentially technical problems.

Participant (unobtrusive) observation on Mars would present technical problems to the 'sociological costumier' — how to provide authentic-looking wrinkled green skins — and to the language laboratory. With luck residual problems in the language department could be overcome by keeping silent as long as possible. Other technical problems to do with the researcher's incompetence at native interaction could perhaps also be solved by *interacting as little as possible with the natives*. The spirit in which the language and the natives' way of life is learned is the same as the spirit in which the green skin is donned. That is, it is the spirit of donning a 'costume', a disguise, and a persona.

Of course, the investigator will have to do some interacting with the natives or he/she will be noticeable by his/her inactivity. Above this minimum, however, the less interacting is done, the less likely are the inadequacies of the costume to be revealed, the less likely is the observer to be spotted as a stranger, and, still more important, the less likely is the observer to affect what would have happened if he/she had not been there.

It is clear that the unobtrusive observer would like, ideally, to be the proverbial fly on the wall; the fly can observe everything without disturbing the situation in any way. In unobtrusive observation, participation is only used (or should only be used) when the investigator cannot think of another way of observing that social setting that is of interest. Participation with its technical problems, is a nuisance. It is clumsy and full of risk. What is more, even the most careful unobtrusive participant observer may disturb the situation without realising it, so the observations can never be assumed to be completely free of distortion.

Unobtrusive observation includes 'surreptitious observation'. That is its most perfect form. However, it also includes observation where the sociologist/anthropologist identity of the observer is known to the subjects but the observer (hopefully) ceases to be obtrusive or disturbing after a time because he/she keeps a 'low profile' and becomes an unnoticed part of the environment. Unobtrusive observation also includes all those methods of observation where the observer's presence is unknown to the observed. These include spying, bugging and 'unobtrusive measures' (Webb et al., 1972). In all these cases the distinction between observer and observed is absolute. This description of the method is well illustrated in Festinger et al.'s book. The book is concerned with a small 'millennial cult' which produced a specific prediction of the date of the ending of the world. Festinger's accomplices infiltrated the group and observed and recorded happenings before, during and after the night of the predicted flood. Quotations from the methodological appendix to the book show the nature of the method as conceived by Festinger and his coauthors:

> Our basic problems were then obtaining entrée for a sufficient number of observers to provide the needed coverage of members' activities and keeping at an absolute minimum any influences which these observers might have on the beliefs and actions of members of the group. We tried to be nondirective, sympathetic listeners, passive participants who were inquisitive and eager to learn whatever others might want to tell us . . . . our initial hope − to avoid *any* influence upon the movement − turned out to be somewhat unrealistic ... (p. 234).

The authors then go on to explain that they felt that they had in fact had an unintentional reinforcing effect on the group's belief by virtue of the fact that entry of the observers constituted a sizeable apparent increase in membership of the group. Also they felt that the stories, concerning psychic experiences, that the observers had to concoct in order to gain membership without revealing their sociologist identities, themselves reinforced the belief system of the group. Further, in maintaining their membership of the group, the observers were sometimes forced to act in ways that had some effect on the group's actions:

> Most blatant was the situation that one of the authors

encountered on November 23 when Marian Keech [the group leader] asked him, in fact commanded him, to lead the meeting that night. His solution was to suggest that the group meditate silently and wait for inspiration. The agonizing silence that followed was broken by Bertha's [an important group member] first plunge into mediumship, an act that was undoubtedly made possible by the silence and by the author's failure to act himself. Twice again during that long meeting Marian Keech asked the author if he had 'brought a message' for the group. By the time of his third refusal to act, he began to be concerned lest his apparant incapacity should injure the carefully nurtured rapport he had established in the group (p. 241).

Similar crises occurred when the observers were asked to leave their jobs, to take a stand during divisions of opinion within the group, to answer telephone enquiries about the group and so forth. On another occasion Bertha embroidered a neutral response from one of the observers into a privileged glimpse of creation. The authors comment: 'Against this sort of runaway invention even the most polished technique of nondirective response is powerless' (p. 243). The authors sum up their role as follows:

we had to conduct the entire inquiry covertly, without revealing our research purpose, pretending to be merely interested individuals who had been persuaded of the correctness of the belief system and yet taking a passive and uninfluential role in the group (p. 249).

The last sentence is especially revealing. The observers had to *pretend* to be persuaded of the correctness of the belief system. They were not actually interested in the belief system itself. Indeed their whole project would have collapsed if they had become persuaded of the belief system and they could not maintain their 'objective' stance. (See Collins and Cox, 1976, for elaboration of this point.) Fortunately, the belief system was fairly irritating to the observers:

The job was frequently irritating because of the irrele-
vancies (from the point of view of our main interest)
that occupied vast quantities of time during the all night
meetings, the repetitiousness of much that was said, and
the incoherence of the congeries of beliefs that went
into the melting pot of ideology. This last aspect was
not only exhausting because of the strain imposed on
attention and memory, but irritating because the
observers felt responsible for *keeping it all straight* and
setting it down as accurately as possible at a later time
(p. 247, my stress).

Participant comprehension

For an example of participant comprehension I will refer to
a study conducted by myself and others which was concerned with the experimental testing of children's ability to
bend metal paranormally, after the style of Uri Geller.[4] There
is an irony in using this example in that the design of the
experimental test that we did ourselves in order to become
participants involved the use of unobtrusive observation.
That is we observed the *subjects of our experiment* — the
young children — while we were hidden behind one-way
screens. Thus we interacted with the subjects of the experiments as little as possible. However, as sociologists we were
only *observing* the subjects because we were interested in
the outcome of these experiments as participants. What we
were trying to *comprehend* were the scientists who did the
experiments and to that end we became scientists ourselves.

In participant comprehension, participation is not an unfortunate necessity which presents difficult but technical
problems and participation would not be avoided if some
other method could be thought up to replace it. It is not
risky or full of pitfalls. It is central, irreplaceable and, indeed,
the essence of the method. In participant comprehension,
the participant does not seek to minimise interaction with
the group under investigation, but to maximise it. Native
incompetence is not a technical problem to be overcome at
the outset at the 'sociological costumiers' and the language

laboratory (though these may have a part to play), but rather the development of native competence may be the end point of participant comprehension (see Halfpenny, 1979). Also, there will be little point in surreptitious behaviour. If the attainment of native competence is the end point of the exercise then incompetence, and therefore visibility is inevitably the starting point. Attempts to remain invisible by minimising interaction will defeat the object of the exercise. In participant comprehension seemingly incoherent 'congeries of beliefs', should they be found among the group under investigation, would not be treated as an irritating nuisance but, at least initially, as a sign that native competence had not yet been achieved. Comprehension will have been achieved when what once seemed irritating and incoherent comes to follow naturally.[5] The investigator has no responsibility to 'keep it all straight' nor to be able to reproduce the details of all the interactions that are observed. On the contrary, the investigator *him/herself* should come to be able to act in the same way as the native members 'as a matter of course' rather than remember or record the details of *their* interactions. It follows that minute-by-minute record taking, as stressed by Festinger et al., is far less important in principle. The stress is not on recording events (though this may be necessary for other aspects of the project in hand) but on internalising a way of life. Once this has been achieved, observation may as well be done on the investigator as other native members, for he/she should be like a native member. We might call this 'participant introspection'. In this method, then, the distinction between observer and observed is blurred.

In using the experiments of myself and others to illustrate participant comprehension, I am going to take certain liberties with the rhetoric of the account. That the work could be done was the result of lucky coincidences involving collaborators, allied with an instinctive sense of opportunity. Where the account suggests that the work was meticulously planned at the outset, and then cold-bloodedly carried through, it is less than honest. Things worked out much too well to have been planned that way, as anyone with experience of fieldwork in practice will see at a glance. It would have been sanguine indeed to have *planned* to do a series of

experiments, in a non-sociological field, to have an account
of them published in a scientific journal, for this published
account to attract newspaper and television publicity which
resulted in a longer-term experimental collaboration with the
key scientists in the field and to result in the investigators
being treated as middle-range experts in the field. Nevertheless, if we had planned to do participant comprehension of
the area we were interested in, this is what we would have
had to plan to do.

The experiments in question took place between May
1975 and the autumn of 1977. The first series were carried
out between Collins and Dr Brian Pamplin of the Physics
Department of the University of Bath. Pamplin was the
instigator of this project, and invited Collins to participate
because he knew of Collins's interest in the paranormal.
(I had done earlier sociological work on parapsychology.)
Pamplin wanted to test the powers of the children, who had
come forward following Uri Geller's appearances on British
television, claiming similar abilities to Geller. He advertised
in the local paper asking for any children who lived locally,
and felt they could repeat Uri Geller's paranormal cutlery
bending, to contact him if they were prepared to be scienti-
fically tested. Several children did come forward, and after
observing some *prima facie* evidence of their abilities we
decided to test them further under laboratory conditions.

Presumably, given these opportunities, the unobtrusive
observer would endeavour to interfere with Pamplin's work
as little as possible and would help out with the experiments
just to the degree that would ensure that the observer was
seen more as a help than a hindrance. In this investigation,
however, Collins played as large a part as possible in the
experiments. Collins was mainly responsible for the decision
to use the one-way-mirror set up, in order to avoid disturbing
the subject. Also, Collins designed the experimental protocol
intended to minimise the credibility of any accusations of
fraud that might be directed at us should we achieve positive
results. This protocol was pressed on Pamplin and other
collaborators. During the experiments, Collins kept a laboratory notebook, took many still photographs, tried to direct
the videotaping of the experiment, made suggestions for

stopping, starting, taking breaks and so forth, and in general played his part as an experimenter, not just an observer of experimenters. Collins was co-author (with Pamplin) of the experimental report that was published in *Nature* in September 1975 that described our experimental results. As a result he experienced the associated publicity, 'confronted' Professor John Taylor on television and was able to set up a further series of experiments with Professors Taylor and Hasted — at the time the leading experimentalists in the field. Again, in these experiments Collins (and later Pinch when he joined the experiment as research officer, in October 1975) played as large a part as possible. Subsequently, as the reputation of the Bath experiments grew, our laboratory was used as the site of challenge tests of 'spoonbenders' when we worked with leading sceptics in the field. As a result of this work, we sociologists became scientists in our own right and can comment on the experience of doing this type of experimentation from our own experience, as well as from the experience of others with whom we shared a small segment of our lives.

The most significant and noticeable pay-off from this was our experience of the asymmetrical pressure to interpret ambiguous experimental results as null results rather than interpreting them as yielding evidence for the existence of the paranormal powers claimed by the child subjects. Though resistance to fringe science has been well documented in the literature, the subtle permeability to outside pressure of day-to-day laboratory observation would be very difficult to understand without experiencing it. Other pay-offs which can be documented easily include the experiences of inter-action with the media, with the subjects of the experiments and with scientific colleagues. All these experiences, which emerged from our role as experimenters rather than as observers, presented surprises to us in the form of unexpected pressures to act one way rather than another. For example, the media demanded black and white findings irrespective of whether they were positive or negative. The lure of the media in terms of both financial reward and flattery was especially highlighted by the astonishing vituperativeness of colleagues who had no idea of what we were up to except that it had to do with the paranormal. This reaction helped us to realise how much the academic relies on support from colleagues in the normal way, and helps to explain the undignified flirtations with the media that parapsychologists occasionally engage in — it may be the only form of recognition left for a parascientist. Our subjects demanded always to be represented in a positive light and could operate the sanction of withdrawal of experimental co-operation if we refused. This made for very strong countervailing pressure to interpret doubtful results as positive. On the other hand, the way that our rather mild null conclusions were interpreted by sceptics was quite surprising, and the lack of subtlety in the war between the parapsychologists and their critics needed to be experienced to be believed.

However, though these results are easy to document, it is less easy to document the development of unspecifiable native competence that came about as a result of the work, and enabled us to interact with other scientists in the field with confidence and write up our results with confidence. Of course, this leads to a difficulty, for while the unspecifiable native competences are the crucial point of this paper, their very unspecifiability makes it difficult to see how knowledge of them can ever be extended beyond the narrow group who actually share them. We claim that we have extended the knowledge belonging to one group to a sociologist or two (ourselves) but can we possibly get this knowledge across to anyone else? For this purpose participant comprehension may have to use techniques that are not essential to the method itself. For example, at the stage of *presentation*, detailed notes recorded at the time of the fieldwork, written up in such a way as to try and put over the feel of the situation, after the manner of a 'writer' rather than a scientist, may be a useful rhetorical device. Unobtrusive observation, of course, has no problem of presentation, for the observer never leaves the frame of meaning which he shares with his fellow sociologists, but merely hides it beneath his 'costume'. Thus the notes the unobtrusive observer takes at the time of his fieldwork are already appropriately packaged for the audience. Indeed, to tamper with them in such a way as to increase their dramatic impact would be to risk distorting the exact account they embody.

Objectivity and replicability

A final difference between unobtrusive observation and participant comprehension lies in their claims to objectivity. The ambition of unobtrusive observation is to compare in *accuracy* with other methods of sociological research. Hence the literature on 'participant observation' is filled with comparisons of the method with other methods and discussions about validity of the method (see, e.g., McCall and Simmons, 1969; Filstead, 1970). Participant comprehension does not aim to compare in accuracy with other methods, as there are no other methods that seek to do the same thing. Both methods are replicable in principle, though confusion is widespread on this point. Clearly, it is expected that any unobtrusive observer should observe the same things if placed within the same social setting. What is not recognised is that the same applies in participant comprehension. Native members, and these include the investigator at the conclusion of participant comprehension, *share* a way of life and should therefore experience it in similar ways. Thus, in principle, they should all report it in similar ways. A later investigator should share, and report, the same native way of life as an earlier investigator. It is often thought that participant comprehension makes no claims to replicability. (Actually it rarely does make such claims in practice, as replicability is part of the rhetoric of positivism, but there is no reason why it could not.) The crucial difference between unobtrusive observation and participant comprehension on the question of replicability lies in the qualifications of potential replicators. In unobtrusive observation any professionally qualified sociologist/anthropologist is a potential replicator and his/her qualifications for the job can be readily inspected by professional peers. In participant comprehension an additional (a different?) qualification is required before competence can be claimed, namely the acquisition of native competence, and this qualification can only be judged by the investigator through his successful matter-of-course interactions with native members — this qualification is not therefore objective.[6] Thus, while 'there is no objective external index of success in understanding' (Collins, 1979) participant comprehension is no less replicable than unobtrusive observation.[7]

Summary of differences between unobtrusive observation and participant comprehension

Unobtrusive Observation	*Participant Comprehension*
Positivist tradition	Interpretivist tradition
Observer and observed clearly distinct	Observer/observed distinction blurred
'Observer effect' a serious problem	'Observer effect' does not arise
Participation is clumsy and risky, use other method if possible	Participation is essence of method
Attainment of native 'costume' is technical problem to be solved at outset	Attainment of native 'competence' is end or near end of project
Surreptitiousness preferable	Surreptitiousness pointless
Minimise interaction as far as possible	Maximise interaction as far as possible
Incoherence of native beliefs irritating	Apparent incoherence of native beliefs is *prima facie* evidence that goals not yet achieved
Detailed records essential	Detailed records may be *rhetorically* useful
No problem in presenting findings	Presentation of findings seem very difficult in principle. 'Scientific' rhetoric inadequate
Any professional can replicate	Only competent natives can replicate

Concluding remarks

If this way of looking at participant observation is accepted then certain practical problems will be solved for the fieldworker. He or she will know how to think about, for example, how many notes to take and how detailed they should be and what purpose they will serve. There may be different answers in precisely the same fieldwork locations depending upon the ideal at which the fieldworker is aiming.

This way of looking at participant observation will also have a reorientating effect on our view of the relationship between participant observation studies. For example, if we represent the old 'continuum view' diagramatically we would find *When Prophecy Fails* to be an account of a study that was located at the extreme participant (left) end of the continuum. From this viewpoint Festinger's study and the study of the Geller phenomenon which we describe look very similar. Indeed Festinger's study is somewhat further to the 'left' than ours since in his case the researchers disguised themselves as natives whereas we were honest about our sociologist identities. To that extent we could be seen as less complete participants.

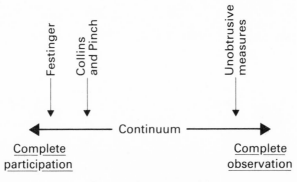

Old continuum model

On the other hand, from the viewpoint of the 'ideal-type-with compromises' model of participant observation the Festinger study lies at the extreme right-hand end since the researchers' disguises were so good that they were forced into making very few compromises indeed. They hardly disturbed the situation. This perspective makes the Festinger study almost indistinguishable from a study which used unobtrusive measures. Our study, on the other hand, is far to the left, quite unlike Festinger's. This difference is extreme in spite of the fact that our respective fieldwork locations were comparable — i.e. we spent a fair amount of time with groups whose native culture was not far removed from our own — Anglo-Saxon millennial cultists, and Anglo-Saxon scientists respectively.

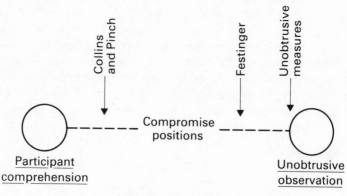

New ideal-type model

The fieldworker is rarely or never in the position to choose a method of research free of the constraints of time, money, social skills and linguistic resources. One advantage of the continuum model of participant observation is that it makes it possible to make a virtue out of the necessity of a forced choice. Any choice has a legitimate place on the range of possibilities presented by the continuum view. Each point on the continuum can be justified. The ideal-type model makes more apparent the nature of the compromises involved in most research decisions. It need not, thereby, sterilise research initiatives but should give answers to practical fieldwork problems while maintaining the visibility of the limitations of methods and consequent findings.[8]

Notes

1   For a recent, and very useful, account of methodological diversity in sociology see Halfpenny (1979). Halfpenny distinguishes four approaches to sociology, positivist, interpretivist, ethno-

methodological and structuralist. In this paper I am concerned only with the first two.

2   The term 'participant observation' is an 'oxymoron', as Tonkin (1979) points out. My paper may appear to favour 'participant comprehension' as an ideal, but this is probably because it is the aim which I adopted. The paper is intended to be symmetrical as regards the choice of philosophical presupposition.

3   See Friedrichs and Lutke (1975) for a positivist oriented account of participant observation. See Bruyn (1966) for a 'humanistic account'.

4   For a full account see Collins and Pinch (1982). Though I report my own fieldwork at some length, I am not here *recommending* its particular style to be adopted at the expense of other possibilities. I am only trying to clarify the issues. Few real studies will be able to locate themselves in any ideal field role. For a discussion of the necessary limitations on fieldwork see Collins, H.M., 'The Investigation of Meaning Frames in Science: Complementarity and Compromise' (1979).

5   I am aware of the point made by Gellner (1970) about over-charitable interpretations of native culture. That is why I say only that incoherence should be treated as a sign of investigator incompetence 'at least initially'.

6   Holy (1979) makes this latter point quite nicely.

7   It would be more correct to say that participant comprehension is no more replicable than unobtrusive observation, for neither are likely to be replicated in practice. Even in the hard sciences, replicability plays a very different role to that put forward within the conventional positivist/empiricist epistemology. (For replication in general, illustrated with an example from physics, see Collins, 1975. For replication in community studies, see Bell, 1975.)

8   For a *positive* use of methodological sensitivity of this type see Pinch (1981). He argues that responses of scientists to his questioning varied systematically according to their perception of him.

4

'It's great to have someone to talk to': the ethics and politics of interviewing women

Janet Finch

Janet Finch's chapter explores some of the ethical problems involved in interviewing women. Drawing on her own work in which she interviewed clergy wives, and mothers involved in playgroups, she looks at the development of trust in the interview situation, and the exploitative potential of this. As she points out, if you are a woman sociologist, reasonably skilled in the arts of qualitative research and semi-structured interviewing, it is the easiest thing in the world to get women to talk to you. While traditional methods textbooks encourage the development of rapport (while deploring any 'over-rapport'), there is little discussion, as Oakley (1981) and McRobbie (1982) have indicated, of the difficulties that can arise from this. Daniels (1967) in an illuminating discussion of the low-caste stranger in social research discusses one set of problems which can arise from the social relationships we have with those we interview. Janet Finch, in a rather different situation, discusses another. In the case of clergy wives, she was interviewing her peers; in the case of the playgroup mothers, women more powerless than she — an ambiguous situation as she rightly recognises. The mechanisms that relatively powerful individuals may be able to use when being researched discussed in Scott's chapter were not open

70

to Finch's playgroup respondents. As Sjoberg (1967, p. xii) suggests, the ethical dilemmas in this sort of situation cannot be achieved through the repetition of the formula 'I am objective'. What we must do is to examine the impact of ethical and political decisions on social research.

The issues which I discuss in this chapter have been raised by my own experience of doing social research of a qualitative variety. In particular, my experience of interviewing has raised a combination of methodological, personal, political and moral issues, upon which I find it necessary to reflect both as a sociologist and as a feminist. These issues have become focused by considering the extreme ease with which, in my experience, a woman researcher can elicit material from other women. That in turn raises ethical and political questions which I have found some difficulty in resolving. One reason for this difficulty is, I shall argue, that discussions of the 'ethics' of research are commonly conducted within a framework which is drawn from the public domain of men, and which I find at best unhelpful in relation to research with women.

I shall illustrate and discuss these issues by drawing upon two studies in which I was the sole researcher, and did all the interviewing myself. These are firstly, a study of clergymen's wives and their relationship to their husband's work, which was based on interviews with 95 women; secondly, a study of 48 women (mostly working class) who were running and using preschool playgroups.[1] In both cases, the interviews were arranged in advance. I contacted prospective interviewees initially by a letter which introduced myself and the research, then made an appointment to interview them in their homes at a pre-arranged time. All the interviews were tape recorded unless the interviewee requested otherwise, and were based on a list of questions to be covered during the interview, rather than upon a formal questionnaire. In the study of clergymen's wives, the interview was the first occasion on which we met. In the playgroup study, I had met some (but not all) of the interviewees during the preceding two years, when I had made observational visits to the playgroups themselves.

The woman-to-woman interview

Both the clergymen's wives and the playgroups studies were concerned entirely with women; in both I used qualitative techniques including in-depth interviewing; and in both I talked to women in their own homes about aspects of their lives which centrally defined their identities as women — marriage, motherhood and childrearing. My consciousness of the special character of a research situation in which women talk to another woman in an informal way, and about these issues, was heightened by reading Ann Oakley's (1981) discussion of interviewing women. Oakley takes the view that formal, survey-type interviewing is unsuited to the production of good sociological work on women. She prefers less-structured research strategies which avoid creating a hierarchical relationship between interviewer and interviewee. That sort of relationship, she argues, is inappropriate for a feminist doing research on women, because it means that we objectify our sisters.

I share Oakley's preference on both methodological and political grounds, and my own research has all been of the type which she recommends. I have also found, quite simply, that it works very well. Initially I was startled by the readiness with which women talked to me. Like every other researcher brought up on orthodox methodology textbooks, I expected to have to work at establishing something called rapport (Oakley, 1981). In my experience, such efforts are normally unnecessary when interviews are set up in the way I have described. Women are almost always enthusiastic about talking to a woman researcher, even if they have some initial anxieties about the purpose of the research or their own 'performance' in the interview situation. Their intentions are apparent, simply from the hospitality which one characteristically receives — an aspect of the research experience which Oakley (1981) notes is seldom mentioned in reports. In my study of clergymen's wives, I was offered tea or coffee, and sometimes meals, in all but two instances; the same happened in the majority of interviews in my playgroup study. One is, therefore, being welcomed into the interviewee's home as a guest, not merely tolerated as an inquisitor. This particular contrast was demonstrated to me in graphic form when I arrived at one interviewee's home during the playgroup study, only to find that she was already being interviewed by someone else. This seemed like the ultimate researcher's nightmare, but in the end proved very much to my advantage. The other interviewer was in fact a local authority housing visitor, who was ploughing her way through a formal questionnaire in a rather unconfident manner, using a format which required the respondent to read some questions from a card ('Do you receive any of the benefits listed on card G?', and so on). My presence during this procedure must have been rather unnerving for the housing visitor, but was most instructive for me. I recorded in my fieldnotes that the stilted and rather grudging answers which she received were in complete contrast with the relaxed discussion of some very private material which the same interviewee offered in her interview with me. My methodological preferences were certainly confirmed by this experience.

I claim no special personal qualities which make it peculiarly easy for me to get people to talk, but women whom I have interviewed often are surprised at the ease with which they do talk in the interview situation. One woman in my playgroup study (who told me that she was so chronically shy that when she had recently started a new job it had taken her a week to pluck up courage to ask how to find the toilet), said after her interview that she had surprised herself — it had not really felt, she said, as if she was talking to a stranger. Another woman in this study said that she found me an easy person to talk to and asked, 'Where did you get your easy manner — did you have to learn it or is it natural?' I quote these instances not to flaunt my imputed skills as an interviewer, but as instances which demonstrate a feeling which was very common among the women I interviewed in both studies — that they (often unexpectedly) had found this kind of interview a welcome experience, in

contrast with the lack of opportunities to talk about themselves in this way in other circumstances. Some variation on
the comment 'I've really enjoyed having someone to talk to'
was made at the end of many interviews.

How far does this experience simply reflect the effectiveness of in-depth interviewing styles *per se*, and how far is it
specific to women? It seems to me that there are grounds for
expecting that where a woman researcher is interviewing
other women, this is a situation with special characteristics
conducive to the easy flow of information. Firstly, women
mostly are more used than men to accepting intrusions
through questioning into the more private parts of their lives,
including during encounters in their own homes. Through
their experience of motherhood they are subject to questioning from doctors, midwives and health visitors; and also from
people such as housing visitors, insurance agents and social
workers, who deal principally with women as the people with
imputed responsibility for home and household. As subjects
of research, therefore, women are less likely than men to find
questions about their lives unusual and therefore inadmis-
sible. Secondly, in the setting of the interviewee's own home,
an interview conducted in an informal way by another
woman can easily take on the character of an intimate conversation. The interviewee feels quite comfortable with this
precisely because the interviewer is acting as a friendly guest,
not an official inquisitor; and the model is, in effect, an easy,
intimate relationship between two women.

Thirdly, the structural position of women, and in particular their consignment to the privatised, domestic sphere
(Stacey, 1981), makes it particularly likely that they will
welcome the opportunity to talk to a sympathetic listener.
The experience of loneliness was common to women in both
my studies. The isolation of women who are full-time housewives has been well documented by Dorothy Hobson, in a
study of women whose circumstances were very similar to
those in my playgroup study (Hobson, 1978, 1980). The
loneliness experienced by clergymen's wives is less obvious
at first sight, but in fact it has a very special character. Many
of them adopt a rule that they should have no friends in the
locality, for fear that they might harm their husband's work

by being seen as partisan (for discussion, see Finch, 1980). The consequences of this were described to me by one Methodist minister's wife as,

> I agree if it's going to hurt people, if it's going to harm her husband's ministry, it's better not to have friends nearby. But I think it's terribly difficult, because I think a woman needs a particular friend. I've always tried not to make particular friends but as I say, you can't help being drawn to sòme people. But as I say, I try not to show it. I never sit beside the same person in a meeting. I never visit one more than anybody else.

The friendly female interviewer, walking into this situation with time to listen and guarantees of confidentiality, not surprisingly finds it easy to get women to talk. In one instance, a clergyman himself thanked me for coming to interview his wife because, he said, *he* felt that she needed someone to talk to. It is not, however, only in the few cases where one is clearly being used as a social worker that women's need to talk is apparent. Almost all the women in my two studies seemed to lack opportunities to engage collectively with other women in ways which they would find supportive, and therefore they welcomed the opportunity to try to make sense of some of the contradictions in their lives in the presence of a sympathetic listener. There seems no reason to doubt that most women who similarly lack such opportunities will also find such an interview a welcome experience.

For these three reasons, the woman-to-woman interview (especially when conducted in the settings and in the ways I have described) does seem to me to be a special situation. This is not to say that men can never make good interviewers, although practice in research teams does suggest that research directors often regard women as especially suited to this task, as Scott points out in her chapter. Men, as social workers or as counsellors, for example, can be very effective in getting both women and men to talk about intimate aspects of their lives. But systematic comparisons of men and women interviewers, in a range of research situations, are not possible because we lack sufficient studies or accounts of the research process which consider the relationship of the gender of the interviewer to the research product. That is an interesting and important methodological issue; but my point about the special character of the woman-to-woman interview is as much political as methodological, and has particular reson- ance for any sociologist who is also a feminist. However effective a male interviewer might be at getting women inter- viewees to talk, there is still necessarily an additional dimen- sion when the interviewer is also a woman, because both parties share a subordinate structural position by virtue of their gender. This creates the possibility that a particular kind of identification will develop.

In my own research experience, I have often been aware of such an identification, as women interviewees have begun to talk about key areas of their lives in ways which denote a high level of trust in me, and indicate that they expect me to understand what they mean simply because I am another woman. One example taken from each of my studies — both concerning the interviewee's experience of marriage — should serve to illustrate this. The first extract comes from the inter- view with the wife of an Anglican clergyman, living in a huge and decaying vicarage, in a mill village on the Yorkshire moors:

> One big problem in being a clergy wife I feel is, at the odd time which happens in every marriage — and it hap- pens in clergy marriages as much as it happens outside — is that when you get the big bang in a marriage, when you get some sort of crisis, and I don't think a marriage ever gels until you've had a crisis in a marriage, where do you go for advice? If you're like me, you can't ask your mother because it's an admission of defeat that you have a problem — a big enough problem to seek advice on — in your marriage. You can't ask the vicar or the vicar's wife because you are, by definition, criticising his curate. You cannot ask the bishop or the archdeacon because, again, you are casting some sort of slight on one of his priests who cannot manage his own marriage. So who do you ask?
>
> I was very fortunate in that I knew the widow of a

clergyman who had no sort of direct tie with the church but had sort of been through the lot herself and could help me. I find this sort of person invaluable, but how many people manage to find her? Other than that, just who do you go to?

The second illustration is from the interview with a 24-year-old mother of two daughters under school age, living on a run-down council estate on the edge of an east Lancashire town,

> *Self*: I know that the children are sort of small at the moment, but do you ever have any sort of hopes or dreams about what they might do when they grow up?
> *Interviewee*: Yes, I'm always — Don't get married for a start. (To child) Not to get married, are you not! And have a career, with some money. And don't have a council house. Bet there's no such thing as council houses when they get older. But I don't want them to get married.
> *Self*: No.
> *Interviewee*: No but I don't, because I think once you get married and have kids, that's it. To a lot of women round here — when you see them walking past — big fat women with all their little kids running behind them. And I think, God. That's why I want to go to College and do something. But fellas don't see it like that, do they? Like, he thinks it's alright for me just going back to work in a factory for the rest of my life, you know. But I don't want that. (To child) You have a career, won't you? Prime Minister, eh?'

Comments of this kind — albeit very differently conceptualised and articulated — would not have been elicited in a formal questionnaire nor if I, as interviewer, had been attempting to maintain an unbiased and objective distance from the interviewees. Nor, I suggest, would they have been made in the same way to a male interviewer. Comments like 'fellas don't see it that way, do they?' and 'you can't ask your mother because it's an admission of defeat' indicate an identification between interviewer and interviewee which is gender specific.

That identification points to a facet of interviewing which I experienced strongly and consistently throughout these two studies: namely that the ease with which one can get women to talk in the interview situation depends not so much upon one's skills as an interviewer, nor upon one's expertise as a sociologist, but upon one's identity as a woman. In particular, I found that there was some unease in the interview situation if an interviewee was in some doubt about how to place me in relation to the crucial categories of marriage and motherhood. For example, during the three years when I was conducting the observational and interview phases of the playgroup study, I changed both my name and address. With several women who ran the playgroups, I noted some hesitation in their approach to me (comments like, 'You've moved, have you?') until I clarified that this was indeed because my marriage had ended. Other researchers have similarly reported that interviewees wanted to 'place' them as women with whom they could share experiences (Hobson, 1978; Oakley, 1981). Male interviewers of course may also be 'placed' (by their occupational or family status, for example). But again, being 'placed' as a woman has the additional dimension of shared structural position and personal identification which is, in my view, central to the special character of the woman-to-woman interview.

The basis of trust and its exploitative potential

From an entirely instrumental point of view as a researcher, there are of course great advantages to be gained from capitalising upon one's shared experiences as a woman. The consequences of doing so can be quite dramatic, as was illustrated to me in my study of clergymen's wives. As an anxious graduate student, I agonised over the question of whether I should reveal to my interviewees the crucial piece of information that I myself was (at that time) also married to a clergyman. Wishing to sustain some attempt at the textbook, 'unbiased' style of interviewing (which Ann Oakley, 1981, has so effectively exposed for the sham it always was), I initially merely introduced myself as a researcher. I found however, that before I arrived for the interview, some people had managed to deduce my 'true' identity. The effects of this unmasking so clearly improved the experience for all concerned that I rapidly took a decision to come clean at the beginning of each interview. The consequence was that interviewees who had met me at the front door requesting assurances that I was not going to sell their story to a Sunday newspaper, or write to the bishop about them, became warm and eager to talk to me after the simple discovery that I was one of them. Suspicious questions about why on earth anyone should be interested in doing a study of clergymen's wives were regarded as fully answered by that simple piece of information. My motives, apparently, had been explained. I rapidly found this a much simpler strategy than attempts to explain how intellectually fascinating I found their situation. The result of course was that they talked to me as another clergyman's wife, and often they were implicitly comparing their own situation with mine. The older women especially made remarks such as 'possibly you haven't come across this yet' or 'of course I suppose it's a bit different for you younger ones now'. The general tone of these interviews often made me feel that I was being treated as a trainee clergyman's wife, being offered both candid comment and wise advice for my own future benefit. In several cases, the relationship was reinforced by gifts given to me at the end, and I became quite good at predicting those interviews where the spoils were likely to include a chocolate cake or a home-grown cabbage as well as the tapes and fieldnotes.

One's identity as a woman therefore provides the entrée into the interview situation. This obviously was true for me in a rather special way in my study of clergy wives, but that does not mean that only interviewers whose life circumstances are exactly the same as their interviewees can conduct successful interviews. It does mean, however, that the interviewer has to be prepared to expose herself to being 'placed' as a woman and to establish that she is willing to be treated accordingly. In the case of my playgroup study, my life situation was rather different from my interviewees': I did not have young children, and by the end of the study I was not married either. However, this seemed no real barrier to encouraging women to talk freely in the interviews. In the previous two years, through my visits to the playgroups, I had already established myself as a figure on their social scene, and they had taken the opportunity to make key identifications of me as a woman. Once these identifications are made, it does indeed seem the easiest thing in the world to get women to talk to you.

The moral dilemmas which I have experienced in relation to the use of the data thus created have emerged precisely because the situation of a woman interviewing women *is* special, and is easy only because my identity as a woman makes it so. I have, in other words, traded on that identity. I have also emerged from interviews with the feeling that my interviewees need to know how to protect themselves from people like me. They have often revealed very private parts of their lives in return for what must be, in the last resort, very flimsy guarantees of confidentiality: my verbal assurances that the material would be seen in full only by me and the person transcribing the tapes, and that I would make any public references to them anonymous and disguised. These assurances were given some apparent weight, I suppose, through my association with the university whose notepaper I used to introduce myself. There were, in fact, quite marked differences in the extent to which my various interviewees requested such guarantees. None of the working-class women in my playgroup study asked for them, although one or two of the women in my middle-class comparison playgroup did so. A number of clergymen's wives asked careful questions before the interview, but I found that they were easily reassured, usually by the revelation that I too was a clergyman's wife, rather than by anything I might have tried to indicate about the professional ethics of a sociologist. With them, as with the women in the playgroup study, it was principally my status and demeanour as a woman, rather than anything to do with the research process, upon which they based their trust in me. I feel certain that *any* friendly woman could offer these assurances and readily be believed.

There is therefore a real exploitative potential in the easily established trust between women, which makes women especially vulnerable as subjects of research. The effectiveness of in-depth interviewing techniques when used by women researchers to study other women is undoubtedly a great asset in creating sociological knowledge which encompasses and expresses the experiences of women (Oakley, 1981). But the very effectiveness of these techniques leaves women open to exploitation of various kinds through the research process. That exploitation is not simply that these techniques can be used by other than *bona fide* researchers: but it is an ever-present possibility for the most serious and morally upright of researchers, feminists included. It seems to me that the crux of this exploitative potential lies in the relationship established between interviewer and interviewee. I would agree with Oakley that the only morally defensible way for a feminist to conduct research with women is through a non-hierarchical relationship in which she is prepared to invest some of her own identity. However, the approach to research − and particularly to interviewing − which this requires can easily be broken down into a set of 'techniques', which can then be divorced from the moral basis in feminism which Oakley adopts. These techniques can be used to great effect to solicit a range of information (some of it very private), which is capable of being used ultimately against the interests of those women who gave it so freely to another woman with whom they found it easy to talk. The prospects for doing that clearly are magnified when (as is so often the case) women interviewers are not themselves the people who will handle and use the data they have created. In those circumstances, women interviewers and research assistants may find that the material which they have created is taken out of their control, and used in ways of which they do not approve and which seem to them to be against the interests of the women whom they interviewed. I have never been in that situation, but I have found that the issues are by no means avoided in research settings such as I have experienced, where I was both interviewer and sole researcher.

Ethics, morals and politics in research

Moral dilemmas of the kind to which I allude are commonly
discussed in research textbooks under the heading of 'ethics'.
These debates have been well summarised by Barnes (1979).
They are formulated in terms of the rights to privacy and
protection of those being researched, which are sometimes
thought to be assured by adherence to a code of professional
ethics. So, are the moral dilemmas raised when women interview women to be resolved by a greater sensitivity to women's
right to privacy? Or perhaps a special code of ethics for
feminists to adopt if they choose? I think not. I find the
terms in which these debates about ethics are constituted
unhelpful in relation to women, and it is instructive that the
issue of gender is rarely mentioned. Barnes's own discussion
conceptualises it as an issue of the rights of the 'citizens' —
certainly an advance upon the term 'subject' or even 'respondent' for the people being researched. None the less, 'citizen'
is a concept drawn from the public domain of men, in
particular from the political arena, from which women have
always been excluded (Stacey and Price, 1980), and it implies
a framework of formalised rights and obligations, along with
procedures of legal redress. Women are unlikely to feel comfortable with such procedures, and do not necessarily have
access to them. Barnes is, however, reflecting the essentially
male paradigms in which most debates about 'ethics' are
conducted. For example, most such discussions tend to focus
upon the point of access or of data collection rather than
upon the use of the material. These discussions implicitly
assume that research 'citizens' can *anticipate* potentially
harmful uses to which such data can be put, and take action
accordingly. Most women are unlikely to be in a position
where they can anticipate the outcome of research in this
way, since they have little access to the public domain
within which the activity of research can be contextualised.
When discussing ethical issues about the use of research data,
Barnes argues that the tension is between, on the one hand,
the desire of citizens to protect their own interests in the
short term, and, on the other hand, the long-term interests
of sustaining informed criticism in a democratic society,

which suggest that the results of research should be published whatever they are. Presumably few male research subjects are wildly enthusiastic about having their short-term interests sacrificed to this latter aim, but women are especially vulnerable. The 'democratic society' where this critical discourse is conducted is of course the public domain of men, where the 'debate' is largely conducted *by* men, in their own terms. As Hanmer and Leonard point out in their chapter, the specific interests of women are unlikely to be voiced there and therefore little protection is available to women once the outcome of research has entered the public 'debate' at that level. The sociologist who produces work about women, therefore, has a special responsibility to anticipate whether it could be interpreted and used in ways quite different from her own intentions (an issue discussed in Platt's and Roberts's chapters).

This highlights a point which is often overlooked in discussions of research ethics, but which is crucial to a feminist doing research on women: namely that collective, not merely individual, interests are at stake. The latter may be relatively easily secured with guarantees of confidentiality, anonymity, codes of ethics and so on. It is far more difficult to devise ways of ensuring that information given so readily in interviews will not be used ultimately against the collective interests of women.

In both my playgroups and clergymen's wives studies, I was very aware that aspects of my data could be discussed in such a way as potentially to undermine the interests of wives and mothers generally, if not necessarily the specific people I had researched in a direct way. For example, many clergy wives expressed satisfaction and contentment in living lives centred around their husband and his work (in which they essentially acted as his unpaid assistants). This could be used to argue that *most* women would be much happier if only they would accept subordinate and supportive positions instead of trying to establish greater independence from their husbands. My developing commitment as a feminist made me very unwilling to see my work used to support such a conclusion. Similarly, in my playgroup study, the character of the playgroups which I was studying certainly was in most cases wildly divergent from bourgeois standards of childcare and pre-school developmental practice. This evidence, I feared, could be used to reinforce the view that working-class women are inadequate and incompetent child rearers. Again, I felt that I was not willing to have my work used to heap further insults upon women whose circumstances were far less privileged than my own, and indeed for a while, I felt quite unable to write *anything* about this aspect of the playgroup study.

In both cases, my commitments as a feminist raised moral questions for my work as a sociologist. In both cases, however, the consequences were that I was pressed into looking more carefully at my data, into thinking through the dilemmas I had raised for myself as intellectual as well as moral issues, and into contextualising my problem in ways which I might not otherwise have done. In both cases, I eventually resolved the moral issues sufficiently to be able to write about these studies.[2] Briefly, in the case of the clergymen's wives, I found that I had to look more closely at the structural position in which these women were placed, and to make a clear distinction between structural position and women's own experience of it. This enabled me to see that evidence of women successfully accommodating to various structural features of their lives in no way alters the essentially exploitative character of the structures in which they are located. In the case of the playgroups study, I eventually saw that I should really be taking more account of the culture and character of the formal educational system, for which the playgroups were intended (in the eyes of the mothers who used them) as a preparation. Rather than focusing on the apparent inadequacies of the groups run by working-class women, I needed to locate the disjuncture between playgroups and schools as part of the continuing cultural imperialism of bourgeois practices within formal schooling itself. In neither case would I claim to have found perfect solutions to the dilemmas which my own work raised for me. But, given that the period covered by these studies was also a period when my own commitment to feminism was developing, partly as a result of radical changes in my own life, they were quite simply the best solutions I could manage at the time. I am also certain that in the process, I was producing better sociology.

The dilemmas which I have encountered therefore raise the possibility of betrayal of the trust which women have placed in me when I interviewed them. I do not really mean 'betrayal' in the individual sense, such as selling the story of someone else's life to a Sunday newspaper. I mean, rather, 'betrayal' in an indirect and collective sense, that is, undermining the interests of women in general by my use of the material given to me by my interviewees. It is betrayal none the less, because the basis upon which the information has been given is the trust placed in one woman by another. In such a situation, I find sanitised, intellectual discussions about 'ethics' fairly irrelevant. I have preferred to call my dilemmas 'moral' ones, but in fact they are also, it seems to me, inherently political in character. They raise the 'whose side are we on?' question in a particular form which relates to gender divisions and to the study of women in that context.

It has become commonplace in discussions of research ethics to distinguish between research on powerless social groups (where rights to privacy, protection, and so on, are of great importance) and research on the powerful, where such considerations can be suspended, on the grounds that the groups concerned already have enough privileges or are well able to protect themselves, or have exposed themselves to legitimate scrutiny by standing for public office (Barnes, 1979; Bulmer, 1982). If one takes the view that the powerful are fair game for the researcher, then the issues of gender inevitably must be raised: in a patriarchal society, women are always relatively powerless. Women, therefore, with perhaps very few exceptions, can never be regarded as fair game. Further, precisely because issues of power are central to gender relations, one cannot treat moral questions about research on women as if they were sanitised 'ethical issues', divorced from the context which makes them essentially political questions.

A feminist sociologist of course will be 'on the side' of the women she studies. This stance is entirely consistent with major traditions in sociological research, in which — as has been acknowledged from Becker onwards — the sociologist sides with the underdog (sic.) (Becker, 1967; Gouldner, 1973;

Barnes, 1979). One essential difference, however, is that a feminist sociologist doing research on women actually shares the powerless position of those she researches, and this is often demonstrated in the research context itself, for example through the under-representation of women in the institution which sponsors the research, and their location often at the most junior levels in her department, her section, or the research team. This experience of shared powerlessness between researchers and researched is seldom paralleled for men unless they are, for example, black sociologists doing work on race, or disabled sociologists researching disability. Siding with the people one researches inevitably means an emotional as well as an intellectual commitment to promoting their interests. How else can one justify having taken from them the very private information which many have given so readily? I find rather unconvincing an argument which says that I should be content with having added to the stock of scientific knowledge. Rather, I would endorse Oakley's position that, as a feminist and a sociologist, one should be creating a sociology *for* women — that is a sociology which articulates women's experiences of their lives — rather than merely creating data for oneself as researcher (Oakley, 1981). How far this has been accomplished is the criterion which I would apply to my own sociological work on women, and to that of other people. This seems to me a more fruitful way to address the moral and political dilemmas I have identified than, for example, writing a separate code of ethics for feminists to follow.

This moral and political position which I (and other feminist researchers) have adopted may provoke the charge that we are not serious sociologists, but merely using our work to promote our politics. Our credibility may be questioned by those who see feminist (and indeed similar) commitments as incompatible with good academic work. Helen Roberts already has produced a convincing answer to such charges, showing that a commitment to taking people's experiences seriously *is* essentially a political activity but is not peculiar to feminist sociologists, nor do we become less professional or rigorous as a result (Roberts, 1981a). Indeed, it seems clear to me that *all* social science knowledge is intrinsically political in character (Bell and Newby, 1977), and is undertaken from a standpoint which embodies some material interests, whatever the claims of the researcher. As Maureen Cain and I have argued elsewhere, this does not mean that the knowledge we produce cannot be evaluated and appraised by others. Indeed, recognising the intrinsically political nature of both theory and data means that the sociologist has a great responsibility to be open and scholarly about her procedures and her conclusions (Cain and Finch, 1981). It does mean, however, that sociologists who are also feminists need not be defensive about the relationships of our political commitments to our work, nor embarrassed when we resolve the moral dilemmas which it raises by frankly political stances. In so doing, I would argue, not only do we avoid compromising our feminism, but we are likely to produce more scholarly and more incisive sociology.

Notes

1   The study of clergymen's wives was undertaken for my PhD, partly funded by an SSRC studentship. The fieldwork was undertaken mainly in West Yorkshire between 1971 and 1973, and covered wives of ministers in four denominations. An account of the study and my conclusions can be found in Spedding (1975) and Finch (1980). The playgroup study was funded by an SSRC grant, and was conducted in Lancashire between 1978 and 1980. It was a study, based on two years' observation followed by interviews, of five self-help playgroups, four of which were in inner urban areas or on council estates, and the fifth was a comparison group in a middle-class suburb. An account of this study can be found in Finch (1981, 1983b, 1983c).

2   Discussion of the points referred to briefly here can be found in Finch (1980, 1983a, 1983c) for issues arising from the clergymen's wives study; and Finch (1981, 1983b) in relation to working class women and preschool playgroups.

5

Incidence or incidents: political and methodological underpinnings of a health research process in a small Italian town

Ronald Frankenberg

This chapter seeks to explore by example how methods of social research and intended methods of political action are related. Frankenberg argues that a concern for subjective meaning has to be combined with a concern for social process and that both may be shown through the use of a direct observational 'dramatic incident' approach. These themes are expounded through the discussion of the in-the-field planning of a medical sociology/anthropology research project currently in progress in a small community in Italy. It seeks to provide a critique of the value and limitations of a survey/questionnaire epidemiological 'target' approach without totally rejecting it. It explores the possibility in the specific environment of a small Italian town of combining reformist interests of administrators and a necessary cultural focus on the family and the state with a consciousness raising (for both investigators and investigated) marxist and/or feminist critique.

Public/private: incidence/incidents

It is now commonplace that the data produced by research is

88

a function of the problems posed and the methods used. Contributors to this volume are committed to helping to change fundamentally the social processes of private and public life. To bring about such a change itself requires methods of political and social action. This chapter seeks to illuminate the relationship between methods of research and methods of action.

Elsewhere in this volume, Hilary Graham suggests, correctly in my view, that 'male' social surveys represent power, and the rendering of the social, individual. They miss the point and meaning of women's lives. I want to put the argument in a different way. Surveys at least in isolation miss the point of everyone's life. It has taken the determination of women to understand and change their own lives to make this apparent to sociologists. They have begun in a more constructive way than mere phenomenological critiques to drive sociology back to a concern with meaning *and* process of classical empirical writers like Thomas and Znaniecki (1918). (They made good use of émigré's letters to their mothers!)

Much British social anthropology never lost this concern (Frankenberg, 1982) and the Ardeners' apparent feminism referred to by Graham arises from their consistency as anthropologists more than from any political commitment.

Public structures are in fact always lived through private processes, for men as well as for women; for managers as well as for workers; for doctors as well as for patients. The research contribution is not to tell women their lives are miserable, workers their production is alienated or patients that their sickness is poorly treated. This is merely impertinent in both senses. Successful research and politics makes clear the connection between the private experience and the collective reality. Women, workers or patients can then act collectively to change their situations. This outcome was not the aim of the great reformers of the past. From Chadwick through Sidney and Beatrice Webb to Goldthorpe and Halsey they were concerned with reform by fiat. They sought to let the governing class know what was going on (or themselves to become the governing class) in the hopes, not always forlorn, that the rulers would then see the necessity for change. This could be a holding operation against more

dangerous realities such as self-understanding and a struggle
for autonomy. For such reformers from above the social
survey is ideal; it raises hopes but not consciousness. At its
worst it does no harm; those subjected to it may never hear
nor see their aggregated individual responses. At its best it
achieves reform which may be welcome even if objectively
inadequate. And at its very best and given the right conditions and theory it may make possible the exposure of the
contradictions that lead to revolutionary change (Marx and
the Blue Books, Lenin and the Zemstvo statistics, modern
Italian feminists and the labour market, Women's Aid Federation of England (WAFE) and the proposed survey on male
violence). Independent of investigators of all kinds, there
are always moments, even whole periods, when the opaque-
ness of social connections becomes transparent. These are
moments of dramatic intensity; the strike, the riot, the
sit-in, the eviction/squat, the battered woman alongside
Women's Aid experiencing the near impossibility of individual solution, the social experience of childbirth, the recol-
lected drama in the surgery of patients' stories (Stimson and
Webb, 1975). These, rather than the carefully posed interview, are the ideal stuff of social research. Even they, however, do not allow us to apply solutions but merely to participate in the process by which people in groups find their
own. Nor should we suppose that each research project let
alone each research act can always and in isolation have
immediate effect.

An Italian research project

A method based on observing and participating in such
dramas is easier to apply in some societies and social situations than in others. Turner (1969, 1981) shows how sickness in one area of Zambia, especially amongst women,
is dramatised through ritual, spirit-possession ceremonies
and what he calls cults of affliction. This dramatisation
enables the sufferer to see sickness as a social as well as
an individual problem. It also enables the observer from

outside and eventually from within to see something of the distribution of power between categories of person classified by age and gender, origin and occupation. Others with more or less radical intent (Lewis, 1971; Young, 1976) have generalised these findings to illuminate the processes of subjection of women in a way not possible to the survey (Boserup, 1970; Little, 1974). Similarly, while surveys of differential wages and work experience begin to reveal the structure of gender relations, only studies like Whitehead's (1976) painful pub participation make transparent the processual relationships needing to be changed.

In 1982 I was awarded an SSRC grant on the recommendation of the then existing Social Anthropology Committee to study the dramatisation of sickness in a part of industrialised semi-rural Italy. The object was to give empirical substance in a European context to my concern to map some of the differences in the nature of dramatic incidents in different societies. The details of these general arguments are set out elsewhere (Frankenberg, 1982; Young, 1982). Here I summarise. In 'pre-capitalist' Africa, even in peripheral Lusaka, the cast of the ritual drama of sickness can be assembled in one place at one time. The healer can and does orchestrate technical/biological, social and individual elements. The sufferer recapitulates publicly and symbolically what she has learned in a lifetime about the social significance of sickness, about the relationships of generations and of affines and about the position of women in society. The recapitulation reinforces, at the same time as it opens to question, what has been learned. In more fragmented industrial capitalist society the moment of consultation is privatised yet relatively impersonal. One speaks of going to see the doctor rather than a named person. A medical visit is furthermore just one incident in a very long play which may have started in childhood. It includes not only oral tradition (Stimson and Webb, 1975; Falassi, 1980) but also the specialised glossy health magazine, the women's journal quiz (the individualised, individual survey *par excellence*), the televised images of *Dr Kildare, General Hospital, MASH, Emergency Ward 10, Angels*, etc. It is related to experience of work, work-risk and injury, authority and power. Unlike the traditional healer, the hospital doctor, primary health care physician and even nurse may not be aware that there is a set of experiences to be orchestrated. Their biological training may have deprived them of the ability to perceive, the desire to act and the skills to do so.

The research problem is to bring out the complexity of the relationships brought to therapeutic encounters and to reveal their importance for the individual and for society. This is also the political problem and it most often has to be resolved in a research or political situation in which different actors have different aims and different degrees of consciousness. Nor can it be assumed that the researcher's consciousness is superior (see Hanmer and Leonard in this volume). For these reasons I am currently engaged in the early field stages of a research project in a small (6,216 inhabitants) Italian town. It is officially an eighteen-month project and I write in the sixth month. As we all know such time scales are unrealistic. I planned my part at least for another eighteen months before and it will not be finished for me, my collaborators or the townspeople when a final report is filed at SSRC. It may not develop at all in the way I presently intend and foresee. It is being done in loose association with a local health unit (USL) and a team within it of an administrator, a medically qualified health educator, a former nurse and a sociologist. I am conscious of several reasons for choosing this particular town.

It is the chief town of a comune (local authority) which is one of the six comunes which make up one Unita Sanitaria Locale of a Province (Firenze) of the Tuscan Regione. It is in the red belt which is ruled at regional, provincial and communal level by left coalitions dominated by the Communist Party (PCI). I expected to find local leaders sympathetic and I was not disappointed. The time is in many senses ripe. It happened to be more or less convenient for four life projects, namely mine, Pauline Hunt's, our pre-school son and an unborn child, condemned to be a participant observer of Italian maternity services. (In the (dramatic) event, Rebecca Frankenberg made a suitably marginal observer's entrance into Italian society. Reflecting the midwives' uncertainties as to the desirability of home as against hospital delivery, she was born in a car on a motorway verge halfway between the two. She challenged with her first breaths the hospital's classification of places of birth as home, hospital or ambulance and the *Anagrafe's* of private address in comune or hospital in Florence. Her clinical case notes — 'born in ambulance' — and her birth certificate will thus for their lifetimes reinforce her parents' scepticism about the reliability of official records as research data.)

It is three years since the formal inception of the Italian Health Service and is seen as a time to take stock. There are already published evaluations from left and right (Berlinguer, 1982; Gruppi Parliamentari, DC, 1982.) There has been a regional stocktaking three-day school of political directors of USL and recently the PCI announced that it was conducting two regional surveys by questionnaire (!) one of a sample of the population and the other of a sample of health workers. The local USL with which I work has its own action research programme as a guide to what it ought to be doing and saying. The administrators, political and technical, are genuinely committed to bringing about fundamental change. They are, however, like myself and other contributors to this book constrained by structures; occupational, national/cultural and political/administrative. One reason for my easy access to and involvement in this particular local health unit is the presence within it as part-time workers of an English married couple resident in Italy — a retired GP and a former practice nurse. They have always seen it as part of their role to encourage outside, relatively short-term, research workers. They did not suggest the current project but they have sustained it in various ways. They have on several occasions in the past been able to crystallise trends of thought into action by bringing in outside, expert support at a crucial moment.

The state, democracy and the family

The conscious aims of the USL personnel are an efficient and democratic health service within the appropriate laws. By efficient they mean responding to the needs of the people on the ground in the comune. Democracy and legality as concepts carry more popular weight in Italy than in Britain for historical reasons which are complex. (The Socialist Party claims to be the party of Garibaldi; most of the Communist Party would prefer not to be the party of Stalin; the Catholic right fears the ghost of Mussolini; the laws are the modified code of Napoleon; the eponymous past hangs heavy!)

The older leaders of the PCI have personal memories of the anti-fascist struggle in the countryside. The Italian state machine still works on Christian Democrat (DC) patronage. An unholy alliance of interlocking gangsters, terrorists and wildcat capitalists continuously, violently and through plots threatens political stability. Italian revolutionaries of every shade recognise the importance of the battlefield as well as of the battle. In Italy, if I say I want to help in changing power relations within the health service, it is immediately clear that I am supporting the (democratic) state. I do not think researchers in England are as aware of having taken such a stand. In Italy there are also counter-examples of social scientists and others who consciously choose totally to reject the state in both their professional and their private lives. Giovanni Senzani, criminologist/ sociologist from Florence, is awaiting trial as the theoretical strategist and practical tactician of one wing of the Red Brigade. Aldo Semerari, criminologist/anthropologist, was decapitated allegedly on the orders of perhaps the only woman Camorra underworld boss, Puppetta Maresca, for being too helpful to her rival Raffaele Cutolo. Some Italian feminists challenged the view I am adopting in a different way when they boycotted demonstrations in favour of continuing legal abortion. They did this on the grounds that to support legal abortion was to support the right of the state to say what happened to women's bodies.

The nature of the local state in Italy is also crucial. The comune (while like all local governments under financial control and constraint from the centre) has considerable power over local citizens. It really matters who controls the comune, who controls the province and who controls the regione. Left coalitions have made real progress and faced real problems in attempting to use local control to counter national impotence (Pridham, 1981). Tuscan USL administrators, unlike US radicals and many UK community activists, think of democracy as working alongside the comune, not against it from below. At another level nothing in the social reality of central Italy leads them to question the family as the health action unit, both acting and acted upon. In this particular area of Tuscany the productive role of the family as a whole is very evident. Each afternoon the old and middle-aged women of the town sit in their garages, on their balconies or at the windows of their sitting rooms sewing the uppers of shoes, finishing jeans, stitching, packing and boxing the products of small or middle sized, artisan or petty capitalist production. Boys help their fathers in carpenters', ironworkers' or leatherworkers' shops and daughters-in-law serve customers while their husbands and fathers and brothers bake the bread, carve the wood or care for the barrels of oil and wine in the rear. Mezzadria (a form of sharecropping) was finally ended by law only on 1 May this year. Within the last ten or fifteen years most inhabitants of the town will have worked within or alongside a system where size of family could be a crucial determinant on whether or not an annual mezzadria contract would be renewed (Da Cecco, personal communication; De Martin, 1982).

Massimo Paci (1982), Laura Balbo (1979) and others have shown how crucial is family support to even partial success of the welfare state. This is especially true in Italy and in its central regions.

In the general context I have described, what research is possible, feasible, useful and likely to happen? As elsewhere, while the central state may control through education and other means the supply of researchers, it can exert little effective direct control even when most hostile. Social research does not in any case need to be prevented. It can merely be ignored or distorted. As in Britain, newspapers and parliamentarians can seek to ridicule, and ministers to cut funds and destroy institutions, but direct censorship is hard to apply. In Italy, as in the United States, local autonomy may be a powerful weapon in the hands of central power. Thus in structurally determined battles between regional and national statistical bodies, one formal weapon in the hands of the latter is paradoxically the control of demographic data by the comune. We were delayed in starting our research because the university statistician who had access to the census tapes could only let us use them when he had received permission from each of the six individual comunes concerned.

Social surveys and epidemiological targets

Social surveys are a familiar part of local and national culture. One television journal for a time published weekly surveys telling readers who, by age, sex and social class, in which region, likes which singer and wants what changes in national and local TV. The comune itself has just published a book based on a survey of workers carried out by a local communist as part of his degree requirements (De Martin, 1982). The PCI carried out a national random sample survey on people's attitudes to terrorism. Direct observation of people's lives and biographies is, however, only usually considered interesting for the well known — 'i big' in colloquial Italian. Similarly the conventional wisdom of service-oriented epidemiological research is the health indicator survey. This suits the bureaucratic requirements of international organisations for comparable data on member states. An Italian regione also has officials who feel stronger if they can say to those of other regiones we differ from you objectively in various ways. Thus the USL had urged upon it the use of an EEC pro-forma and the choice of producing data which were comparable but not useful or useful but not comparable. They chose the latter. It was this decision which made our choice of starting point the identification of target syndromes (McCarthy cyclostyled, 1982.) McCarthy suggests for British Health Authorities ten such targets namely: coronary heart disease, lung cancer, disability requiring hospitalisation of the elderly, low birthweight, child accidents, bad teeth, minor surgery, delay in provision of abortion, mental handicap and mental health. He suggests that the adoption of such targets would shift emphasis from administration (as the source of problems to be overcome) to the epidemiological reality. He concludes (p. 15):

> These ten targets cover several common medical concerns. Improvements in outcome will depend on changes in medical practice and the distribution of resources. There are broadly two themes of practice arising from the targets. The first six require doctors to concern themselves with prevention, whereas the latter four show that efficiency is also important.
>
> Each target is in a medical subject area using substantial resources. To initiate improvements in the targets, the Health Authority might assess current practices and discuss these with clinicians. It may be that clinicians suggest alternative targets, which can be judged according to their relevance and practicability. Change will be faster if clinicians are closely involved in achieving the targets for themselves: ready feedback of relevant statistics will assist this process.

Britain has District Health *Authorities* whereas Italy has Local Health *Units*, the authority lies elsewhere. McCarthy is clearly asking that the authority is used but that the co-operation of clinicians be sought so that at least they do not use their countervailing powers of autonomy and abstention. The targets are objects, the Chinese might call them the Six Diseases and the Four Inefficiencies. It is a doctor's view, the patients as active subjects are absent.

From our viewpoint in Chianti this view needed sociological expansion to overcome the lack of social relations and what seemed to us an implied assumption that people themselves, even as individuals, did nothing about their own ills save to consult the appropriate expert. We sought therefore to identify different social situations in which different people (women and men, single and married, old and young, 'barren or dwelling in their houses the joyful mothers of children') met and coped with suffering and difficulty. So sensitised, we could then seek to get them to tell us when, in what circumstances and from whom they felt they needed help and did not get it. This exercise involved us not merely in asking questions and listening to the answers of people on their own but also in groups. Such groups obviously cover health workers including clinicians, trade unions in general, groups of women (there are no women's groups), young people, and members of the political parties, the church and of voluntary organisations like the Misericordia. This last provides the only ambulance service and the only collection of blood donations. The major grouping, however, remains the more or less extended family.

The fact that we are critical of the division of sex roles and the disastrous effect of marriage/motherhood ideology on the autonomy of young Italian women and on the behaviour of Italian men of *all* ages cannot wish away the family's crucial role in protecting and meeting the difficulties of male and female wage workers. This is especially true of those who in the expressive Italian terms have jobs as 'precarii', with short-term security, and 'pendolari', commuters to local towns. Again it is only the family which makes possible the escape route from precariosità and pendolarità provided for a large minority of local inhabitants by small-scale artisan enterprise. As the terms of discourse of the successful struggles for abortion, contraception and divorce show (Caldwell, 1982), the distinction between Catholic ideology of the idyllic family unit — working, praying and playing together, protecting each other from the gross immoralities of a materialist world — and a marxist and/or feminist perspective of understanding the family in order to transcend it, is not easy to make in practical terms. We hope not to fall into facile reformist Bethnalgreenism and urge the kind of argument that because housing and home depend on mum in the inner city, so the local authority should see that they can do so in the suburb or housing estate.

Investigation: social or individual

We did not see it as enough just to move wholly or partially from individual to group as the subjects of our enquiry (providers of our information). We felt it necessary also to theorise the nature of intervention.

Often even social and preventive medicine is seen in individualised terms and medical or non-medical interventions by state and non-state agencies, by kin and non-kin are conceptually collapsed one into another. We wished to recognise that different social processes are generated by different types of intervention by various agencies of differential degrees of sociality. This can be illustrated from the interventions surrounding pregnancy, labour, birth and early infancy.

As seen by clinicians, the individual's problems in this area are the possibility of genetic handicap, low birthweight, neonatal, perinatal and maternal mortality and family spacing. These can be seen as social problems subject to planned prevention in the community through the creation of a favourable social environment. This in turn can be seen either as something given from above or fought for and won from below. Or in a stricter sense, they can be seen as individual problems soluble by personalised clinical intervention by tests, analyses, examinations, abortion, and individual contraceptive advice. Here, as Tudor Hart (1971), Black (1980), and Townsend and Davidson (1982) have pointed out, the presence or absence of personalised clinical intervention is itself not independent of other social realities. Quite specifically some individual interventions are only made possible by earlier social struggles in which physicians and other health workers played a minor part. There is, however, a tendency to see health like British parliamentary socialism — a short period of intense struggle in which all are involved and none is authoritarian expert, followed by a long period in which the experts re-establish control and act on the passive, powerless patient.

The family: a suitable unit for study?

The medical provision by the state of classes, clinics, advice centres, domestic and central obstetric and contraceptive services and the social welfare provision of help with problems arising, for example, from migration or commuting treat the problems as social. This is an advance, because it provides the arena for action dialogue which creates the possibility of more and explicitly social provision. This in turn opens the chance of a shift in the nature of non-state, non-medical intervention from familial to something more. The social environment of the extended family, with its emphasis on male power and the desirability of male children, backed by the church, and perpetuated by advice, economic and housing and ideological control by senior generations, may be modified or changed by the group of pregnant peers. Shared social experience at clinic and exercise class may lead not only to changed attitudes but to new forms of social organisation. In so far as family and clinical ideology are reactionary and mutually reinforcing they can thus be undermined not by frontal attack but by perceived increasing irrelevance.

The individual and clinical approach, on the other hand, enhances the importance and power of the ideological set, especially since the very process and logistics of individual consultation is preceded and carried out by family discussion, organisation and fund-raising. It is this kind of dynamic of personal politics which is overlooked by analyses like Stark's (1982) stark contrast of radical and materialist approaches. Even in this area, however, the survey which was the starting point of USL concern has not become entirely irrelevant. Birth rates, infant mortality, maternal death rates, monthly and annual birth rates and stillbirth rates, population change, family size, and accidents in the home are still statistics needed to plan and shape services and to defend them from political enemies. The information required is no longer dictated by the administrative considerations decried or the clinical requirements decreed by McCarthy but by an understanding of, and sensitivity to, social process.

The stratified sample originally proposed for the health status survey is still useful, but will now be supplemented both by the group interviews already mentioned and by more informal dialogue discussion in depth with the families in it. In this way we intend to get a picture of biographical experience both in terms of life cycle and crucial personal experience and to try to understand what the survey and its questions meant to those subjected to it. This is made easier by living in the community, using its services and observing its dramas and their impact. I have here illustrated our thinking by outlining our approach to the social processes surrounding pregnancy and birth. We have treated other phases in the life cycle and life events in a similar way. We have literally charted theoretical approaches to experiences shared by virtually all (school, adolescence, work, marriage, middle and old age,) and others specific to only some (chronic illness, migration, shift from country to town). We have paid attention to those negative experiences which involve the individual in social processes of sociological and potentially health relevance — not moving from country to town, not marrying, not being heterosexual, not having children and even, in Italy, not taking a holiday in August.

As I have argued above, to understand individual life-cycle crises in their full social significance they need to be seen as scenes within a play within a cycle, within in fact the dramatic expressions of the whole social setting — the public conflict, the demonstration, the council meeting, confrontations, formal and informal. The officials of the USL, and especially its president, do in fact appear on many such occasions, but only daily living in the community enables moments of drama to be seen in their context. This context is often determined by socially based differential perception of time and space. At one local Festa de l'Unita (a seven-day festival in the village square devoted to raising social and cultural support for the communist press, see Pridham, 1981, for wider political significance) in a remote village an evening debate on the health reform was included. The major topics raised by the people to their mayor and the president of the USL were the shortage of water, the lack of public transport and the neglect of local roads which it was said made courting, visiting patients in the local hospital and getting cervical smears highly hazardous procedures. For the USL and even the comune a year was not a long time to improve the waterworks; and a village 3 miles off was an improvement on Florence as the site for medical services. To villagers a miss was still as good as a mile and an inaccessible clinic 3 miles away no better than one 25 miles away. To villagers the different cultural attitudes symbolised a difference in attitude of town and country which has always worked to their disadvantage.

In the end administrators and revolutionaries, and those who want to be both simultaneously, have to make their own mistakes and successes. I think it is still sometimes useful to them to have an outside view from a sociologist who comes, if only temporarily, to reside within. A view of the outside is also useful in the sociologist's own home society. Laura Balbo's work (1979 and summarised in English by Pinto, 1981) compares welfare in several European countries and the US and uses this to illuminate the Italian experience. Ida Susser (1982) has consciously applied the ideas of social drama and process here advocated to a study of welfare in Brooklyn.

The social survey seems to me to move from outside view to outside view. The questions are devised outside in accordance with externally imposed ideas of relevance and, as Hilary Graham argues, made to fit an individualist but public framework. There is no real interaction, indeed, as Wright Mills (1959) pointed out long ago, there may typically be no meeting between researcher and researched at all. On the other hand, the direct observer is forced into a dialectic of meaning with the members of society and in the current example with self-appointed, state, party- and church-appointed agents of change. I come into this situation carrying, like the surveyor, externally imposed problems, but here they are being put to the test and their inadequacies painfully revealed. The famous anthropological dictum of becoming a pupil by working in a foreign language has wider relevance than my own struggles with colloquial Tuscan Italian and newfound sympathy for overseas students. I shall leave this town (but always incompletely) in yet another painful process of making sense of what I have learned in terms of my own future actions, professional and political. Unlike the survey sociologist's hopes, I cannot rely on readers' acceptance of my views for I cannot legitimate them by faultless technique or precise calculation. All I can offer is an invitation that others might consider the problems of other people and other groups in other societies in a similar way. I can invite people in Tuscany to test my outsider's view against their own insider's experience, past, present and future.

I hope the political implications for intellectuals and politicians are clear. Democracy requires more than the consent of the governed. It requires their participation and their control of their own fates. To challenge power, sociology has to move in the same direction. Compromise is often necessary, but the key question must always be: Do my methods exclude even a possibility that my subjects are condemned for ever to be objects, and never, before, during, or after, the event answer back?

Notes

1   This research is being carried out with financial support from the University of Keele and SSRC grant no. G0023/0016. It has been facilitated by USL 10/H and the Comune authorities. The paper has been beneficially discussed with Hugh and Marian Faulkner and Pauline Hunt. I am responsible for its errors.

6

Surveying through stories

Hilary Graham

As the introduction indicates, we believe that stories about, or reflections on, social research are a useful way of discussing the politics, problems and practice of research. In this chapter, Hilary Graham further claims that stories are a good means of collecting material in the first place. Graham has argued elsewhere (Graham, 1983) that survey research occupies a central but highly ambiguous position within contemporary sociology; that social surveys have provided the empirical base for the development of mainstream 'masculinist' sociology, but have also provided the empirical data on which a feminist critique of this sociological tradition has been constructed. Graham does not reject the survey approach, but suggests that interviewers who are too interventionist in the research process tend to get brief, stilted and unhelpful answers. Drawing on the research which she and Lorna McKee did on the experience of early motherhood, she explores the use of narrative in survey research, arguing that such a device can be used to overcome the tendency to 'fracture women's experiences' through a more structured question-and-answer approach.

Narratives, in the specific sense of stories told in the first person, have long had their place in the construction of knowledge about the social world. My interest in story-telling was fired during the course of a survey I conducted with Lorna McKee. The survey was concerned with the experience of early motherhood, and was based on a sample of 200 women whom we followed from pregnancy into the first year of their babies' lives. Since completing the study, I have thought more and more about the methodo-logy of story-telling, and the possibilities it offers to re-searchers, who find themselves, and their respondents, trapped within the survey method. I have reflected, parti-cularly, on the kind of relationship which the telling of stories establishes between an informant and her researcher. The sections below explore this relationship further, looking at the crucial questions of exploitation and misrepresentation in survey research. The exploration takes three directions. Firstly, the chapter describes the use of narratives within the campaigns and enquiries launched over the last hundred years on behalf of those who live their lives 'hidden from history'. Secondly, it examines the use of narratives within the sociological tradition, illustrating the potential of per-sonal stories as a data-collection instrument in contemporary studies of women's experiences. Thirdly, it explores some of the wider epistemological issues raised by feminist research, and the contribution of stories to a sociology for women.

Telling it like it is: the role of narratives in social research

In 1915, a book was published which claimed to tell for the first time 'the real problems of maternity as seen through women's own accounts of their lives' (Llewelyn Davies, 1978, p. 3). The book, launched by the Women's Cooperative Guild, was part of the campaign to secure state provision for working-class women. It was, in its own time, and ours, an unusual book. It consists almost entirely of letters, 160 of them written by the 'voteless and voiceless' women of England (ibid., introduction) who give 'in their own words the working women's view of their life' (ibid., p. 3). Endowed with neither vote nor voice, the women were able sufficiently to impress an MP (who evidently possessed both) to write a foreword to the book. Here he observes that the letters give 'an intimate picture of the difficulties, the troubles, often the miseries, sometimes the agonies that afflict millions of our people' (ibid., preface).

Between 1939 and 1945, a different kind of social enquiry was launched by the Mass Observation Project. Again, the aim was to discover more about the 'real lives' of the people. Nella Last, a Lancashire housewife, participated in the inquiry, keeping a diary through the war years (Fleming and Broad, 1982). It is recognised to be 'a vivid and intimate testimony of the dual war that women fought during that period ... the story of women's response to the crisis and scarcity of war in their homes and their community' (Francis, 1982, p. 8).

In 1982, the findings of another investigation were published (McLelland, 1982). Like the 1915 volume from the Women's Cooperative Guild which appeared seventy years before, *A Little Pride and Dignity* is a book of letters from women. Reflecting the times perhaps, the letters were solicited not through a grass-roots working-class organisation, but through the national newspaper, the *Sun*. The inquiry concerned readers' opinions about child benefit. Although based on questionnaires, over 700 readers wrote letters which they attached to their forms. In these letters, 'mothers themselves make the case for child benefit. The message ... comes through loud and clear' (ibid., p. 4).

The three studies are examples only. There are many others, where ordinary people have been invited to speak for themselves. There is the legacy of working-class autobiographies, for example, where men and women write down and talk over their experiences (Lambert and Beales, 1934; Armstrong and Beynon, 1977). There are the records, too, which women have made of their lives (McCrindle and Rowbotham, 1977). While differing in origin and orientation, these inquiries share a common methodology. Firstly, in each, the informants are asked to record their experiences through a time-honoured medium of communication. They are invited to write letters, to keep diaries and, in the age of the tape recorders, simply to talk. The data is bio-graphical, yet the enquiries do not rely on secondary material. Letters, diaries and conversations are constructed for the inquiry. Participation therefore does not depend on personal archives, on resources of which women, and working-class women in particular, traditionally have been deprived. As Glastonbury notes (1979, p.72), the literary tradition is inevitably an elitist one, resting on the existence of wealth and property. It requires space; 'not just a drawer to put the manuscript in, but vaults and attics in which to store love letters, pictures, trophies and mementos of family and friends, all the slowly-maturing symbolic property which distils in writers a sense of the value of their existence and the importance of what they have to day.' The narrative tradition, by contrast, is a popular tradition. It presumes only that the speaker has a story which she is prepared to share with others.

This popular tradition stands in contrast, too, to the more aggressive techniques associated with scientific research. In the folk media of stories, letters and diaries, the emphasis is on telling rather than asking. The investigative style is not that of the clip-board and questionnaire, where the researcher seeks to control the release of information (Oakley, 1981, p. 33). Instead, the style is more akin to ethnography, with the investigator seeking to record the culture as it is lived and spoken. Yet there is a crucial difference. Unlike ethno-graphy and observation, story-telling is not a covert method of data-collection. The narrator knows she is providing information: the story marks out the territory in which intrusion is tolerated. This is a feature to which we return, for it sets limits on the possibility of manipulation and exploitation which haunts social research.

The traditional narrative techniques demand a particular receptivity on the part of the investigator-listener. This receptivity is associated with a second methodological feature of story-based studies. The surveys of the Women's Cooperative Guild and the *Sun*, and the diary of Nella Last, acknowledge the validity of self-knowledge. They are con-structed as vehicles through which this self-knowledge can be presented to sceptical outsiders. In these studies, we can glimpse what E.P. Thompson calls 'histories from below', everyday histories of struggle and resistance. The histories shed light on the shadowy areas of our social world, the lacunae traditionally untrodden by social scientists. Illuminated in particular is the nature and organisation of human reproduction: the poverty within the family, the social relations of gender and generation which determine the experience of caring. As McClelland notes in *A Little Pride and Dignity* (1982, p. 8), the writers speak of a situation which they feel is 'being hidden; that people don't know how difficult it is to budget on a low income, and what a constant struggle it is'. In her editorial capacity, McClelland is summarising other people's histories: it is the history-makers themselves who tell it like it is. The *Birmingham Mail* (C. Lewis, 1982) invited its readers to write to the newspaper and share their experiences of being unemployed.[1] One woman began her letter by stating 'I feel as if I've waited a thousand years to tell my story of survival on the dole'.

Speaking 'from below' demands courage. The informants remind us that they are opening doors on their private lives (although some, of course, may remain firmly shut). One contributor to the Women's Cooperative Guild survey (Llewelyn Davis, 1978, p. 59) noted: 'I know it is a most delicate subject and great care must be used in introducing it, but still, a word spoken sometimes does good.' Other writers are less equivocal. A respondent in the *Sun* survey returned her questionnaire with the comment (McClelland, 1982, p. 9): 'Of course I've filled up the enclosed form. As a housewife and mother, its my duty to voice my opinions about government proposals. I say mums of Britain speak up or we will never be heard.' Letters, it seems, furnish the mums of Britain with a powerful medium through which they can make themselves heard. Like other autobiographical forms, they provide social scientists with a way of representing the lives of the silent majority within their investigations. This question of representation, too, is one to which we return.

So far, we have considered studies conducted outside mainstream sociology. However, the idea of speaking up through stories is not alien to the discipline. Indeed, the need for culturally appropriate ways for people to talk about their experiences has been a major theme in the sociological research literature. The search for naturalistic methods has been most closely associated with the school of symbolic interaction. A naturalistic mode of inquiry, according to Denzin (1978, p. 1), seeks to 'yield a penetration into the everyday worlds of interaction'. In this penetration (an uncomfortable metaphor), the participants' 'self images and identities, the meanings they assign to social objects, the social situations they enter into, and the social relationships they form must all be described, analysed and fitted within a theoretical framework which reflects the everyday realities of the participants' (Denzin, 1978, p. 2). Such a programme has much in common with Llewellyn Davies's, with that of the Mass Observation Project and the Child Poverty Action Group. Not surprisingly, we find the place of respondent-generated accounts is well-established in the naturalistic tradition. Narratives, written and spoken, have achieved a particularly prominent place, identified under the rubric of 'the life history method' (Becker, 1978). This is described by Armstrong (1982, pp. 7, 19, 20) as follows:

> The life history method attempts to locate individuals in their overall life experience as well as their broader socio-historical backgrounds against which they live. . . . There appear to be two main alternatives. . . . [The] complete life history attempts to cover the entire sweep of the subject's life experiences. It is inevitably long, many-sided and complex. . . . The alternative would be to collect multiple biographies within the same or similar area of research. . . . The multiple biographies approach, by abstracting dominant themes, makes it possible to generalise to one type by showing that certain biographies have, for all the idiosyncrasy, some common elements.

In terms of Armstrong's schema, it is possible to locate the three studies in the second category. They each draw on the autobiographical accounts which their informants provided

about one aspect or period in their lives. It is this style of
history-taking that is explored in this chapter.

While most actively colonised by sociologists working
within the interpretative paradigm, biographical methods are
incorporated into both qualitative and quantitative research.
The use of 'multiple biographies' features, for example, in
survey design. Social surveys are typically concerned with
the measurement of behaviour over time. They may describe
long time-periods; employment careers, reproductive histories
and family background. Or their focus may be a more specific
one: the status passage of pregnancy, marriage breakdown,
and illness. Among the available techniques, follow-up
surveys and panel samples are well-established procedures for
tapping this time dimension (Hakim, 1982, pp. 109 and
151). Time-budgets and diaries, too, figure prominently in
survey design. Cullen (1979, p. 118) highlights the way in
which researchers can construct 24-hour retrospective diaries
for their informants which are finely adapted to 'the what,
when and where of everyday life'. When coupled with interviews, he argues, they can be used to pin-point the structures
which individuals perceive as constraining their daily lives.
While diaries, like panel samples and longitudinal surveys,
all have their place in survey research, 'the commonest
method is retrospective questioning of informants about
their behaviour or experiences over a defined period in the
past' (Thomas, 1981, p. 2). While this retrospective questioning can be tightly structured in line with the researcher's
interests, recall is facilitated when the informant determines
the shape and content of the story. As Thomas (1981, p. 7)
notes, 'it is generally thought most reliable to elicit histories
in the form of a "narrative", attaching dates to significant
events as one goes along.'

For this kind of exploratory interviewing, Goode and Hatt
(1952) advocate the use of an 'interview guide'. Unlike the
more precisely formulated interview schedule, this guide
introduces themes and issues on which individuals are encouraged to reflect at length. As Dobash, Cavanagh and Wilson
note in their study of battered wives, the interview guide
aids the telling of experiences in the biographical context
in which they occur. It 'allowed for maximum recall, since

[the respondent] was allowed to speak about an issue or event as a whole rather than answer isolated questions which to her might appear to be inappropriate or inapplicable' (1976, p. 4).

It is not only survey researchers who have recognised the place of narratives in social research. The use of biographical material has been formally incorporated within observational methods, too. Zimmerman and Wieder (1977), for example, describe what they call a Diary-Interview method similar in many ways to Cullen's Extended Diary Method, outlined above. Such a method, they suggest, is particularly useful when observers wish to understand the experiences of those occupying 'diffuse roles' in which activities are typically pursued alone. Such roles present obvious difficulties to participant observers. These difficulties Zimmerman and Wieder illustrate with reference to housewives. They note that the housewife 'who typically spends much of the day in solitude or in the company of young children, would have, in the presence of the ethnographer, an adult companion with whom she could constantly interact as she went about her day.' To meet this exigency, Zimmerman and Wieder asked their respondents to keep a diary, or an 'annotated chronological log' about aspects of their lives. The log then became the basis for intensive interviewing, with the resulting diary-interview compensating for the limitations of participant observation.

From this brief review, we can conclude that the methodology of story-telling is well integrated into the design of social inquiries. Surveys and interviews, in particular, appear to be grounded in the chronology of people's lives. Yet narratives have served as an implicit methodology, present in the practice rather than the principles of survey research. Where this research has concerned the experiences of women, however, the practice of story-telling is brought into clearer focus. The section below explores the role of stories in surveys of women's lives.

It's the way she tells them: surveying through stories

Over the last two decades, the study of women's experiences has featured strongly on the agenda of empirical sociology.

Two themes have characterised the accumulation of this empirical data. Firstly, research has been oriented to the interior of women's lives. It has described the activities of women who do the housework, become mothers, go out to work, become ill and see the doctor. This orientation is consistent with a feminist perspective which sees in these seemingly mundane activities the forces which shape women's identity. Feminist researchers thus have sought to record 'the dull thud of the commonplace' and 'the small everyday moments of dismissive encounter' (Glastonbury, 1979, p. 171; Rowbotham et al., 1979, p. 27). Secondly, the survey has been the dominant method of inquiry. Most empirically based knowledge on women's lives is survey-based knowledge. What we know about women's lives is gleaned either from large-scale government surveys plotting macro-trends or from small-scale surveys which map the social processes which lie behind the national statistics. By comparison, little sociological knowledge has been generated through participant observation and ethnography, and the battery of techniques associated with a naturalistic mode of inquiry.

In surveying women's experiences, feminist researchers have become aware of a tension between subject and method. The act of conducting surveys on women's oppression is experienced as 'a contradiction in terms' (Oakley, 1981, p. 49). The nature of this oppression is seen as one which resists neat encapsulation in the categories of survey research. The tensions are felt most acutely at the moment of data-collection itself: when the feminist surveyor confronts her sisters in the field. The possibility of manipulation and misrepresentation, latent in all social research, appear in sharp relief when sociologists begin to investigate 'the very personal business of being female in a patriarchal society' (Oakley, 1981, p. 49).

Firstly, feminists engaged in survey research have raised the question of exploitation. Westcott (1979, p. 427), for example, argues that sociologists have made commodities out of women's suffering. They have turned oppression into books and articles which can be sold on the market-place. In this disturbing scenario, the ease of access enjoyed by feminist and non-feminist researchers is a measure of the extent to which women have only their knowledge to lose. McRobbie (1982, pp. 56 and 57) argues forcefully that 'sociology does not prepare us for the humility of powerless women, for their totally deferential attitude to the researcher, "why are *you* interested in *me*, I'm only a housewife?" . . . Their extreme involvement in the research could be interpreted as yet another index of their powerlessness.' Individual efforts by feminist sociologists to create a more equal and reciprocal relationship with their informants fits uneasily within this political reality. As Acker, Barry and Esseveld (1982, p. 15) note, 'the researcher's goal is always to gather information, thus the danger always exists of manipulating friendships to that end.'

Exploitation is not the only problem for those who research into women's lives through the medium of the social survey. Feminists have been concerned with a second and closely related issue. Surveys are seen to mask or misrepresent the position of women in patriarchical societies in important ways (Graham, 1983). The social order of the survey is one of 'units' and 'cases'. These units, which in everyday life function as individuals, households, streets and nation-states, are assumed to be islands entire of themselves (Galtung, 1967, p. 28; Townsend, 1979, p. 114). Such an assumption, however, is a profoundly un-sociological one. As Ackroyd and Hughes (1981, p. 63) observe, it is a 'crucial postulate underpinning all the social sciences that individuals are related through associations and groups of various kinds'. In obscuring 'the group life in which individuals actually live and interact' (ibid.), surveys restrict access to the very everyday social processes which feminist researchers most want to tap. For it is here, in the everyday relations of gender, class and generation, that the ineluctable dimensions of women's experiences are to be found.

The tendency to obscure and ossify group processes is compounded by another feature of the survey method. Surveys assume that the outputs of the units under study — the facts, experiences and opinions about the person or household — can be communicated in words. Surveys work to the extent that individuals can formulate the required information as answers to questions chosen by the investigator. Aspects of our social life which cannot be shaped into answer-size pieces are inevitably lost to posterity. There is considerable evidence to suggest that women's experiences are peculiarly resistant to such shaping (Ardener, 1978; Spender, 1980). Their experiences remain 'unspoken and unspeakable' (Rich, 1980, p. 199) within the language of the questionnaire and the interview.

Exploitation and misrepresentation may be impossible to eradicate from social research. None the less, those engaged in surveys of women's lives have attempted to temper these tendencies. The aim has been to design data-collecting instruments in which women can participate as subjects in the research process. As Acker, Barry and Esseveld (1982, p. 6) explain:

> Our intention is to minimise the tendency in all social research to transform those researched into objects of scrutiny and manipulation. In the ideal case, we want to create conditions in which the object of research enters into the process as an active subject.

How can we create these conditions in the heart of a survey tradition that denies them? How can we guarantee that, in encouraging women to enter actively into the research, we do not find that what they say is 'taken down in evidence and used against them'? (Glastonbury, 1979, p. 174).

It was with this fundamental question that Lorna McKee and I set off to survey women's experiences of motherhood (Graham and McKee, 1980). Our solution seemed modest, and inadequate to the task. We designed our survey around a series of semi-structured interviews. These were composed of open-ended questions which, in following the trajectory of pregnancy and motherhood, we hoped would encourage our informants to take on and take over the interview as their own. Our approach was neither an original nor a radical departure from conventional survey practice. Nevertheless, it is the one adopted in most contemporary surveys of women. The use of semi-structured interviews has become the principal means by which feminists have sought to achieve the active involvement of their respondents in the construction of data about their lives (see, for example, Finch, this volume; Oakley, 1981; Hunt, 1980; Acker, Barry and Esseveld, 1982). While qualitatively different to fixed-choice questionnaires, semi-structured interviews are still, as the label suggests, structured. The structuring, moreover, is one designed by the researcher, albeit to facilitate the active participation of the respondent.

We conducted three such interviews for the 200 mothers in our survey: during the sixth month of pregnancy and during the first and fifth months after childbirth. In addition, we made another visit to the women's homes in the week after they left hospital. This visit was designed as an opportunity for the researchers to offer their congratulations and for the mothers to recount their experiences of labour and delivery. The visit, however, soon assumed the proportions of an interview, at least with respect to length. The notion of 'dropping in' was abandoned as we found ourselves staying for several hours. With extra data on our hands, we developed an interview schedule to contain it. However, because the collection of detailed information on childbirth lay beyond the formal boundaries of our research brief, we were less rigorous in our adherence to the schedule. The result was two types of data about the same experience. Some informants were invited to tell of their experiences through topics introduced by the interviewer. Others spoke through a different interview format. It could also be described as semi-structured, but the structure was imposed by the informant. The structure was that of a story, to which the researcher was invited — occasionally — to contribute.

The difference is best conveyed through examples. In the extracts below, three mothers, all having their first baby, are discussing the role of their husbands during labour. The first and second extracts are taken from two transcripts in which the respondents answered the questions contained in the interview schedule. The third account is drawn from an interview in which the informant was invited to tell the researcher what happened when her baby was born. There was no schedule, no questionnaire; the mother was simply asked to provide as much detail about her experiences as she felt she wanted. While all three agreed that they wanted their husbands there, we seem to learn more from the story-teller about his contribution and the structure of lay and medical roles which shaped their experiences.

Extract 1

I. Was your husband with you?

R. Yes, well, he went home for his tea but apart from that he was with me all day.

I. Were you glad he was there?

R. Oh, yes it made the day. I couldn't have beared it by myself I don't think.

I. Did you find it painful?

R. Oh, yes, but it was only for a short while you know.

Extract 2

I. Did your husband stay?

R. Yes he stayed the whole of the time.

I. Did you find it a help having your husband?

R. Oh, terrific, yes.

I. So you feel it's worthwhile having him?

R. Oh, yes, he was marvellous with back rubbing, ter-rific really. He was marvellous telling me what to do, to keep blowing out and to stop pushing, and I'm sure that made it much quicker you know.

Extract 3

He said he wanted to go, not to see her being born, but just to see I was all right. Somebody to look after me, and I appreciated him being there. I don't know, its just nice. I wouldn't have liked to have gone through it on my own. They [the midwives] just sort of flitted in and out. And then it was getting really bad at the end, he said 'I'm going to get someone, I'm going to get some-one.' So I said 'It's all right' and I got my hand on the buzzer and I was pressing it for ages and ages and no-body was coming. And he had to go out in the end and look for somebody. And I'll tell you what got me, they wanted to take me machine away, me air and oxygen, because I found I was getting times when they were really bad and I'd faint, and me legs give way, and me hands go dead white with cramp. I felt stupid you see and Bill kept getting a flannel and flapping it across me face and a nurse came in and said 'Oh good gracious, I think you'd better take the machine away, she's having too much of that.' Anyway I grabbed the mask and I wouldn't let her have it. I don't know what she thought, I bet she thought 'Cor blimey' and she vanished again. And I said to Bill to tell her next time he saw her that she can't have my machine, I get like this when I get me periods. I could hear him in the distance telling somebody this and she said 'Oh that's very strange! . . . [But the gas and air machine remained in situ beside her bed]

It may be argued that childbirth is peculiarly amenable to encapsulation in a narrative. Other areas of life may lend themselves less easily to story-telling. The fourth extract, therefore, deals with a different issue: the feelings commonly described as 'the baby blues'. In the account below, the mother has reached the point in her story where she is in the post-natal ward with her new baby, experiencing the intimate connection between physical and mental health. Here, again, the narrative form seems to capture the personal reality of being a British Mum.

After he was born, heavens, I was pretty miserable actually because I felt so bad. There was, I think, eight of us in the ward, we helped make the beds and we helped set the tables and everything and quite honestly I didn't feel up to it. You know it was really quite exhausting. And I got a bit depressed with it because I found that, you know, I was constipated. I didn't go to the toilet until I'd been in there six days and, oh, I felt dreadful with it because the toilet was right at the other end of the ward. It was really quite a way to get there and it seemed as if everything was such an effort. And I had a palaver with that because I didn't want suppositories — I'd got Jeff to smuggle me some liquid paraffin

in because it always worked before. But that didn't
do me any good either. And I didn't want these suppositories. I think it was because I was so sore, I didn't
want this thing and I had to have them in the end and
they didn't do me any good — I had two of them and
they didn't work. So I was pretty miserable actually
in hospital afterwards. I think I wouldn't have had the
depression otherwise, but I was very depressed, but I
think because of that. Yes, I had tears a few times. But
I think it was because I felt so exhausted, you know,
fed up with everything . . .

The use of such examples is clearly problematic. Case
studies occupy an ambiguous position in a scientific discipline which emphasises the need for data to meet the criteria of external validity. From these extracts it is not possible for the reader to explore the influence of other variables. The reader may object that in the first two examples
the interview schedule was badly designed, rapport was poor
or the respondents simply had little to say. Without a pro-
perly constructed case-control trial involving a larger number
of informants, it is not possible for me to prove the power
of story-telling in survey research. However, it is possible to
indicate a link between data and method; between what
women tell and the way they tell it.

In making this connection, we can look to the narrative
tradition for empirical support. This tradition, reviewed in
the previous section, relies on folk methods of communication to illuminate the hidden landscapes of our social
world. In so doing, story-telling provides a way of confront-
ing the crucial issues of misrepresentation and exploitation
which bedevil those who work in the frontline of social
research. It thus offers an alternative to the (researcher
designed) semi-structured interview, currently favoured in
survey investigations. Stories, as we have seen, provide the
basis for informant-structured interviews, diaries and letters,
all of which can be incorporated, singly or together, into the
framework of a sample survey. In several respects, story-
telling offers advantages over traditional interviewing, more
effectively safeguarding the rights of informants to parti-

cipate as subjects as well as objects in the construction of sociological knowledge.

Firstly, story-telling counteracts the tendency of surveys to fracture women's experiences. As we've seen, social surveys encourage respondents to reduce their experiences to fragments which can be captured in a question-and-answer format. Stories, by contrast, provide a vehicle through which individuals can build up and communicate the complexity of their lives. Stories can be used to illuminate the uncertain, dynamic quality of experience, being themselves part of the process by which individuals make sense of past events and present circumstances (Stimson and Webb, 1975, p. 90). While surveys 'tear individuals from their social context' (Galtung, 1967, p. 150), stories are pre-eminently ways of relating individuals and events to social contexts, ways of weaving personal experiences into their social fabric. Moreover, stories provide a vehicle through which the existence and experience of inequality can be described. Stimson and Webb noted the potential of stories in their study of *Going to See the Doctor* (1975, p. 90): 'The story is a form of communication .... in which some redress is made for the inequalities in the relations between the client and the professional.'

Stimson and Webb suggest that stories, told afterwards to those not present to the interaction, are a means by which patients can describe and deal with the power of doctors. They note how story-telling was fashioned to meet the exigencies of the medical encounter: here, we argue that story-telling may well be adopted by other social groups who find that the dominant vocabulary robs them of an adequate way of communicating their experiences. Stimson and Webb's observation that 'all our stories were collected from women' whose doctors were mainly men, points to the possibility that women telling stories in a patriarchal society indeed has a methodological significance beyond medical sociology.

Secondly, stories, in providing a self-structured format for the interview, can counteract the exploitative tendencies of social research. In researcher-structured interviews, the respondent becomes a repository of data, while interpretation and analysis remains the prerogative of the investigator.

In stories, data and interpretation are fused, the story-line providing the interpretative framework through which the data are constructed. The story, moreover, marks the boundaries of what the individual is prepared to tell. The narrator can spell out from the start the terms on which information is to be exchanged: the interviewer, anxious to protect the integrity of her informants, can use the story to guide her questioning. The opportunity for fabrication, for 'telling tales' in a pejorative sense, is present in stories as it is in conventional question-and-answer techniques. The opportunity for avoiding the truth is commonly regarded as a major problem of survey research. But perhaps we should welcome the space it provides for those who receive researchers into their lives. The switch from the personal testimony to the extravagant tale is not difficult to detect, yet it provides the teller with a way of controlling the release of information about herself. In a situation of inequality, both honest stories and fabricated tales are resources by which informants can redress the balance of power.

It is (or should be) a *sine qua non* of social research that informants have a story to tell. The integration of 'multiple biographies' into survey design provides a simple and direct method through which they can tell it. It is a method, too, consistent with a feminist research programme which seeks to involve women in the faithful recording of their experiences. This programme has as its objective the construction of a sociology for women. It is to the construction of this new sociology that we now turn.

Narratives and a sociology for women

It was 1961 when Dennis Wrong spotted *homo sociologicus* stalking the landscape of western sociology. Twenty-two years later, and there is powerful evidence to support the contention that *homo sociologicus* is indeed a man. A series of disciplinary critiques conclude that what passes as sociological knowledge is knowledge that illuminates the position of a gendered and not a generic 'man' (Smith, 1974, 1979; Stacey, 1981; Elshtain, 1981). The theories and methods of sociology, it seems, derive from the visions of the social world afforded to men in western society. The discipline furnishes knowledge which supports the interests of those who manage and control society, providing 'a conceptualisation of women which is consistent with continuing male domination' (Acker, Barry and Esseveld, 1982, p. 2). Thus, while a place can be found for a sociology of women, 'it never quite makes sense to do a sociology of men, nor is it clear how it would differ from the sociology we do' (Smith, 1979, p. 159).

The recognition that *homo sociologicus* is not a woman has prompted feminists to reassess 'the sociology we do'. Some have abandoned the discipline altogether, convinced that working within sociology is incompatible with a commitment to work for the liberation of women. Academic sociology is seen to de-politicise women's experiences, transforming them from a political issue into a social problem whose boundaries can be neatly contained by those seeking a career in the social sciences. However, in general, the reassessment of sociology has not resulted in a wholesale evacuation of the discipline. Instead, it has been identified as a crucial territory to contest. Like other public services, academic sociology is seen to relate to the communication of patriarchal values and the administration of capitalist society. In common with other service-providers, the response has been to rebuild sociology from within (London Edinburgh Weekend Return Group, 1979). Westcott (1979, p. 422) explains that this response involves feminists in dialogues and debates of a particular kind:

> These dialogues are not debates between outsiders and insiders; they are, rather, critical confrontations among those who have been educated and trained within particular disciplines. The feminist debate arises because some of these insiders, who are women, are also outsiders. When women realize that we are simultaneously immersed in and estranged from both our own particular discipline and the western intellectual tradition generally, a personal tension develops that informs the critical dialogue. This tension, rooted in the contradiction

of women's belonging and not belonging, provides the basis for knowing deeply and personally that which we criticise.

It is not only criticism but reconstruction that has emerged from this dialogue within the discipline. Fundamental to this reconstruction is the idea of a 'sociology for women' (Smith, 1979; Westcott, 1979, p. 428). A sociology for women is contrasted with the sociology of women which traditionally has characterised the discipline's approach to gender. The commitment is to a sociology in which women are subjects and not objects in the research process; a sociology which enlightens and emancipates. According to Smith (1979, p. 123):

> We might attempt to develop analyses for women them- selves, descriptions and understandings of their situa- tion, of their everyday world and of its determinations in the larger socio-economic organisation in which it is articulated.

In a similar vein, Elshtain argues that sociologists should 'search for the female subject', to discover how she 'sees herself, or would, were she given the opportunity to provide a spoken account of her existence' (1981, p. 304). Like Smith, Elshtain identifies self-understanding as a central objective, with the sociologist constructing 'new meanings' so that women, becoming 'more intelligible to themselves', can oppose their social condition more effectively (1981, p. 311).

The construction of a feminist epistemology has been debated largely in theoretical terms. Yet it is a profoundly practical undertaking. Searching for the lost female subject involves us in re-searching, in its literal sense. We have to return to the world and begin again to observe, listen and record. A sociology for women is inevitably and funda- mentally an empirical sociology. However, it is not a socio- logy which eschews abstraction and theory. Abstraction and theory are essential if 'new meanings' are to be welded between the personal and political domains. It is, however, a sociology which places a particular emphasis on experience and subjectivity as the route to theory. The questions we ask of women relate to our lives as women: in interpreting the answers we listen carefully to 'the language of silence' (Rowbotham, 1973, p. 30). As Rose (1982, p. 368) explains:

> feminist methodology seeks to bring together subjective and objective ways of knowing the world. It begins and constantly returns to the subjective shared experiences of oppression. It is important to stress shared, as the purely personal account of one individual women's oppression while casting some brilliant insights, may tell us more about the essentially idiosyncratic character of her unique experience than the generality of the experience of all or even most women. Nonetheless within feminist theoretical production, the living participating 'I' is seen as a dimension which must be included in an adequate analysis.

Workers' inquiries and community surveys provide models in which 'the living participating I' is incorporated into the collection and analysis of data. Like narratives, they have a long history beyond and within the social sciences (Marsh, 1982, p. 19). Their explicit intention is to invest control over the process of generating knowledge firmly in the hands of their informants. As one recent inquiry concludes, 'a workers' investigation . . . is not only one carried out by workers themselves for themselves, but is also one that insists on the legitimacy of their "own way of experiencing and understanding".' Like group discussions and group interviews to which they are linked, such investigations are grounded in the collectivities and networks in which people 'actually live and interact' (Ackroyd and Hughes, 1981, p. 63). Social structure and process are not obscured: rather, they provide the framework in which the study develops.

Self-surveys and group inquiries provide a standard by which we can assess social research. However, they lie beyond the reach of the majority of social scientists, locked into institutions committed to the more conventional research techniques. Their room for manoeuvre is highly restricted:

their mode of intervention must therefore be all the more effective. It is in this context that narrative-based methods offer a way of working for a new sociology within the confines of the old. Specifically, as we saw in the previous section, it offers those who labour here a way of working In and Against the survey method.

Story-telling clearly does not answer every feminist's prayer; but it may help revive the faint-hearted. It indicates that there are areas left in which feminist practice can take root within empirical sociology. In somewhat visionary terms, it can be seen as a methodological catalyst: something which can aid the transformation of the research process without compromising our feminism. More modestly, it provides a simple, low-tech procedure through which we can involve women in studies of their lives without, at the same time, oppressing them.

Note

1   I would like to thank Lorna McKee for drawing this report to my attention.

7

A postscript to nursing

Nicky James

This chapter can be approached in at least two ways. It is an immediate account of doing fieldwork in a situation that most of us would find extremely stressful. It is full of insight into all the difficulties of role adoption, data recording, subjectivity and detachment that would be routinely faced by any 'participant observer'. Nicky James was 'really' working (albeit for free) as a nurse in 2 hospices for five months and trying to make sense of her experiences. Matters of dress and demeanour become central, not marginal, to the research. Access has to be negotiated and research positions maintained — and almost hourly negotiated. She, unlike some of the other contributors to this book, has of necessity to write herself into her account. The immediate comparisons, as we make clear elsewhere, are with Collins's and Jenkins's contributions. It is also an account of beginning postgraduate sociological work that others in this situation will find invaluable. How to start? What is a problem? Is it doable? What are theories? What are data? What is their relationship? In what ways is this really work? (especially in this case in comparison with the 'real' work of nursing). This chapter should also be read alongside Sue Scott's on sociology postgraduates' more general experience. That post-

graduate work in sociology can be a genuine educational experience as well as 'research training' is made marvellously clear from Nicky James's chapter.

Fieldwork: on a late shift, September 1981
Staff Nurse in charge of a continuing care unit

That evening I served out only the main courses, and left whoever was around to serve pudding. I gave only one person a mouthwash, instead of the normal 5 and practised what I was going to say when I phoned Andrea. How do you tell a 19-year-old that her father is about to die? Michael Mills, the social worker, rang and said he'd come if Andrea wanted him. She was to phone him. I thought: 'That'll muck up his Friday evening at home.' When I did get through to Andrea my words did not come out as calmly as I wanted. Without swamping her I wanted to find out if she was by herself, would she manage, how would Susie be, and how prepared was she for his death? I didn't want to frighten her, but I wanted her here quickly. I told her about Michael Mills and asked her if she wanted me to contact any of her relatives.

Life in the rest of the unit was going on like clockwork, though Fran said: 'I was so happy when I came on . . .but this place today. It's going to be a hard shift.'

I went with Anna to make Ronald Saunders look as comfortable as possible, as much for Andrea and the relatives and us as for him, then went for my break with everyone knowing that I wanted to catch Andrea for a chat before she went in to see her father. Change in appearance can be a shock.

On the 6p.m. drug round Ethel (92) gave us a smile and a grouch as we fed her the medicine, which restored a sense of an ordinary day, and poor Mrs Straw, the day's new admission, was so nervous and scared she needed somebody just to sit with her for a while. But we didn't have time. Mrs Harrison refused the extra dose of diamorphine we offered her to make it easier to turn her. Retrospectively we decided that she managed her pain much better than we did, positively and usefully to make herself feel alive. We thought that we wanted her to have more medicine for our benefit not hers.

Andrea timed it beautifully and arrived as we finished the drugs. I took her to the quiet room, and left her to ring her aunt and uncle before she saw her father, intending to go in with her, but she found the new room by herself. I didn't know whether to intrude or not.

Fran passed me and said: 'Gawd Nicky, you're actually doing some work today. But you're managing all right. Not getting upset about it.' I was pleased that my performance did not reflect my inner disorganisation.

Mr Saunders died without anyone in there, which seemed a pity. But you can never predict the exact moment and can hang around for hours. A friendly doctor from the adjacent hospital came over to certify him dead, and encouraged Susan, the enrolled nurse, and me to use the opthalmascope to look into his eyes to see the changes that occur with death. It was educational, and incongruous with our affection for Ronald. I fumbled the words as I told Andrea and her aunt and uncles in the quiet room, and asked them if they wanted to see the body. She did not, but they did.

Anna and I laid Ronald out, while Susan filled in all the forms. I was surprised at Anna's determined efficiency. Instead of the usual grin she was grim and quiet. It stopped my flippancy to see how much his death mattered to her despite the many she had seen. Tending to be guided by whoever I was with, sometimes we behaved as if the body was still a person to be treated with gentle attention. Other times it was an empty shell, and comments on being witheld entry at the pearly gates because the paper knickers were on inside out were not irreverent, because the person had gone.

We washed him, dressed him in clean pyjamas and between us sorted out the uncertainties of what to pack in the black plastic bag to go home and what to throw away. Imagining the wrench of things being unpacked the other end. You know what to do about half-used bottles of orange squash and flannels. You chuck them. And the teddy bear lent by

the 6-year-old would go back, with the cards wishing him
well. But used pyjamas and their father's well-worn razor we
wanted to throw away and knew we couldn't. I took the
property to Andrea and asked her to sign for it, which she
did without opening the bag to check it. And then: 'Do you
know if you want him to be buried or cremated?' What a
question to ask within an hour of the death! But it makes a
difference to the certification. To my immense relief the
question did not jar, and there was a plot next to his father.
I suspect it is easy for nurses to overestimate their importance at these times of numbness, but there is a fear that you
might say the key wrong thing and make their sorrow worse,
and perhaps your own.

Taking the uncles along to the room, I asked if they thought
Andrea and Susie would manage all right, whilst thinking to
myself, do I stay in the room with them, and for how long,
or just go? I stayed for moments as they reflected on his
life, and then left them. They remained only minutes longer,
went back to the quiet room, and all of them left together.
The tin trunk[1] was ordered from the porters for after the
visitors had gone at 8p.m.

Before writing the Kardex[2] and day report on each person's
condition, I nipped in to see everyone first. Otherwise,
especially in a unit like this, you can write that Mrs X is
satisfactory, and then find that it is not so. In the men's
4-bedded room Mrs Whyte, visiting her husband, asked what
had happened to Ronald. She was upset when I told her.
It was a great temptation just to say he was very ill with
the hope that she would not ask again, but then an endless
circle of evasion and half-truths can start.

At about 8.15 the nurses had a public and unofficial tea-
break at the nurses station, in the middle of the unit. Anna
had brought in apple pie for us all, and after the patients
had been given the drinks they wanted, we helped ourselves. Since things had quietened down, this delightful
ritual continued as usual. Susan offered to write the day
report, but I said I would, and suspected myself of unrea-
sonably asserting my status. They went back to work while
I carried on writing. I hadn't finished when the three night
staff arrived together, early, just after 9p.m. for 9.15. Anna

and Fran went off, leaving Susan to answer the patients' bells while I gave report. We discussed what had happened during the day and I gave details of the new lady in more depth before we talked at length about Mrs Harrison and Mrs Benedict.

By 9.45 Susan had left and I'd finished the writing. On the way off I want to say goodbye to Mr Benedict, who was in the quiet room and going to stay the night. His son was there. I was introduced and we talked of this and that and Mrs Benedict. Bill, the son, was smashing with Mr Benedict, letting his dad be proud of him and arguing with him occasionally about army stories. They seemed extraordinarily normal. Billy said to me that I must want to go home — which I did because I was tired, but I didn't know how to get away without being heartless or offensive. An awful thought was that Mrs Benedict would die soon, and I did not want to be there. You want to make each person's death as personal to the family as possible, but sometimes you run out of steam.

At 11p.m. I left the unit to drive home, thinking I hadn't managed well, because a measure of that is that you are off on time. It was the saddest shift in 8 months of field-work — the kind that would become folklore — and I felt wrung out.

When I got home I delivered a monologue on the day. In turn, I was told of the party of primary school kids taken round the big farm we lived on. They'd spent hours seeing the cows, feeding the bull, looking at the chickens, in the dairy, whilst draped over the adults, squealing and excited. Somehow that seemed to balance things out, a bit.

'Nicky, you're sort of like a P.S. in a letter. Not part of the main body of the nursing team, but still important.'
Night nurse at the hospital.
'This is our pet sociologist who's working on the unit and studying us. She's found out all sorts of interesting things.'
Continuing care unit Sister, introducing me to an outsider.

A beginning

Armed with a title of morbid imprecision, 'Death and Dying in Britain', I began a project which came to be about nursing the dying. A reflection on what was done and why will be shaped by using the facets of learning the job of researcher that I found to be most tantalising. Whilst emphasising one theme, like searching for sociology, pick a problem, laughing with death, or facts about feelings, would simplify making concise points, in the end it fails to convey the essence of doing the research since it was the combination of those stimulants that made the project what it was and continues to affect the writing up. Instead, in mingling them, doubts and ambiguities, easy to mellow or miss, are clarified — at the loss of a tidy account. The suggestion of grave misgivings as to what I was trying to achieve or of responding to outside pressures to change the research, contribute to a sense that the project was 'unscientific', perhaps with the implication that it was therefore not worth doing. Having spoken to other, mainly female, researchers of various guises who shared some of my uncertainties and lack of confidence gives me a sense of permission to expose the naivety and doubts which influenced perhaps not only this project, but others as well.

My intention is to imagine a rough split in my three-year PhD project, between the university-based first year, the second, which consisted mainly of fieldwork, and the reflection and reorientation for the write-up of the thesis of the third year; a time to consider the passage of learning to be a researcher on the job.

Chronologies can be a misleading way of accounting for the end products of research, tending to imply a straightforward and considered passage from beginning to end, with a few hiccups to show it was not easy all the way. Instead, for this project, it seemed that beginnings and ends were rarely clear, but that periodic re-assessment, often forced by the giving of a seminar, or the need to account to the SSRC gave a sometimes fictitious form to the study (as my supervisor put it, with light cynicism), which gradually became incorporated into it. This is one such undertaking.

Since definite statements convey a certainty that is more persuasive and therefore useful than steady qualification, learning to be convinced and convincing about the study, and balancing it against overstatement, was one of the unanticipated facets of being a researcher.

Narrowing down the task

Not knowing how the research system worked granted me the luxury of submitting, unperturbed, an outline, both vague and short, which managed to supply me with a department from which to work, and an initial two years' money from a central fund, with the possibility of a third year. The department was where I had done my undergraduate degree, and the mixed blessings of familiarity saved at least some of the groundwork of establishing myself. My supervisor, a vital ingredient whose importance I had not recognised, had overseen the undergraduate dissertation from which the postgraduate study was to develop. We agreed with minimal discussion to continue with each other. Approachable and non-directive as he was, he left me to discover a problem that interested me from reading which included spiritualism, psychoanalysis, census data, ethics, medicine, government reports, and so on. Somehow from this bewildering wealth, a question had to be chosen that could be followed up to reach some kind of conclusion. The distractions of philosophy held no more appeal than the abstractions of grand theory, so it was fortuitous that I was able to build on the tensions I found between being an academic and being a nurse.

Nurses *do* things as their work, hence Fran's reference to me at the beginning of this chapter. If they are not doing something physical they are not working, and to be in a sociology department concentrating on the written word and discussion seemed egocentric and indulgent. Thus one of the easiest decisions on how to solidify the nebulous thesis was to make it empirical, using previous knowledge. Such a decision had a huge impact, far from clear at the time, because it not only structured the projected three years into a manageable timetable, but to me implied a particular way

of thinking, which excluded number crunching and hypothesis testing — both, then, sociology of derision. Thinking
in terms of interpersonal relations, I wanted to know how
people affected each other in looking after the dying (which
at the time I took to be a passive event for the patient) and
where the power of decision lay.

Intertwined with considering more specifically what I
wanted to do was the input from others. During the initial
weeks I discovered there were different groups of people
relevant to the project — outsiders, university staff,
other postgraduates and friends. Needless to say, these
shifted categories over time. I also worked on the basis that
there were two types of problems, acceptable ones you feel
you can ask about and unacceptable ones which are more
difficult to ask and which are matched more carefully against
the audience.

The staff, whom I already knew, although unclear on the
resources available for postgraduates ('ask the secretary' see
Scott's chapter and Moss Kanter, 1978) were a source of
endless suggestions of people to see and expansive lists of
books and articles to read. Knowing that they could not all
be seen or read, it was difficult to evaluate which to choose.
To optimise their proferred help required knowing what I
was doing at the very time I was least sure.

The list of references grew alarmingly in inverse proportion
to the clarity of the problem. Some friends were intrigued
enough to be useful sounding boards, asking questions which,
in encouraging me to explain simply, helped sort the irrelevant from the necessary to the enlightening. Others were part
of the network keeping me informed of radio and television
programmes, talks and newspaper articles, also providing light
entertainment when the dark side of death was looming large.

In January, four months after starting, I attended a multi-
disciplinary terminal care course with nurses, social workers,
clergy and a few doctors. From taking embarrassingly more
notes than anyone else, and feeling like neither nurse nor
researcher, it occurred to me that spoken repetition on the
course of written phrases in the literature, which encapsulate
'good' terminal care, such as 'teamwork', 'individual patient
assessment', 'death with dignity', could be used as categories

of observation. Sociologically this carried all the dangers of using language generated within and by the groups being observed, but they were of value because commendable as ideals, though I thought there might be some obstacles to their practice. They also served the useful function of giving credibility to a study within the medical settings in which I thought it might be pertinent to work.

A few weeks later when 'the role of the nurse[3] in the care of the dying' had been achieved as the working title, I began to formulate the kind of fieldwork I was going to do, and devise ways of becoming acceptable to nursing administrators — hoping to use the sway of past nursing training. So 'staff' spread from academics to National Health administrators.

Despite the profoundly good advice of an anthropologist who told me that projects should be limited to take home life into account, it took a formal discussion with three nursing hierarchs to alter my grandiose schemes. The meeting was a fascinating struggle between my two roles of nurse and researcher, with the former winning. Although medical sociology was well established locally, I had thought that being introduced so officially to people I wanted to work with on the wards might make me a threat. Instead, using old nursing contacts, I made my own way.

In the proposal to the nursing administrators, submitted before I went to see them, I tried to 'sell' myself by predicting what they would like, and also what they would dislike, so that it could be counteracted. The proposal was deliberately left flexible so that there was room for manoeuvre, but my main doubt was that they would tolerate an observer. Why should they? To try to overcome that, I made a commitment to working free, instead of being an onlooker, and the more I thought about it the more I thought it would provoke interesting data. I also felt that this might alleviate a problem encountered by MacIntosh (1977) who noted how awkward he felt when the cancer ward he was studying was busy.

As it was I totally misjudged their reading of the proposal. Instead of being flexible it looked as though I did not know what I was doing, and though they welcomed nursing research, there was some anxiety over someone who wanted to be integrated. The effectiveness that the authority of nursing administrators can have on those they train showed, and I acquiesced to their suggestions that I drop totally the community part of a scheme which had included time to be spent in a community, in a hospital, and in a hospice.

In the report on the meeting I noted that; 'I went in optimistic and came out feeling like a grilled sardine — small, squashed and hot.'

Having given me their tentative support, the administrators continued to meet me intermittently, and they helped devise the proposal to go before the Ethical Committee. At the time it caused enormous concern since the project could be stopped, but once it was accepted the whole thing vanished as unimportant, with the exception that they made me have a nurse supervisor. A senior tutor at the Infirmary Nursing School, she not only let me talk at her, but eased my way into the nursing school, allowing me freely to use the library and video facilities, and by the end setting up interviews with other nursing tutors and a forum for discussion of what I was doing. It was part of my integration back into the nursing establishment.

Not until the end of the first year with a methodology summer school, did the relief and revelation come that other postgraduates had trouble with their filing systems, how to take notes, and how to distinguish fact from opinion in their own writing, let alone other people's. I found that everyone struggles to write, or avoid it, that their theoretical base was not the clear shining light illuminating their path that I assumed it should be. Indeed other participant observers, like me, were at a loss to know how data fits theory or theory fits data. That these were not necessarily difficulties solved as an undergraduate indicated that some of the questions I had thought to be too obvious to ask about were part of learning research. Others too suffered from degrees of lack of professional confidence that I had not formerly thought commensurate with the status of a postgraduate, and as we chatted over the minutiae of our research problems, informally as much as in guided sessions, so our academic contacts grew to good effect and came to be renewed at future conferences. I found this invaluable.

A one-month hospice course during the first year had firmed up my supposition that there was a gap between the rhetoric of 'good' terminal care, and what happens when it is practised, and also indicated some of the future problems of participant observation. As the time for the bulk of the fieldwork was approaching, I anticipated difficulties in writing at the end of a shift. I therefore devised a limited number of A4 forms (to allow for later adaptation) — partly numbers and cases, and partly descriptive, to ease the way into getting the shift into some kind of perspective. To this were to be added tape recordings of what the shift had felt like, although it was only once the fieldwork was underway that sheets of 'odd thoughts' developed. They made no attempt to be a coherent part of the data, but just seemed brilliantly insightful at the time.

Another aspect of preparation was to introduce myself and the study to the hospital ward and the continuing care unit where I was to work — ostensibly to ask their permission, although I felt they had little choice once the doctors and the Ethical Committee had agreed to it.

The Sister on the medical ward which was used mainly for heart patients was exceptionally open-minded, forward thinking and relaxed, but saw little point in having a researcher into dying on the ward when there were not that many deaths — which was difficult when the numbers of deaths apparently went up when I was there. The common quip about me being a Jonah had something of an edge to it. In contrast, the Sister on the continuing care unit, a place known as something of a deathhouse, was anxious to present the staff and patients as a happy and unified family — which I did not believe, but had qualms at the prospect of exposing. In both places I sat in on the report when all the nurses on duty regularly gather together, to explain what I wanted to do, neither wanting to appear an academic know-all nor to make them feel like the objects of study. (In the end, one of the ways I was accepted was to be thought of as clever (only clever people are at university) but a bit dim at practical things.) I could only explain in general terms what I intended to do, pointing out that the outcome of the research was unclear — it was exactly why I was going to do the study —

and so like many researchers, deliberately or not, I failed to convey what the research was about.

To maintain my identity as a researcher, what I wore to work (it was noticeable that I used 'work' to describe nursing but rarely to describe writing or university events) became of symbolic significance. I was in a quandary, as I did not want to deliberately obscure my identity to pretend I was not doing research, but also wanted to be accepted as one of the team, though the administrators wanted me to be visibly different. The white coat was discarded in favour of a nursing dress, but I was not to have a hat or epaulettes which denote the stage and type of training. As was intended these careful omissions generated an awareness of my difference, but by the end of fieldwork in the hospital, before I started in the unit, I had acquired both. Usually reluctant to wear uniforms, not feeling I belonged was disquieting and I made the effort to be allowed the privilege of wearing a white paper hat, and the pink epaulettes of a staff nurse. Going native.

Which is the right information?

The great day came. The proper start of fieldwork. On for an early shift, I got up at 5.30a.m. after a terrible night's sleep, drove with jumbled thoughts to the hospital, changed in the sisters' locker room (a measure of my confusing status to administrators as well as to myself), and went down early to the ward where my name had been added to the nursing rota. (Despite my being on the rota, no nurse was to be displaced as the result of my being there. It would have caused union problems as I was unpaid. It was also to my advantage because most nurses are reluctant to be 'lent' when there are too many nurses on the ward, and it could have created bad feeling.) The shift was a daunting muddle to me. We had report and unlike the others, I was not allocated to work with someone but left to find my own jobs. The Sister thought she was being helpful, but I felt lost. A few remarks from my fieldnotes:

I didn't know what I was doing, and the lack of routine

was very undermining, or rather the lack of knowledge of the routine was very undermining to me. I felt that I had no independence on the ward because I nearly always had to ask people if I wanted to do, or thought I ought to do, something.

One of the problems all during today has been the vast input of possible information, and not knowing how to select it. I'd already decided that for the first couple of days I'd concentrate on my own socialisation, the acquiring of the routine, learning about the ward and so on to be able to write down the timetable of the nursing day, but even so.

Confusion and doubt is part of any nurse's move to a new ward, but I had forgotten that and I found it difficult to make sense of things as a nurse, let alone a researcher. Even as I settled down to doing auxiliary-nurse-type of work, though still having coffee in Sister's office, I was casting about for what it was that I was trying to discover. Good social scientists manage to establish valuable facts. My observations seemed to lack that authority. And as Shaffir says: 'field researchers always live, to some extent, with the disquieting notion that they are gathering the wrong data, that they should be observing or asking questions about another event or practice, instead of the present one' (Shaffir et al., 1980, p. 17).

Truth, objectivity and bias loomed large in my thinking throughout the fieldwork, and increasingly quantitative research seemed to hold the enticing allure of being 'scientific'. It was not until I was well back out of the nursing that what had been written during it looked as though it had any purpose or explanatory use.

It was intended that the research would generate its own emphases, but I had needed not only a product to sell to the people whose aid I wanted to enlist, but also to give some direction to my thinking — as for instance in the forms I made.

In submitting the proposal to the nursing administrators I had made a mental note to beware that I did not get taken in by my own propaganda, to remember that my interest was skewed to people who were thought to be ill and people who helped look after them, rather than patients and nurses, that I was being a nurse merely as a means to research. Once involved, that seemed heartlessly instrumental. When they went to supper, work stopped for them, as they assumed it did for me, and their trust, which I wanted, was discomforting. Occasionally passing outrageous remarks to make it clear that I was not one of them, giving them a chance to defend themselves against me, did little but salve my conscience. However, as they were subjects of study to me, so to some extent was I subject to study and use by them. In attempting to keep free enough from the restrictions of hypotheses to let the data indicate the important issues, so I was open to be buffeted by the most powerful influences and friendships. The result is that the majority of quotable quotes came from few people, and my preoccupations were those of the places and people with whom I worked. A useful bias.

I had been concerned at not being allocated to an oncology ward (they had recently been overstaffed and there had been complaints from the nurses. The wards had also been the subjects of other research) and that despite proposal claims that I would not make 'direct' comparisons, I would not be able to make the best use of the deaths that I saw. Instead, and to my advantage, the different types of death from the dramatic adrenalin-driving emergencies, to people who had suffered four heart attacks now living on the edge of the fear of sudden death, to the release of the expected fading away, were a superb reminder of how nurses cope with different deaths and that the ideals of the hospices must be translatable to different circumstances. For example, when a man due out the next day had a cardiac arrest and died later, having witnessed his roommate die suddenly and unexpectedly that day, it was gone over time and again by the staff as those involved at any stage tried to work out if they were to blame, what else could have been done and how to live with it. The Sister rang me up to tell me. When Charlie (82), a ward favourite − the only one allowed to lie on the bed with his boots on − died, there was sadness but just gentle memories we recalled with a sense of affection and loss for the skilled fiddle-playing old codger, with the knowledge that it had been his time to go.

Unanticipated and useful additions to my knowledge were also made as my status changed, on the hospital ward, but more obviously so in the continuing care unit. In both places I tried to fit in by doing what was asked of me, but not taking leading decisions, and I had thought that I would work in the background with the auxiliaries. Not only do the auxiliaries not stay in the background, but I was known to be a staff nurse. By the fourth day in the hospital, when I asked a student nurse about doing something, she said: 'You decide, you're in charge.' When time was short and the drug round was due, I was qualified to do it, and to take charge of the drug keys when other trained staff were off the ward. Adopting different roles in the hierarchy is what everyone but the most senior do everyday, and that on one shift I could be in charge of the continuing care unit and the next be cleaning the sluice − auxiliary territory − pointed up just how conscious and specific the hierarchies are.

After a year looking at the literature, my general knowledge of the terminal care movements was greater than almost anyone I worked with. Having been warned by the methodology books, I was duly concerned about observer effect. When a hospital consultant asked, in some depth, my opinion on the way to organise the last months of a patient who was terminally ill with cancer, even though I suspected him of wanting to show me that he cared for his patients in a way that I would approve of, it would have been wrong to withhold any help I could give. By the time I was working in the smaller, closer-knit group in the continuing care unit, I had accepted that, like other nurses with their own idiosyncrasies, I would affect the care and work, not just as an observer, but actively, as a participant, without knowing exactly how and where. It was only after fieldwork finished that I discovered from one of the auxiliaries that she would groan if she was working with me (as senior) because I would sit out some of the very heavy patients who would normally have stayed in bed.

As my time at the hospital came to a close, I decided that

a longer and perhaps more reflective discussion on the
nurses' thoughts about their work would be a helpful addition to the remarks and brief debates that I heard as they
organised and cared for the patients. On night duty there
had been more opportunity to talk casually and at length,
but on days it needed to be arranged beforehand. I went to
Betty's house as researcher and workmate, but after a five-
hour rambling conversation which included her husband
and child, interspersed with lunch and afternoon tea, the
difficulty of remembering what had been said made a tape
recorder an attractive proposition just to leave running. I
asked the Sister if she minded me having one there as she and
I talked round a few subjects, and she was relaxed enough to
ignore it. I did not do enough taping at the hospital before
I left to take account of the kind of effect I was having.

During a two-month break from nursing for a reappraisal
of where I'd got so far, I gave a seminar paper in the department which, though not obvious then, became one of the
main outlines for the final thesis. This, together with the
regular meetings with my supervisor throughout the fieldwork, allowed some of my thoughts on terminal care nursing to coalesce. When I went to work on the purpose-built
continuing care unit I hoped, somewhat deviously, that
getting people to talk about their thoughts on how care of
the dying should be approached would give a helpful comparison with what could be observed of their practice of it.
I postponed doing this until I was better known, but when
an excellent nurse was about to leave, I was provoked to
start. People knew me and my ideas too well for me to be
able to interview them, and although there were four general
areas I wanted to ask about, having a 'conversation' was more
appropriate. Taping saved intrusive scribbling. I anticipated
that everyone worked with me and teased me well enough
for the conversations not to bother them too much. They
were either at people's houses or at the unit, whichever they
preferred, but the variations in how easy people found it,
and their fluency in the more formal talk, were enormous.
Until I listened to the tapes retrospectively, I did not realise
the resistance, despite familiarity, of the power structure
between interviewer and informant. In some cases I got the

power balances quite wrong even when I had learnt to sit through the silences, though in others they organised them-selves to make it easier. I arrived at Mary's to find that she had invited Jessica round so they could do it together, and we all had lovely afternoon tea. This in itself was good data, not to be missed out and whilst it was part of the 'gossamer of ideas' (Brody, 1981) on how nurses control their circum-stances, I was constantly concerned as to its validity (to whom?) and acceptability (to whom?) as social science, prompted by what I thought to be its unacceptability within medical circles. They obviously talked over the conversations with each other as they happened, and inevitably the discus-sions gave pause for reflection — I was told so several times — but how they affected behaviour was impossible to detect.

The unit was something of a showcase, built as it was with money from the local community and with the purpose of providing care for cancer patients. The Sister in charge was therefore more involved than most in showing visitors round, thereby, with some anxiety, putting herself on show. She looked after me as thoughtfully as she looked after the others, giving me time in the quiet room to write up notes, and I suspect she was both pleased and somewhat disquieted to have me there. Although we were both careful in our management of it, it is possible that I may have been a threat to her, and as far as I can remember, despite being there for five months, I did not publicly air my views in front of her as vehemently as I did in other chatting groups. Mutual support is an important contribution to maintaining a happy atmosphere in terminal care units, feared and criticised as they often are by outsiders, and stressful within. My criti-cisms, through regular discussion and deliberate distancing, were more succinct than most, and it was something of a dilemma when asked my opinion.

A dysfunction built into the research, for which I had made inadequate provision, was the constant prodding at the defence mechanisms which are a means of continu-ing at the unit. If I pushed the others too far they would evade, avoid or tell me to shut up, but my own defences were also under scrutiny and the more I was perturbed by exposing them, the more my reluctance to write up at the

end of the day grew. I was enjoying the nursing. For the
research, philosophy, the structure of the National Health
Service, and numbers became easier lines of thought. None
of them had anything to do with people.

Getting the balance in writing

By the time the main fieldwork was over, the unit was in the
turmoil of four established staff leaving together, taking
with them their assurance and the unit's sense of coherence.
As one of those going, there were times when it seemed a
more attractive prospect to stay, especially as I battled with
the misgivings of writing about people who had confided
in me. A hagiographic account would be useless. The place
was not perfect. Yet it seemed an act of disloyalty and
arrogance to expose their private and work lives to outsiders and presumption to explain their living with dying.

The initial difficulties of devising a problem were still
there, taking the form of what to write in and what to leave
out. Could and should the detail of decision-making in nursing — who to get up first — be put with the effects of a
national charity organisation working with the NHS, and if
so, how should it be balanced? I had been taught that it is
less the data and more how it is used that is significant, and
I was aware that such analytical skill is hard to acquire.

An infrequent conference attender, I found the allure of
them was strong, and the BSA medical sociology conference
came at a beneficial time. The distancing from the unit,
the different perspectives and stimulation of the papers,
served to sharpen my academic interests, not only through
the printed agenda but with the pleasure of discussion
amongst the gathered circus of friends, acquaintances and
unknowns. Being a sociologist was not mistaken for being a
social worker, and some there were even willing to talk
about pain, death and loss. Even the gnawing fear that someone was doing the same research as me and I hadn't found
out about it was partially cured. They were, but I still thought
I had something to say. As I grew away from the unit,
almost imperceptibly the major themes and their place

under chapter headings were emerging.

At the outset of the three years my supervisor offered suggestions which I thought were obscure. He said that I would be surprised how the themes I had started out with would thread through the work, and that looking back I would be able to trace them. Also that the issues to be written about would become clear as I went through the fieldwork. They seemed contradictory remarks, as the first implies some kind of formulation of the problem before I began, and the other that the problem would become manifest. Baldamus (1972, 1976) notes that there is a progressive double fit between fact and theory. That this was happening despite my incredulity, suggests that I had begun with firmer ideas than I thought and that from this base, observations interesting enough to pursue could emerge.

The academic influences on the project were not exclusively those selected for it. One of the great benefits of working in the sponsored individual PhD system is the freedom to follow divergent lines of thought. When I began reading and attending women's studies discussions, it seemed an indulgence that could be justified in terms of knowledge of current sociological thinking, but not in terms of the thesis. I had wanted to understand the interactions and negotiations in stressful practical work which happened to be almost exclusively by women. Here splits by profession rather than gender were important, and one of the foremost hospices in the country had female leaders for doctors, social workers, nurses, physiotherapists and volunteer workers. Regardless, my indulgence continued. Later, out of fieldwork and unaer pressure from a friend to use all my reading materials, I began to see the explanatory value of gender relations in what I was doing, and the indulgence became so redefined as to be a significant part of the analysis. Had it been there from the beginning, the study would have been quite different.

If an egocentric research diary used to record basic information like dates of meetings as well as frustrations, was a framework to reflect on events, recording what I read showed a more haphazard pattern. As I thought about writing the project up, I rediscovered the limitations of written words.

To capture the essence of a particular experience rather than social science, I read literature where webs of relations can be dealt with fluently, dynamically, vividly, lightly or intensely. Writing about the shift in a journalese/story form was a means of trying to retain some of the wealth of events, affection, pressures, humour, motives and life of the unit, but it has limited use for translating passing thoughts and actions into an analysis.

Scurrying hurriedly round other hospices, with little time to do anything other than ask questions, indicated some of the significance of what I had learnt taking part in the work. I also noticed that participant observation gives an appearance of personal choice in the selection and presentation of what is observed to be significant, which was less obvious by the time my inquiries were in question form. How to retain the integrity of my participation in the work became a major stumbling block.

The information I gleaned convinced me, of course, of the validity of participant observation as an approach but also confirmed the drawbacks and rewards of working in familiar settings. In the end, in the attempt to justify my involvement, I concluded that the involvement does not invalidate my analysis, it merely marks the project as structured within one kind of sociological tradition, which itself will alter as different emphases are required of it.

Conclusions

One of the absurdities of chronological reporting on projects is that they manufacture unreal endings. This thesis could still change, and the future uses and adaptations of it and the research training it provided are unclear — to be swayed by the context in which they are received. This essay is offered as part of the story so far.

In answer to the embarrassing questions of what is sociological information and what is academically acceptable research, a vulgar answer is that it depends on who assesses and pays the researcher to do what, and subsequently how the researcher can manipulate it to their own ends. Within research systems, the sponsored individual PhD, with its implications for the training of postgraduates, is the freest and therefore perhaps the most difficult research process of all, carrying with it the responsibility to produce and the struggles of deciding what to produce. It allows the liberty of a genuine education, of invaluable academic growth and practice, generating its own enthusiams and with the stumbling discoveries that are useful heuristic devices. On the other hand, working with money given for the purpose of furthering sociology makes it awkward to question openly the directions in which sociology ought to go, and how to get there. This can make it a lonely task.

Writing an essay of this kind is a measure of optimism. It assumes that the variations in traditions and the debate and criticism within social science are vitally interesting and strong enough to withstand evaluation. A problem in making it public is that critics of the system are given the ammunition they want to undermine it, and as social research for social policy becomes a survival tactic, assessors like to have precisely measured results for their financial backing as Bell indicates in his chapter. Postgraduate training schemes exclusively along the lines of apprenticeship in leader-dominated units, offer an attractive proposition to those who enjoy the predictability of uniformity (see for example Illsley, 1981). Yet the provoking content of sociology is richer than those who would make it only a fashion dictated by economics can allow.

One of the supreme tools sociology has given me is the means to look beyond predominant explanations of policies and their effects. I find it deeply reassuring of the value of sociology that some of the alternative explanations it provides invoke emphatic disagreement.

Notes

I would like to thank Eleanor Forbes, David Oldman, and Rory Williams; the editors for their help with this essay, and Alice Lovell for nagging me about it so beautifully.
All names used in the chapter have been changed for obvious reasons.

1   The 'tin trunk' is a deep trolley covered with a sheet and pillow to make it look ordinary, in which the body is taken from the ward to the mortuary.

2   Kardex is a reporting system, filled in each shift for each patient, to give a running commentary of the patient's condition and care. It belongs to the nurses rather than the doctors.

3   References to nurses include auxiliaries, sisters, pupil, student and staff nurses.

8

Bringing it all back home:
an anthropologist in Belfast

Richard Jenkins

Anthropologists, especially as they have 'come home' now, face fieldwork dilemmas that are in many ways very similar to those experienced by sociologists who have done, say, community studies in this country. Richard Jenkins's account of doing anthropological fieldwork in a Belfast housing estate is especially valuable because he was neither a real 'local' nor a complete 'outsider'. In the extremely difficult situation that exists in Ulster it is perhaps surprising that this sort of fieldwork is possible at all. Certainly his role was 'checked out', and maintaining his credibility could have been quite literally a matter of life and death. He discusses with great insight 'the importance of the identity of the researcher in the eyes of his or her research subjects in constraining or creating the possibility of effective access to particular situations and groups' as well as the limitations in the very method of participant observation in allowing (or not) access to certain areas of social reality. He is very sensitive to the limits and constraints that he, a male fieldworker, was working within in regard to access to the lives of the young women and to the more 'private' aspects of family life. William F. Whyte — in many ways Jenkins's mentor — said, in Street Corner Society, *that he was build-*

ing a sociology based upon 'observed interpersonal events'.
To the extent that not all interpersonal events are observable
and that not all we are interested in is interpersonal, there
are some apparent limitations to this method, and great
strengths too, as this chapter illustrates.

Discussions of the fieldwork experience, the ethnographer's
rite de passage, have almost become a sub-literature within
the anthropological tradition, Eleanor Bowen's *Return to*
Laughter (1964) being one of the better-known examples.
More recently, these revelations have achieved a more intimate character with the publication of Malinowski's field
diary (1967) and Margaret Mead's letters from the field
(1977). Given the typical anthropological research site of
'Bongo-Bongoland', most of these reflections on the participant observation experience have concerned themselves
with the impact on the researcher of immersion in a more
or less alien and exotic social world. Even Whyte, one of the
few anthropologists who discusses the experience of urban
fieldwork (1955, pp. 279-358), was a cultural outsider in
Cornerville, having to learn Italian in order to get by. The
topic of this chapter is slightly different, being an attempt
to come to terms with some of the problems involved in
doing anthropological fieldwork in an urban environment
in which, although not a local, the researcher is certainly not
an outsider either.

This is a subject which has, for obvious reasons perhaps,
attracted more attention to date from sociologists. It is, in
fact, something of a paradox that at a time when some social
anthropologists, formerly the classical exponents of the art
of participant observation, are beginning to embrace quantitative approaches and are adapting the methods accordingly,
there is a strong movement within British sociology in the
direction of ethnographic fieldwork. With this upsurge in
interest from sociologists has also come an appreciation of
some of the problems and possibilities associated with the
participant observer role in the United Kingdom (i.e. Burton,
1978, pp. 164-79; Hargreaves, 1967, pp. 193-205; Willis,

1980). It should be pointed out, however, that participant observation, as I shall discuss later, still remains very much the characteristic anthropological method.

In this chapter I shall discuss some of the possibilities and problems as they presented themselves to me during anthropological fieldwork in a Belfast housing estate. Bearing in mind that increasingly anthropologists are turning — or, perhaps, having to turn — their attention towards their own cultures, this is clearly an area in which greater dialogue between the two disciplines would be useful. There is some evidence that this is a methodological issue which is being taken more seriously at the moment by anthropologists across the Atlantic (Messerchmidt, 1981).

Author and subject: an introduction

In order to set the scene for the discussion below it is essential to know something about my background and how that background relates to 'Ballyhightown', the housing estate where I did my research. Born in Liverpool, I moved with my family to Larne, a small town about twenty miles north of Belfast, in 1960 when I was eight. Apart from ten months in 1970-71, Larne was my home until 1977, when I left to go to Cambridge. It was a staunchly Protestant town; I went to school there, worked in an engineering factory overlooking the sea, and lived there for most of the period during which I was a student in Belfast. The housing estate where I lived as a child and as an adult, Craigy Hill, is very similar to Ballyhightown, having been built by the Northern Ireland Housing Trust (now the Housing Executive) at about the same time, the ground having been broken for both in the early 1950s. I was, therefore, intimately familiar with the kind of built environment I found myself in during the fieldwork.

The similarities between Ballyhightown and Craigy Hill should not, however, be overstressed. Ballyhightown is very much a part of Belfast, albeit an outlying part, and Belfast is a very different sort of place to Larne. Similarly, 'Hightown' has suffered much more as a result of the Troubles. However, it would be true to say that as a Protestant housing estate there was much about life in Ballyhightown that I felt at home with and recognised.

A more important aspect of my relationship with Bally-hightown reflected the fact that the peripheries of my own personal network extended into the estate and its environs. For example, two of the teachers in the local secondary school had been to school with me, as had one of the hotel managers I contacted during a postal survey of employers. Another local employer, the manager of a small engineering company, had actually lived next door to me in Larne at one time. Similarly, a mate of mine from my days on the shop-floor in Larne worked for another small engineering company near the estate where some of the kids I was interested in also worked. It all helped. Most significant of all, I suspect, I was easy to 'find out about', should anyone have wished to do so. Given the existence of paramilitary organisations and the fact that I, of necessity, asked questions and poked my nose into matters which may well have been no concern of mine, there were people who probably *did* want to find out about me. In this sense it is likely that my identity was easy to check with their contacts in Larne. That I had a good friend in common with a local man who appeared to be 'involved' at a high level undoubtedly helped. As part of my youth work role I also built up a stock of good rela-tionships with those people on the community-work fringe of local parliamentary politics which served me in good stead later. Over and against this, however, there were a significant number of people, both kids and adults, who remained suspicious of me to the last. They remain suspi-cious to this day.

Relationships of this type may be thought to present ethical problems. They undoubtedly do, but the problems are as much about the researcher's relationship with the local community and his or her informants, as the question of responsibility to the under-society. During the period I was there, there was simply no way I could have carried out intensive research in Ballyhightown without establish-ing a comfortable *modus vivendi* with some people whom I believed to be members of paramilitary organisations. This, as we shall see, led to difficulties; it was, however, inescapable if a whole aspect of life in Ballyhightown was not to be missed out. As things turned out, relationships of this nature resulted in one of the most personally rewarding aspects of the fieldwork. Arriving in Ballyhightown with what might best be described as a 'liberal' or 'moderate' set of attitudes concerning Northern Irish politics, generally critical of political violence from whichever quarter, I left feeling that I knew something more about the complexities of the situation, and hopefully rather more understanding of the reasons why people seek their political ends through violence.

The route by which I arrived at Ballyhightown is also important to this account. In May 1976 I was a social anthropology undergraduate at Queen's University, Belfast. I had been offered a postgraduate place at Cambridge to do research on witchcraft in eighteenth and nineteenth century Ireland; that is probably what I would have done had it not been for a bomb attack on a bar near the University at the end of May. Coming hard on the heels of a rapidly disintegrating marriage, the shock of being caught in the explosion and seeing a friend killed made me stop and think. I was granted a year's grace by Cambridge and took a youth-work job in Ballyhightown, more or less to provide the breathing space I felt I needed.

Fourteen months later I did go to Cambridge, the intervening period having convinced me that I wasn't cut out to be a youth worker. Inadequately thought out by the local education authority and characterised by conflict within the organisation and with other organisations, the project was something of a non-event. Furthermore, in my own eyes and in the eyes of the kids and my colleagues, it was clear that I wasn't much of a youth worker anyway.

However, it was not time wasted. I left Ballyhightown with a pile of detailed fieldnotes — which, to this day, I'm not sure why I kept — and my personal relationships with the young people and the youth workers more or less intact. When I did get to Cambridge I was fortunate in having a head of department, Jack Goody, my eventual supervisor, who took an interest in what I had been doing during my year off and encouraged me to capitalise on it, and a supervisor, Alan Macfarlane, who was tolerant of my increased lack of interest in witches and let me go with his blessing. This, therefore, was the succession of accidents and unplanned events which led to my arrival in Ballyhightown in 1978 as a research student interested in the transition from school to work.

The research continued on and off, until the summer of 1979. I do not intend to say very much about the eventual findings nor, indeed, about the estate itself. I have documented the research at length elsewhere (Jenkins, 1981; 1982b; 1983a; 1983b) and to do so here would be redundant. There are, however, two problems which emerged from my experiences in the field which may be either peculiar to, or exacerbated by, the participant observation approach; first, the importance of the identity of the researcher in the eyes of his or her research subjects in constraining or creating the possibility of effective access to particular situations or groups, and second, the limitations of the method itself in permitting (or not) access to certain areas of the social reality under study.

Seeing yourself as others see you: questions of identity

There were several places in Ballyhightown which were important foci for the research. The first was the Youth Centre, which I continued to hang about during the fieldwork. There were also the Hillview Social Club, Ballyhightown Secondary School, the homes of friends and the two flats in which I lived. Just as important were events: the Saturday afternoon trips 'into town', watching Linfield play at home or away, the minibus trip to Dublin to support Northern Ireland in their European Championship match against Eire, evenings spent drinking, local parties and evenings spent simply looking for something to do. These places and occasions formed the framework within which questions were asked and notebooks filled.

Particularly during the period when I was no longer a youth worker, it proved difficult, for two reasons, to establish a new and clear-cut identity for myself. First, I was still working on a voluntary basis, and specifically with an eye towards participant observation, in the Youth Centre. Second, I experienced some difficulty in explaining to people, inside and outside the Centre, exactly what the role of researcher was. Unlike the conventional researcher, armed with an interview schedule or survey and self-evidently seen to do research, the participant observer must — almost by definition — be *not* seen to do research. I didn't appear to have a 'real' job and, although I told them I was writing a thesis about young people from the area, what they actually saw me do for most of the time was hang about the Youth Centre or a couple of the local bars and clubs. Telling them that I was a student didn't clarify matters either. In their experience, that meant either a student teacher on teaching practice in the school or a youth work student on placement in the Centre; they knew that I was neither of those. Some of the kids did appreciate my role to some extent and actively supported the research, but very many more, particularly those with whom I had only superficial regular contact, remained convinced that I was some odd breed of youth worker.

I had several motives for continuing to work in the Youth Centre. First, I hoped to use the Centre's senior youth club and afternoon sessions for the unemployed as research venues. It was important, therefore, given the misunderstanding of my research role by some of the kids, to have some sort of other role in that context. Not being young enough or local enough to participate as a club member, and given my personal history as a Centre staff member, I settled for an identity somewhere between that of observer and youth worker. This entailed trying to get on with the club users in much the same way as I had previously done, while at the same time the staff didn't make the demands of me which they would have done had I been there as a part-time worker. On balance, this was a successful enough compromise in practice.

Second, I participated in some senior youth club activities in a more structured fashion, organising discussion groups on Sunday evenings, sometimes with invited speakers, for a group of senior members who had requested a repeat of the previous year's successful discussion groups. This gave me the chance to record their views on a wide range of subjects, at the same time relieving the Centre's overworked staff of the responsibility for organising that part of the club's programme. Finally, there were personal reasons for continuing to participate in the work of the Centre. I enjoyed it and it helped me to overcome, at least to a limited extent, my feelings of being redundant at best and parasitic at worst. Working in the Centre did not blunt the edge of these self-criticisms; it did, however, enable me to pursue the research without succumbing to them.

Thus, in the eyes of many of the young people, and adults, living on the estate I retained something of my previous identity as a youth worker. Looked at from the standpoint of doing research, this had undoubted advantages. It was a role many people on the estate were sympathetic towards and this may have led to me being told things I might possibly not have discovered had my role simply been that of researcher.

It is, however, equally likely that my adoption of this identity may have militated against my establishing a useful research relationship with those who regarded the Youth Centre as an outpost of authority, 'them' as against 'us', in Ballyhightown.

I suspect that this was, however, offset in practice by the Centre's reputation locally as a rough and rowdy place, a place many 'respectable' young people 'wouldn't be seen dead in'. This might explain the fact that the only outright refusal I encountered during the formal interviewing phase of the research was from one of the 'citizens', the sample of 'respectable' young people.

Role ambiguity of this sort poses serious ethical problems. These I have partly resolved by treating some of the information as confidential, only to be used when suitable camouflage, the alteration of important details, does not diminish their usefulness. Furthermore, in some cases in which I was knowingly privy to information which was sensitive or confidential in a variety of respects, whether as a youth worker or later, I simply decided not to use it at all. In most cases information of this nature was not even recorded. Ethical considerations of this nature are important in all research, particularly when participant observation, however that is defined, is involved. They have even greater urgency in Northern Ireland, where political violence is an integral part of the social reality being studied. In this situation responsibility and careful reporting is of the greatest importance, if only to safeguard the researcher and his/her informants.

This brings me to the second identity-related problem which I encountered. Those local people who did appreciate my role as a researcher saw me as specifically interested in the broad topics of youth, education and the labour market. This was not simply a reflection of my previous existence in the Youth Centre, it was actually how I presented myself to people — that was the subject I was researching and with which I was primarily concerned. However, I was also heavily influenced, through my reading and the pre-fieldwork seminars in Cambridge, by the time-honoured anthropological approach of 'write-everything-down-you-never-know-what-might-be-important-later'. Even the most trivial details of social life become transformed into data.

This has its dangers in a place like Ballyhightown. It becomes even more problematic when, of necessity, you are mixing with people who may have an involvement in violent politics, people who may want to know why you are interested in subjects which appear to lie outside your brief. Related to this is a third problem: when is the participant observer 'off duty'? When *do* you write things down and when not? Even when the appropriate role in a particular situation is that of 'researcher', it is very easy to let your guard down, especially in a society of which you are, to some degree, a member.

A concrete example of the kind of tricky situation which these kinds of problems can lead to concerned a meeting of a local community group. The meeting adjourned after an evening's business to one of the local social clubs and a very heavy night's drinking followed. When I finally left the club I was so drunk that I left my briefcase behind, complete with notebook. The notes were undoubtedly suspicious from one point of view, dealing as they did with matters much wider than the youth-related issues I was nominally interested in. Fortunately, the fact that my social 'credit' was good in certain quarters prevented that evening's indiscretion having any untoward consequences. That the outcome was a happy one says a lot for the good common sense of the people concerned; that the incident happened at all, however, says just as much about my naivety in the initial period of the fieldwork (i.e. while I was a student).

Belfast, of course, is not the only place where researchers may, with complete justification it must be said, be suspected of spying; nor is it the only place in which that might become a very dangerous situation indeed. Correspondingly it may be useful to briefly consider those steps the participant observer can take to reduce the likelihood of such an incident occurring.

In the first place, sobriety obviously has its virtues. Unfortunately, however, it is usually in the kind of situation where moderation is most desirable that it is most difficult to maintain! Second, it should be possible to be reasonably selective about information-gathering. Recording everything possible may be important if the aim is to document the community concerned in the most holistic fashion possible. For most research projects, however, selectivity, like discretion, is much the better part of valour. It is also much fairer to the people who are the objects of the researcher's curiosity. Finally, and on the purely practical level, given that *any* research notes may contain information about individuals which might be embarrassing should other individuals in the community see them, it makes sense to only carry around the current day's notes. This is easily achieved by using a loose-leaf notebook and minimises the damage which can be done by any possible accidental disclosure. Above all, the researcher must constantly be on his/or her guard when the research role is being adopted; when this role is laid aside, however, the researcher should be equally clear about the responsibilities to the community members that this implies.

There are, of course, other problems revolving around the researcher's identity. The first are the problems (real or imagined) attached to being a male research worker with a professional interest in adolescent girls and young women. These problems are serious but they are not insurmountable. The second set of problems are those of over-identification

with one group possibly prejudicing
groups. I shall discuss these problems i
section.

Power and research access: the limits of parti observation

In the above I discussed some problems encountered in attempt to construct a credible and honest research identity as a participant observer. Once this identity was established, there remained the problem of reaching my potential research subjects and persuading them to participate in that research. There were at least four separate aspects of my role in Ballyhightown which affected the access I negotiated with particular sections of the estate's youth.

First, there are the very real obstacles encountered by a male researcher interested in documenting the social reality constructed and experienced by women. Such difficulties may appear to be obvious; it ought to be remembered here that some women researchers appear to consider that girls, particularly working-class girls, are more problematic as research subjects than their male equivalents. The defences of caution and giggles seem to be inordinately hard to overcome (McRobbie, 1978; McRobbie and Garber, 1976). There is certainly a degree of truth in this; given the distinction between the public domain of men and the privatised female domestic world, and the imbalance in power and evaluation which accompanies it (Imray and Middleton, 1983; Rosaldo, 1974), it would be surprising if young men were *not* more accessible than young women.

The difficulties involved in doing research into young women should not be minimised. Those problems which I had, however, seemed to depend on the situation and the research strategy adopted. For example, in undertaking a programme of formal interviews with three samples, the Lads, the Ordinary Kids and the Citizens (see Jenkins, 1983b), I did not feel my sex to be a major disadvantage. Given that the Lads were an all-male sample, the eventual composition of the other samples bear this out to some

...ɔ per cent of the Ordinary Kids and 44 per cent of Citizens were female. One aspect of the interviewing which may have been adversely affected by the fact that I am male, however, was the quality of the rapport between myself and the young women being interviewed. It is difficult to say much about this in retrospect, except to observe that the interviews with the girls in the Ordinary Kids group did not appear to differ in any important respect from those with the boys; they were all very variable. The female members of the Citizens, the 'respectable' sample, however, were very tricky to interview.

Coming to participant observation, there are definite and marked differences in the quality of the material dealing with young men and young women. There were at least two reasons for this. In the first place, I could participate in male activities in a way that I could never have done in the day-to-day life of the girls. This is straightforward and unavoidable; no amount of good, confidential relationships with individual girls can compensate for this *de facto* exclusion from their shared group activities. The second reason relates to the distinction between the public and private domains mentioned above. The 'bedroom culture' of many girls (Frith, 1978, p. 66) is relatively private and correspondingly hard to get at; the boys are simply more publically available. Even in public, the girls tend to be talked down by any males present; 'girl talk' usually closes down at the approach of a man, whether he be a researcher or a local.

The second problem also reflects the dichotomy between the public and the private; my identity as an ex-youth worker placed a limitation upon research into family backgrounds. As a youth worker, I had found it appropriate to only contact kids' families at their specific request — or by chance, of course. This was not because of any hostility on the part of either the young people or their parents. The public sphere of the Youth Centre was a social arena distinct from the private domestic world; by tacit agreement the most comfortable relationship between the two was one of relative insulation. During the later fieldwork, this separation remained important for most of the kids, although there were important exceptions. While I did gather some material on the family, the focus of the research remained firmly outside the household. The strength of the analysis, that of doing 'insider' research, was also its weakness; I remained very much limited to the spheres of action defined by the actors.

My continuing identification with the Youth Centre was the source of another limitation upon my access to all sections of Ballyhightown's youth. My links with the Centre, a 'rough' place to some, may have made the 'respectable' citizens more difficult to interview, particularly the girls. More conscious of their privacy than the Lads or the Ordinary Kids, I encountered one outright refusal, from a member of the Presbyterian Church's Girls' Brigade company (although I did interview her sister). There were, however, reasons for these difficulties other than my past history in the Youth Centre. First, although I was personally acquainted with the members of the other samples, the reverse was true for the Citizens. Second, it may also have had something to do with the greater privatisation of the 'respectable' residents of Ballyhightown.

Finally, my work in the Youth Centre may have confined my interviewing within the network of the Lads to those individuals who continued to use the Centre. This may also be related to the political situation in Northern Ireland. Although I appeared to have come to a tacit understanding with the various political groupings active on the estate, as I said earlier this did *not* mean that I was no longer regarded with suspicion by some people. Some members of the Lads' network may, therefore, have been wary of giving me an interview. There were no outright refusals from any of the Lads, but it would have been a simple enough matter to avoid being interviewed without obviously doing so. The fact that they spent a lot of their spare time downing pints didn't help either. A public bar or a social club is not the best environment in which to try and interview one person, let alone four or five sitting round a table ordering rounds!

Considering all of these difficulties, it is clear that the barriers of gender were not the only obstacles in my path. As a result of these factors my coverage of Ballyhightown's youth in the research was uneven, in both the quantitative and qualitative senses. Furthermore, my connection with

the Youth Centre was a mixed blessing: although it allowed
me to enter a situation which another researcher might have
had difficulty penetrating, within that situation it made for
a certain inevitable patchiness.

These are some of the inevitable weaknesses of the participant observer methodology, weaknesses which relate to the
researcher's position within the locality being studied. There
are other limitations, however. While there may once have
been situations, for example, in which the ethnographer
could write a credible and accurate account of a community
solely on the basis of participant observation, I find it hard
to imagine such a situation obtaining anywhere in the modern
world, let alone in contemporary Europe. In the first place,
the anthropologist is as much a participant in the power
relations of the society under examination as are his or her
informants. This is equally true whether the observer is
a native of the society in question or not. In many of the
situations I researched, for example the light engineering
factory whose recruitment procedures I looked at, I simply
was not *empowered* to observe directly much of what I have
written about. I could not *participate* in the making of
selection decisions at TransInternational Electronics. My
presence in such situations would have been inappropriate
unless I had been prepared in some fashion to associate my
research with the interests of the company. Even had I been
happy enough to do so, such an approach would have immediately closed off other avenues of research to me. I therefore
had to adopt a methodologically promiscuous approach,
relying largely on formal or informal interviews with past and
present employees and company spokesmen. Participant
observation had only a minor part to play, and then only
indirectly in the sense that chance conversations were often
useful. The higher one researches within the organisational
hierarchies of the modern state of industry, the less likely
it is that one will be allowed to do participant observation;
even more rarely are enough decisions made in public to
allow for the construction of an adequate account of what
is going on through observation alone.

Power has a bearing upon another constraint upon participant observation. Society — and most certainly capitalist

society — is constructed in the interaction of collectivities which are often in conflict with each other and this produces difficulties for the erstwhile participant observer. It would not, for example, be possible to construct a full anthropological account of this kind of relationship between criminals and the police: the researcher could not be trusted in *both* social worlds. The same holds good for managers and workers. Furthermore, there are other legal or customary limits to the scope of participant observation. It would, for example, have been impossible to sit in on confidential interviews between social security officers and claimants. Because of the 'negotiatedness' of this kind of research, the researcher is rarely in a position to get round this problem; one negotiates an identity and this identity necessarily colours the rest of the research. By its very nature participant observation *must* lead to partial accounts.

Finally, there are two other limitations upon the usefulness of participant observation in urban, industrialised societies which deserve a mention here: social scale and spatial scale. There are more people, groups and institutions making up these societies than in the more traditional anthropological communities of the third world or the European margins. Not everything the researcher is interested in is routinely available within manageable geographical areas. In addition, the time factor may preclude the use of participant observation, which is both labour-intensive and time-consuming, on the scale which would be necessary to encompass even a small 'slice' of, for example, a medium-sized English town such as Banbury. Participant observation on its own is no longer enough — if, indeed, it ever was.

The future of the anthropological method

Although this chapter has been about the difficulties of one researcher in one situation, it may be appropriate, in closing, to consider the wider implications of those difficulties. Having concentrated on the limitations and inadequacies of participant observation, however, it must be said that there seems to be no methodological approach which is more suited to the task of finding out what people think about themselves and the world, or how they act in complex social situations. It is the limited range of situations in which it is practical which is the problem. Participant observation may be necessary but it is no longer sufficient; it must be viewed as one part of a heterogeneous methodological package if it is to retain its usefulness when western anthropologists come to examine their own societies.

Some anthropologists appear to have recognised this (i.e. Grillo, 1980), but it is clear that participant observation is still widely regarded within the profession, despite the tendency to quantification mentioned earlier, as the thing above all others which distinguishes social anthropology from, for example, sociology. That and an emphasis upon the holistic, on the presentation of a rounded picture of the 'community' or 'group' under study. The result is the preponderance within the anthropology of 'complex societies' of studies of marginal peasant communities or ethnic minorities. This limited range of research topics reflects the very methodological limitations I have been talking about: these are small-scale units which are manageable using conventional anthropological methods.

Participant observation, therefore, remains at the heart of anthropology's model of itself. This I discovered on several occasions in trying to explain to my disciplinary peers a programme of research into the labour market which relied heavily on interviews with managers for its data (Jenkins, 1982a). The typical response to this was that it certainly wasn't anthropology, whatever else it was!

Here, of course, the reader might well pause to ask whether all of this really matters. It does, but probably only to anthropologists, and that for two reasons. First, anthropologists themselves are increasingly dissatisfied with the theoretical adequacy of atomistic models of society based on the 'community' or the 'group' (Boissevain and Friedl, 1975; Ennew, 1980; Grillo, 1980). Many important aspects of 'complex societies' are overlooked: state institutions, multinational corporations and the historical context are but three of the more obvious.

Second, at a time when research in the third world is

becoming both more difficult to arrange, in terms of access, and frequently the subject of competition between disciplines for agency funding, and when resources for social science activity of all kinds in the United Kingdom (for example) are under severe pressure, social anthropology will increasingly be judged alongside other disciplines. Given that sociology — if it is permissible to talk about such a disparate discipline as a whole — increasingly includes the methods and preoccupations of anthropology within its domain of discourse, this is a comparison which may well prove painful for social anthropology.

There is, perhaps, no real reason why it must. There are aspects of the anthropological tradition other than participant observation which might well be stressed in the future; the presentation of holistic accounts of social reality, as discussed above, and a healthy concern with the routine daily life of the participants in that reality, for example. Neither of these necessarily involves participant observation. Indeed, if these objectives are to be pursued at all 'levels' of society, participant observation may be less useful than other approaches such as interviewing, the examination of documentary material or formal surveying techniques.

At the end of the day, a model of social reality must be constructed which adequately comprehends the life-worlds of the people being studied, while at the same time firmly situating those worlds within their broader social context(s). In order for such an anthropology to be genuinely novel, however, those contexts (the state, the labour market, or whatever) should themselves be de-constructed, rendered problematic and examined (Davis, 1975). The prospect for anthropology in pursuing such an approach is a more or less distinctive niche within social science which will enable it to compete on a more equal footing with other disciplines for students and research funding. If this road, or others like it, is not taken, however, and the discipline remains wedded to the participant observation method, anthropology may well end up as marginal or peripheral as some of its traditional research subjects.

Acknowledgments

The research documented in this paper was funded, in the first instance, by the local education authority responsible for Ballyhightown, for whom I worked as a youth worker, and secondly, by the Northern Ireland Department of Education, who awarded me a research scholarship.

9

The personable and the powerful:
gender and status in sociological research

Sue Scott

As Hilary Graham and Janet Finch point out in their chapters, gender is an important dimension of the power relations inherent in qualitative research, and there are problems for the researcher in dealing with gender-based and gender-derived data. In this chapter, Sue Scott looks at the interlocking power structures of gender and status in the research process. Drawing on data collected during a three-year study of postgraduate research in sociology, she examines one dimension of the position of the researcher researching researchers. In Daniels's (1967) terms 'low caste' in relation to some of her respondents, Scott was perceived by others as relatively powerful in a situation in which she was by no means a 'stranger'. In looking at the particular contradictions she and her research associate faced, Scott shows how, to use Dingwall's (1980) phrase, 'personable young women' may be useful as researchers, but face some problems which may not be faced by personable (or otherwise) young men. In examining some of the problems she encountered in interviewing male academics, she moves away from the use of 'male' as a unitary concept, in order to look at the different power locations of the men interviewed, and argues for a reflexive sociology in which those doing sociological

165

research exercise their sociological imaginations a little more
strenuously in order to understand the social relations within
which they themselves operate.

Most sociologists, if asked, would recognise that even within
sociology there exist hierarchies of status, and inequalities
centred around gender. I want to suggest here that my experiences as a researcher studying sociology show that this
recognition is still largely partial and uninformed. As sociologists, most of us spend our lives studying other people; by
coincidence rather than intention, I have spent the last
three years studying sociologists, and I want to suggest,
through a description of some events from those three years,
why it might be useful for social researchers to study themselves and their discipline.

The postgraduate research project

The research experiences and data on which this chapter
draws were collected during a three-year longitudinal study
of the context and process of postgraduate research in the
social sciences, funded by the Social Science Research
Council. The research developed out of discussions between
the Social Science Research Council and the British Sociological Association about the problems facing postgraduates
in general and part-time postgraduates in particular. The
Social Science Research Council showed a willingness to
consider research proposals, and John Wakeford's proposal
was accepted, a decision which caused bad feeling in some
sections of the sociological community (as these things
invariably do), because some people felt that a large-scale
survey was more relevant than the more ethnographic work
which John envisaged. We were to feel some of the ripples
of this discontent later in the project.

The funding began in January 1979, and two Research
Associates, myself and Mary Porter, were appointed, along
with a Research Secretary, Jackie Covill. Although the

research had clearly been initiated by John, he envisaged an egalitarian research team, and in fact, took a back seat for the most part.[1] I was employed from postgraduate research in the same department as John, and Mary came from a recently completed degree in Social Anthropology. It would be over-stating the case to suggest that either of us had a burning interest in the research topic, but we were both in sympathy with the aims of the project, considered it to be useful and sociologically relevant, and were committed to doing a good job.

Home base

It is difficult to separate with any certainty (and this will be a central theme throughout this piece) the influences of gender and of status hierarchy on women's experience in academia. In our case, this was clear in the relationship between the project and the department in which it was located.

John, Mary and I all felt that most other members of the department were not remotely interested in our research. The fact that John had obtained quite a large grant was seen by some as empire-building, and going against the avowedly democratic *modus operandi* of the department (although I'm sure John saw it as a way of creating jobs in sociology and doing some useful research at the same time). There had never been full-time researchers, as opposed to lecturers in the department before, and some people made it quite obvious that they didn't expect Mary and me either to be treated like or to behave like members of staff. At one departmental committee meeting the constitution was produced to see whether the number of student representa-tives would have to be increased because of our presence, and it was suggested by someone that it wasn't really a problem, since, after all, we weren't 'really' staff. At another meeting a piece of paper was circulating inviting staff to a party at a lecturer's home, and when the party-giver saw Mary putting her name on the list rushed over and took the paper away, saying 'oh, I didn't realise you were technically staff'. Needless to say, Cinderella didn't go to the ball.

This sort of response was compounded by our physical isolation from the department. As Diana Woodward and Lynne Chisholm (1981) have described, and in common with many other research workers, our project office wasn't in the department, but on the other side of campus. Allied to this was a tendency in the department to treat Mary and me as one person. We were allocated one pigeon hole, and when we finally managed to get a room in the department (on the grounds that we were doing some teaching) we were given one key between us. The department secretary constantly called each by the other's name, and when we both offered to sit on a department sub-committee one member of staff said that we shouldn't both be on it, implying that this would be unfair, since we would surely have the same views on everything. We did indeed have much in common, but we were certainly not interchangeable, and there was something undermining about being seen as one of a pair, especially in a setting where individual excellence is the order of the day. It is impossible to 'prove', but my gut-reaction was that this response would not have occurred had one or both of us been male. In short, in our own department, where according to our contracts we were members of staff with the same rights and privileges as everyone else, we were treated as young women without status. This is not to suggest that people were nasty to us, indeed some of our colleagues were helpful and sympathetic, but to indicate that as young women not involved in teaching we simply didn't fit.

These initial problems in our own department seemed strange to me at the time, made me much more defensive about the research and often caused me to be overtly critical of it myself. In an atmosphere where theoretical work was the norm, and where teaching and writing books was seen as 'proper' academic activity, where many people felt qualitative methodology to be suspect, and where the research topic was viewed as inconsequential, the fact that two young women, lacking the academic 'respectability' of publications and higher degrees, were not treated as equal is no longer surprising.

My major concerns as I started the fieldwork, then, were that I felt marginal in my own department, that I felt that doing research on research was seen as a second-rate exercise, that those who could do sociology did it and those who couldn't did research on it. Other members of the department, it seemed, thought the research a waste of time, since it was designed to discover what any practising sociologist knew already. During the project however, through meeting other women in similar positions, and through developing understandings of some of the social relations of social research, my own feelings of powerlessness became more readily explicable. They were not simply isolated and individualised responses to specific situations, but were related to the experiences of others and to sets of relations within sociology as a whole. In other words, I became much more sociological about sociology. My experience in my department, however, remains encapsulated for me by a colleague's joking remark at the beginning of our research, 'Haven't you finished yet, you could write that up in ten minutes?'

The fieldwork

Robert Dingwall (1980, p. 881) has noted that it is the conventional wisdom that women make more empathetic interviewers than men: 'It is quite clear that certain sets of data are made more readily available to personable young women ... much as we may regret this on ideological grounds, it is always a temptation to engage such a person, particularly in studies of older men.' Elsewhere, Rosalie Wax (1971) has warned the interviewer to 'remember that a coquette is in a much better position to learn about men than a nun.'

These understandings of the place of women in sociological research overlook an important factor, and that is the experience of the woman researcher herself, how she and her research are affected by gender assumptions, and how these assumptions crosscut dimensions of status and hierarchy. An acute example of such a problem was provided by an interview I arranged with a male postgraduate. The interview was to take place at his home, and I phoned him to arrange a time. During the conversation he mentioned that, unfortunately, the interview would have to take place in his bedroom. My immediate suspicions were allayed when he explained that he had builders in and the rest of the house was a mess, the floorboards were up and so on. When I arrived for the interview, he explained that he had to dash out to the bank, and showed me into the front room to wait for his return. The room, to my disquiet, was in pristine condition, with not a loose floorboard in sight. Waiting for him to return, I went through a rather harrowing time wondering whether he'd insist on me interviewing him in his bedroom when this room seemed perfectly adequate. I'd almost made up my mind to slip quietly away when my interviewee returned, and I asked him why we couldn't stay where we were. Pointing to a cage in the corner, he said 'It's the budgies, once we start talking, they'll chatter right through the interview.' In the end, the interview went without a hitch.

But the problem is not simply that particular interview situations are radically different for women than men, but more than that, the whole process of interviewing, and therefore the data themselves, are coloured by gender considerations. Being forced, in the line of duty, to cross large and unfamiliar cities alone at night by public transport to interview strange men in their own homes is bound to have some effect on the way a woman thinks about the interview process, and on the data collected.

Interviewing peers or the powerful

As sociologists interviewing sociologists, we expected to encounter problems such as those raised by Jennifer Platt (1981) in relation to interviewing one's peers and the status of the data collected. Although we did find that the filtering process created by our respondents' prior knowledge of, and sociological interpretations of our research and its methodology were significant this concern did not become central to the interviewing. This is not to suggest that Jennifer Platt was wrong in her assessment of her respondents as peers, but simply to point out that my structural location was different from hers and this affected my experience of interviewing. What became important was our understanding that the definition of 'peer' is itself problematic. It became evident that we were not interviewing our peers but individuals with different positions and involved in different sets of relations. Our respondents were not peers in the sense that Platt (1981, p. 75) identifies:

> One's peers are in a diffuse sense one's social equals, they are one's equals in role-specific senses, they share the same background knowledge and subcultural understandings, and they are members of the same groups or communities.

Some academics treated me as a peer, some were extremely high-handed; some postgraduates treated me as a peer, others saw me as more knowledgeable and powerful than themselves, and others, notably male part-timers in senior posts, saw me as less powerful. I had an equal relationship with most of the women I interviewed and with some of the men, but only a few. In short, we found that the status of the respondents, and the way this crosscut with their gender, was significantly as interesting as their participation in sociology.

I found many examples of the status of the respondent being used to deny me interviews or to control the interview itself. One eminent male academic simply refused to be interviewed, because he didn't 'believe in empirical research'. One senior woman academic controlled the interview by behaving as if it wasn't an interview at all but just a general chat, and told me very little that I couldn't have discovered from the prospectus. A male professor said he was so busy he could only give me fifteen minutes and then proceeded to fill the time with his views on research training and extravagant claims for the graduate seminars in his department. Presumably this sort of thing was partly to do with prior knowledge of the interview process and how to subvert it or deny it, but importantly the ability of these respondents to do so was because they were not my peers. They were in positions of power which enabled them to treat me as a mere interviewer rather than as a colleague.

Of prime importance in the way the research was affected by our experiences of the interview was the gender of the respondent. It is sometimes difficult to distinguish satisfactorily between the effects of gender and those of status, but in what follows I describe some of the problems which I encountered during the fieldwork which I perceived as being related primarily to the issue of women interviewing men. A major problem which I encountered, and which I think is specific to interviewing both parties to a relationship (in this case supervisor/student) several times over a fairly long period, is the information which is gathered about the person to be interviewed from outside the interview itself, and how the interviewer copes with this. In one instance, I had to interview a senior academic who I had been told by several people in the department was in the habit of putting 'page three' pictures under the glass in his coffee table. In another department I interviewed a supervisor whose female student had complained that he had suggested that their relationship was comparable to a sexual one. What is important here is the way such foreknowledge makes one feel about the person concerned and, given that the qualitative interview should be a social rather than a mechanical situation, the effect that these feelings might have on the way the interview is conducted.

Of course, this also raises the important question of the status of information and what constitutes data. The data which was available to the whole research team were primarily the transcripts of taped interviews, but at an early stage we decided to make notes of things which were said before and after the taped interview. We had no desire to lose such gems as 'oh dear, are you going to tape this, that means I won't be able to chat you up', and a lengthy talk which one supervisor gave on his student's research into impotence, designed we felt, to embarrass us and maintain control over the interview.

Such examples of potentially sexist behaviour made Mary and me much more anxious about possible interview problems and particularly about the necessity, because we were interviewing part-time students, of doing interviews in the evening. In view of this we always made sure that someone knew where we were going and roughly when we were expected back. The common worry for women about being alone with strange men was one which became for us part of the job, part of the interview process.

However, it wasn't simply the worry about crude sexism which affected us in our relations with male interviewees. More refined aspects of the relationship became, if not alarming, irritating. We found that many male academics, and not just those in positions of power, were either overtly or unthinkingly patronising because of our gender. As 'mere' women our theoretical and methodological competence was constantly called into question. Many men attempted to take over the interview and began to interview themselves, one man going to the lengths of summing up the interview and more or less testing the interviewer at the end as to whether it had been done correctly and whether all the data that *he* thought was wanted had been collected. One man actually asked the interviewer, when the interview was being arranged, whether the interviewer knew what she was doing, because he didn't want to 'waste his time with a lot of irrelevant questions'.

I also often found it difficult not to engage in arguments with interviewees who were unwittingly sexist. One part-time postgraduate I interviewed, a vicar, explained that while he was doing his previous degree he had been 'pestered' by his wife, who wanted him to spend some time with her and his children. He had got round this problem this time, he explained, by not telling her he was doing a PhD and pretending that he spent his time locked up in his study writing sermons.

Interviewing peers

Although we found issues of gender and status to be of prime importance in doing fieldwork, Jennifer Platt (1981) is clearly correct in identifying methodological issues which are particular to doing research on a community of which one is a member.

Having made an early decision that *all* the information we gathered about the departments in our sample was relevant data, we often found ourselves in the position of participant observers, at conferences, study group meetings or other professional occasions. Some ethical problems were difficult. At one conference I became involved in a social conversation with a woman which began to turn into a story about the problems she was encountering in her department. I felt that I had to tell her that the department was in our sample and that anything she told me would inevitably become project data. Oddly, ethical concerns such as this never seemed to be much of a problem for many of my colleagues in sociology, a staggering number of whom seemed to think that I would quite willingly gossip about my data. It was on occasions difficult to resist telling stories, and it certainly would have been more difficult if I had been working on my own, but we consistently treated all our information as confidential to ourselves.

A major methodological problem which Jennifer Platt (1981) isolates is that data collected from one's sociological peers is not 'raw' data, but is filtered through sociological understandings. I want to explain in the next section how this difficulty became for me not a problem to be overcome, but something which facilitated insights into the way that sociology is produced and reproduced. I first noticed the importance of the kind of sociological understandings that our respondents brought to the interview in terms of the relationship between different kinds of sociology and the different views on the 'proper' way to do a PhD. I want to suggest that the study of sociology, which is necessary if we are to have any control over how it is reproduced, is precisely the study of those sociological understandings which I was initially worried might affect the validity of our data.

The reproduction of sociology

In previous sections I have described some of my experiences as a researcher in sociology, and have given some examples of the ways that those experiences of sexism and lack of status affected my sense of self and my contribution to the research in which I was involved. It is, however, not enough for women simply to recount their experiences without commenting on the forces that create them and speculating on how those forces may change or solidify. Significantly, my experiences as a researcher bore striking similarities to experiences described to me by many of the women postgraduates I interviewed.[2] Many described feelings of self-doubt about their work, worries about the complexities of the gender implications of their relationships with male supervisors, their feelings of 'separateness' from the ethos and actuality of male-defined academia. I hadn't noticed, until after a particular incident in which I was involved, how many women postgraduates complained to me about their distaste for graduate seminars and the level of cut and thrust competitiveness that they often display, what David Morgan (1981) calls 'academic machismo'. Mary and I were asked to present a paper on our research at a graduate seminar in a department which we had visited to conduct interviews. We had done other seminars and, unsuspectingly, agreed. We gave the paper and asked for discussion. Almost before we had finished speaking the professor leapt to his feet and began a diatribe, during which he evinced not simply disagreement with our presentation and methodology, but anger. He took us to task for writing an article in the British Sociological Association's magazine *Network*, on research training, because this 'made our research worthless' since we had published before completing the research. He launched into a tirade against John Wakeford, almost as if we were empty vessels containing John's opinions, and he capped this by starting to discuss the interview that Mary had carried out with him. We felt that we had been set up as an example of the 'dangers' of ethnographic research so that this professor could play the big man and knock us down in front of his graduate students. We found out later that the professor had been one of those most vociferous in preference for a large-scale survey when our project had first been mooted.

The power this professor was wielding was the power to define sociology, a power that accrues to his status and to his gender; it enables certain definitions of what is and what is not sociology to become accepted and reified, such that, although sociology is often described as a broad church of perspective, its clergymen still insist on the observance of certain rituals. The generalised understandings of what sociology is, understandings which prescribe some things and proscribe others are not simply sets of theories or methodologies linked to movements of thought, but are created and altered within status and gender relations.

This process, the creation of sociology as a particular and boundaried discipline, can be seen within the creation of the 'departmental ethos', and the assumptions, which vary from department to department, as to what constitutes 'good' sociology and 'good' research. It can also be seen in the effects that cutbacks in postgraduate funding are having not simply on the number of postgraduate students but on generalised expectations and assumptions about postgraduate research. A simple cutback in student numbers has actually affected not just how much postgraduate sociology is being done, but the kind of postgraduate sociology being done, and this has occurred through sets of relations between departments, between supervisors in competition for fewer students, within generalised gender relations and within competing theoretical perspectives. Today's funded postgraduate student must have a much more concrete proposal than previously, since this is seen as an encouraging sign that the student will complete. Today's funded postgraduate is more likely to be male and more likely to be working within traditional and concretely defined areas of study. Today's funded postgraduate is more likely to be chosen on the class of degree result, even though there is little evidence that this is a reliable indicator of research ability. Today's funded postgraduate is less likely to have previously been a part-timer in the same department, and upwards of fifteen candidates are now being interviewed for a single quota award to try to ensure that the 'best' student is found.

So, although nothing new is being said by the Social Science Research Council about postgraduate training, or at least nothing that was not said before finance became a serious issue, a simple cutback in numbers has resulted in considerable changes in postgraduate experience and our expectations of them, changes which we have been instrumental in creating and which we do not fully understand, since we fail too often to apply our sociological experience to our own situation and to the complexity of relations in which we and sociology exist.

In suggesting that sociologists research themselves, and in describing my own experiences and reactions to them, I have been concerned to throw light on the ways in which sociology's male-as-norm bias is reproduced. I enjoy being a sociologist and a researcher; I'm not so sure I enjoyed being marginal. Although it certainly wasn't a central part of the remit of the research in which I was involved to gather data and experience of male attitudes and practices in sociology, it did become an increasing concern. As Stanley and Wise (1979, p. 361) suggest, 'no researcher can separate herself from personhood and thus from deriving second order constructs from experience.' My experience of being a woman researcher, feelings of marginalisation and self-doubt, feelings of being seen by others as simply a 'personable' instrument of data collection, feelings of anger and dissatisfaction at subtle and not-so-subtle sexism, are part of my experience of, and my feelings about, sociology as a whole.

There is a case to be made for the powerful within sociology listening more closely to the experiences of the relatively powerless, and not ignoring them or reacting to them in unthought ways. In several departments I interviewed men who assumed (rightly) that I was a feminist and spent a great deal of time assuring me how non-sexist they were and how their department was making huge efforts to 'help' women postgraduates. This would have been impressive if I hadn't been hearing entirely different stories from the women postgraduates themselves. In one department where there had never been any women postgraduates, three women were given grants in the same year, with a great show of 'generosity', which made the women concerned feel even more marginal; there because they were women and someone thought it politically appropriate rather than because they were good students.

My own experiences as a sociologist studying sociologists

and sociology made a reflexive approach inevitable. Over the three years of the project I became more and more concerned about the lack of reflexivity in much sociology. This, it seemed to me, contributed to, and possibly brought about, in part both a continued marginalisation of women and an inattention to the damaging effects of status and hierarchy. My experiences of sexism and the use of my low status against me were not specific to myself, but institutionalised within the discipline. A recognition of the complexity of sexism and status-use, and a recognition that they are not simply damaging to the individuals doing research but also to the research they do is not only useful but necessary.

Coda

Throughout this chapter, names have been omitted to protect the guilty. The examples used should not be seen simply as idiosyncratic and individualised quirks, but as reinforcements of generalised situations and understandings. It should not be thought that this critique of sociology might not apply even more forcibly to other disciplines. I criticise sociology because I am a sociologist.

Notes

1   The bulk of the work on the project was carried out jointly by Mary Porter and myself, with advice from John Wakeford and secretarial and clerical back-up from Jackie Covill. This paper bears a single name since Mary Porter is now living in America and we have divided the writing between us; John Wakeford said at an early stage that he thought it would be inappropriate for him to put his name on papers jointly with us; an attitude which showed a good deal of sensitivity to the position of women researchers with a male research director (see Wakeford, 1982).
2   For a fuller discussion of the position of women postgraduates see S.J. Scott and M. Porter (1983).

10

The *Affluent Worker* re-visited

Jennifer Platt

The Affluent Worker *project was the product of a particular time and place, and the form it took was affected both by the original circumstances and by changes that took place once it was under way. By the time the books were written, both political and sociological events had occurred that in some ways changed the original conception, and made it appropriate to write the data up in ways that took them into account. When the books finally appeared, they were admired and criticised from a variety of perspectives, not all social-scientific; what was it about books and circumstances that made this work such a focus of attention? Why did some of the interpretations made not correspond to the authors' understandings of what they had written? Fairly rapidly it became a 'classic' and an A-level text; other empirical studies have related themselves to it, and it appears in textbooks and in footnotes. What do these show about the meanings that have been given to it and the aspects that have been of interest? Have these changed over time? And how can the patterns be accounted for? In this chapter, Jennifer Platt, who was employed on the project, looks at the reception of the work, and the differing (and sometimes surprising) meanings attributed to the study.*

The *Affluent Worker* project, on which I worked for three years, achieved considerable fame and influence. The work has been widely used by other social scientists, the books have sold in large numbers, it has been used in A and O level as well as university courses, and some interest has been shown in it from outside academic life. Although it has by no means been immune from criticism, it is generally recognised in Britain as a standard work or modern classic. The personal attractions of treating all this as entirely due to the abstract intellectual merits of the work are obvious. None the less, it still seems worth considering what the social processes are which produce such results, since even casual observation suggests that there is a less than perfect general correlation between intellectual merit and the fame or popularity of sociological work. An additional spur to curiosity is the fact that, over the years, some of the attention given to the books has appeared to rest on misinterpretations of what I thought they said; this suggests some process other than simple recognition of clear intellectual qualities. This paper, therefore, explores the history of the *Affluent Worker* study as published. It starts by outlining available data on the work's popularity and use, goes on to consider what it was about the historical context that gave the theme wide appeal and made the books take just the form that they did, describes the uses and abuses made of the publications, and attempts to account for the patterns observed.[1]

The facts

The basic facts about the project are these. The originators of the project were David Lockwood and John Goldthorpe, both then lecturers at Cambridge; the first research assistant was myself, joined the following year by Frank Bechhofer. Numbers of others were involved at various stages in more junior and transient capacities. It was funded for four years, from 1961 to 1965; a number of articles were published, and conference papers given, before the publication of the three books in 1968 and 1969. Three main further articles appeared after the books. (A complete list of project publications appears in the Appendix.) The early articles were, obviously, theoretical statements or critical reviews of the literature; only in 1965, when the data had been collected and analysis had started, were there the first publications based on the project's own systematic data. However, there were earlier conference papers which started the process of diffusion of findings and interpretations before formal publication. After the books had appeared in English, there were French, German, Hungarian, Italian, Spanish and Swedish editions of all or parts of the material.

The peak year for sales of the books was 1970, when just over 10,000 copies were sold, but despite a marked decline since then they were still selling around 2,000 a year at the end of the 1970s. The *Political Attitudes and Behaviour* volume (*PAB*) has regularly sold less than the *Industrial Attitudes and Behaviour* one (*IAB*), and the final volume, *The Affluent Worker in the Class Structure* (*AWCS*), until 1980, sold more than the other two together.

The books were extremely widely reviewed. They were covered in the usual journals of academic sociology (although *AWCS*, oddly, seems to have had only 4 reviews there, as compared with the 7 and 13 of the other two volumes); they also had reviews in rather more of the journals of other social sciences or interdisciplinary social science. More strikingly, perhaps, they were also extensively reviewed in the journals of practitioners of various kinds and in those aimed at the more general public. The practitioner journals were mostly those of industrial management or trade unions; perhaps such periodicals as *International Socialism* should also be counted under that heading. Those aimed at the general public were mostly the quality newspapers and intellectual and political weeklies, though they also mysteriously included the *Nuneaton Evening Tribune*, the *Methodist Recorder* and the *Swindon Evening Advertiser*, to which due credit should be given for the catholicity of their coverage.[2]

Both the articles and the books have been widely referred to in work by other authors. The effort has been made to trace and analyse such references in articles by others from 1969, using the *Social Science Citation Index* (*SSCI*).[3] (Only the major articles published before the books (Lockwood, 1960; Goldthorpe and Lockwood, 1963; Lockwood, 1966; Goldthorpe, 1966; Goldthorpe, Lockwood, Bechhofer and Platt, 1967) have been included in the search, and after 1972 odd-numbered years were omitted to limit the task.) Twenty articles referring to one or more of the works were found in 1969, and 46 in 1980; in between the rise was fairly steady, except for a dip in the late 1970s. (Note that this pattern is not the same as that for book sales.) The largest single group of references is in British sources, although there are also a fair number in US and European sources. From 1970 to 1976, more of the references come from outside straight academic sociology than from within it; for 1978 and 1980, sociology overtakes the other sources. For individual books, the pattern over time is similar, with peaks in 1971-2, 1975-6 and 1979-80, and troughs in 1973-4 and 1977-8; *PAB*, however, is referred to considerably less than the other two, which run neck and neck over the years.

Some of these references are trivial, others substantial; more on this below. There is, however, one category of reference that deserves special mention, and that is the extended critique, of which there have been a number, some quite recent. The major ones traced, excluding those published as reviews, are Daniel (1969), Westergaard (1970), Kemeny (1972), Crewe (1973), Mackenzie (1974), Whelan (1976), MacKinnon (1980) and Grieco (1981).

Finally, there are other research projects that derived more or less directly, in whole or in part, from the project's ideas and data. These are harder to identify clearly, but some at least can be mentioned. The volume edited by Martin Bulmer (1975), *Working-Class Images of Society*, gives reports on the data of six projects which made significant use of the ideas in Lockwood's 'Sources of Variation in Working-Class Images of Society'. In addition to the projects mentioned there, there is the work represented by books by Gallie (1978), Hill (1976), Ingham (1970), Mann (1973) and Salaman (1974); all of these except Hill were research students supervised at least partly by John Goldthorpe. (Perhaps Blackburn and Mann (1979) should also be mentioned.) There were also several projects, started even before the publication of the books, which were strongly affected by the ideas of the earlier papers; these include those of Mercer and Weir (1972), Piepe et al. (1969), Parsler (1970) and Toomey (1969).

Teaching uses cannot be documented for higher education, but were certainly extensive. For schools, it may be taken as suggestive that every Associated Exam Board 'A' level paper from 1968-78 has a fairly obvious *Affluent Worker* question, and that the examiners report frequent use of the material in answer to other questions. All three books are still on the recommended reading list for the 1982 revised syllabus. The Resources Exchange of the Association for the Teaching of the Social Sciences includes several items about the project on its list of materials.[4]

In the absence of comparative data, no precise evaluation can be made of the quantitative significance of all this. One may safely conclude, however, that it showed an exceptional level of interest and attention. The nature and significance of that interest is analysed further below.

What, then, has the project meant to its audience? This can only be understood by placing it in its historical context.

The historical context

The work was originally addressed to a large-scale socio-political issue of widespread interest outside as well as inside the social sciences. It was clear that important social changes were taking place in Britain, and to many semi-popular writers the process of 'embourgeoisement' seemed obvious. A significant part of the argument for this was the successive election victories of the Conservative party, which suggested an irreversible trend. It was to this thesis that the project addressed itself — critically. At the same time there was only a small British sociological community and, although its output of solid empirical research was creditable, not much of it was directly related to large public issues; those works that were, Young and Willmott's (1957) *Family and Kinship in East London* and Floud et al.'s (1957) *Social Class and Educational Opportunity*, aroused comparable general interest.

One of the strongest areas in British sociology in the 1960s was industrial sociology, often addressed to managerial concerns. John Goldthorpe's background in that field led him to draw out the possibilities of relating developments there to the idea of embourgeoisement in a way that few others would have done, and thus made the eventual work of wider interest than it would otherwise have been.

British empirical work had not been very strong theoretically, and so the strong theoretical side of the *Affluent Worker* was immediately recognised as particularly valuable, as well as again making the work seem relevant to a wider audience. This owed a lot to David Lockwood's cast of mind. His contacts with German sociology, as well as those of John Goldthorpe with French sociology, helped both to connect the enterprise with other styles of work with unfamiliar strengths and to give it a more cosmopolitan character; this, of course, increased the likelihood that those with other intellectual backgrounds would be interested in it.

A final feature, in a sense accidental, maximised the potential audience for the work. The working definition of 'embourgeoisement' as becoming similar to the middle class, with 'class' for practical purposes being taken to include almost every aspect of life-style, meant that the data collected were designed to include anything that previous research or general knowledge suggested distinguished working from middle class. Since much previous research, as well as works such as Hoggart's (1957) *The Uses of Literacy*, had dwelt on this, there was plenty to draw on. The books, therefore, whatever their central theme, also provided a quarry from which those so inclined could mine nuggets of information on friendship patterns, conjugal roles, car ownership, bank accounts, and so on.

The historical context of the project's origins had, however, changed by the time the books were written and published, and this had a significant effect on the form they eventually took and on their reception. At the simplest level the psephological version of the embourgeoisement thesis was demolished by the Labour election victory of 1964. As a measure of political change over the period, I offer two personal anecdotes with a certain period nostalgia. In 1963,

I went to a party given by a colleague to celebrate the election of left-winger Harold Wilson as leader of the Labour party. In 1969, at the start of the period of student unrest and the revival of intellectual Marxism, I was astonished[5] to find myself in a mass meeting at Sussex being attacked (by students at least one of whom is now an SDP councillor) for the political errors and bourgeois empiricism of the *Affluent Worker*.

Apart from such external changes, there were also changes within sociology — and, as far as British sociology is concerned, at least some of them were brought about by the earlier stages of the *Affluent Worker* project. David Lockwood, in a recent letter, points out that people have frequently said that after the appearance of 'Affluence and the British class structure' (Goldthorpe and Lockwood, 1963) it hardly seemed necessary to go on and do the research, since this had undermined the theoretical grounding of the embourgeoisement thesis. Clearly a report which was only on the degree of confirmation of the thesis would, by the later 1960s, have lacked topicality and theoretical novelty. Also important in redefining the most significant problems was French work, related to a marxist problematic, around the ideas of alienation and class consciousness; this was not conspicuous to most British sociologists at the time, though there were perhaps connections through *New Left Review*, but John Goldthorpe's French contacts made it salient to him. The appearance of Etzioni's work on types of power and involvement in organisations systematised ideas connected with those already held by David Lockwood and John Goldthorpe, and using a congenially typological strategy, and so articulated well with their thinking; it was important to the development of the idea of 'instrumentalism' and the emphasis on orientations to work. Naturally the ideas of those working on the project also developed over time.

For all these reasons, the book eventually produced differed from those originally envisaged. This is not to say that the embourgeoisement thesis did not still provide a central organising theme; it did. However, I think that marxist themes bulked larger than they would have done a few years earlier, and the final chapter of *AWCS* goes well beyond the embourgeoisement thesis to consider the position of the new working class more generally. Other considerations apart, there were pressures to do this arising from the design of the research; a negative finding, however striking, has less appeal than a positive one — as T.H. Marshall (1970) pointed out in his review, 'it is in the positive that we are all ultimately interested'. (This no doubt contributed to some of the over-interpretations described below.) As he also pointed out, and as others have done too, a design appropriate for a negative thesis may well be inappropriate for a positive one; hence some of the justified methodological criticisms made, especially of the sample as a basis for the conclusions. *IAB* was a by-product of the main project, prompted by unanticipated findings and the sheer bulk of the material as much as by other developments; its appearance before the main report in *AWCS* was to have unintended consequences for the way in which that was received, emphasising the industrial aspects of the work. *PAB* addressed itself strictly to the political aspects of the original theme, and was thus more quickly outdated; hence, presumably, the lesser made of it. It had to be written, but by definition could not show the same sensitivity to changing circumstances. I shall not attempt an authoritative general statement of what the books 'really' said;[6] what did they say to their readers?

Reactions and uses

Initial reviews were in the main highly favourable, even though some important points of criticism were made, and particularly praised the care taken in design and the tightness of argument relating theory and data. In early discussion of the work two coherent lines are particularly prominent, the critique from the New Left and the industrial sociology critique; each is briefly considered.

The critique from the Left was not simply a marxist critique, although there is clearly ample scope for such in the concept of class used. The attack on the embourgeoisement thesis was welcomed, although not treated as very novel, since the Left had never accepted it. Strongly criticised, however, were those aspects of the interpretation which threw doubt on the future prospects of militant working-class consciousness. Westergaard's version of this is a sophisticated one, which sees 'instrumentalism' and 'privatisation' as a new form of embourgeoisement, and offers a reinterpretation of the data in terms of the salience and intrinsic fragility of the cash nexus. He sees contradictions of consciousness as providing potential for change. A cruder version appears in Blackburn (1967, 1969). His central arguments are that it is not sufficiently recognised that consciousness can be ambivalent, that resignation may be disguised as satisfaction, and that the right circumstances may give rise to explosions of consciousness. His strongest piece of evidence is what became the famous Vauxhall strike episode. Presumably it became famous as a result of his use of it; it had an extraordinary currency as an argument at the time, even among those who did not appear to have read the articles or books.

Already in a review in September 1969 Cannon could quote a finalist's use of it. More striking is the extraordinary episode in which the distinguished French marxist André Gorz, lecturing in Harvard, apparently drew only on Blackburn's writings to construct a largely mythical version of what actually happened (in which distribution of *Affluent Worker* conclusions led directly to Vauxhall riots!); others then quoted this in the *New York Review of Books* . . . and so on. One of the more curious features of this critique from the Left is that it is all based on the publications before *AWCS*, and in Blackburn's case entirely on 'Attitudes and Behaviour of Car Assembly Workers' (Goldthorpe, 1966), although his arguments remained in oral currency long after that had come out including both a general discussion more relevant to the issue and an appendix replying to Blackburn's version. (It should be mentioned, however, that Westergaard noted, in an addition at the proof stage, that *AWCS* changed the picture.) It is hard to avoid the conclusion that, whatever the considerable merits of some of the points made, the Left's use of the work contained as much of wishful thinking as it did of close attention to its arguments and data.

The critique from industrial sociology was initially conducted mainly by Daniel (1969), Woodward (1968) and Brown (1973). It focused on two aspects: the 'action' approach and the significance of orientation to work, and the importance to be attached to technology or other aspects of in-plant experience. These aspects are undoubtedly central to those parts of the work concerned with industrial topics, and what it says does indeed lay itself open to criticism and difference of opinion.[7] What is most interesting here, perhaps, is that despite the consensus that the problems raised are important ones, and the continuation of detailed discussion over the years (Grieco, 1981; Mackinnon, 1980; Whelan, 1976), there does not appear to have been any subsequent research, except that of Blackburn and Mann (1979) and Ingham in his PhD thesis (1970) designed to resolve them empirically; we still await a longitudinal study of the formation of orientations to work, or a systematic investigation of the relative importance in determining behaviour of orientations and situational factors. Most of the direct attempts to follow up on industrial topics seem, oddly, to have concentrated on the not specifically industrial aspects of the original work, and to be about 'traditional' workers and images of society (Bulmer, 1975).

Looking beyond reviews and critiques, what other uses have been made of the work? Its use in general works on stratification and industry may be taken as given. A scanning of available British introductory textbooks and general books about British society shows the *Affluent Worker* bulking fairly large, though in very different ways. Some use it only for its central ideas, referred to briefly (Bottomore, 1972; J.E. Goldthorpe, 1968; Halsey, 1972; Wilkins, 1970) or extensively (Cotgrove, 1978; Hurd et al., 1973; Ryder and Silver, 1970), while others use it for a variety of empirical points (Haralambos, 1980; Noble, 1975). It is notable in this context, however, how often the work is in some way misrepresented. The most obvious form this takes is to treat the study as one only of car-workers, who in fact constituted less than half the sample, or even only of car-assembly-workers when there were also other car-workers; this is done by Cotgrove (1978, p. 108), Rex (1974, p. 2), Worsley et al. (1970, p. 219) and Hurd et al. (1973, pp. 181-2) despite the fact that the sample is there described correctly later in the chapter. More subtle is the treatment of interpretations as findings, as when the books are taken to have found that instrumentalism existed (Haralambos, 1980), or findings are over-generalised (Noble, 1975, p. 157, though mentioning the affluent nature of the sample, treats its low rates of union commitment as representative; Haralambos, 1980, p. 62, refers to 'the money model which, judging from the studies of Goldthorpe and Lockwood and Hill, is the dominant image of society held by workers in Britain') or when potentially misleading ways of summarising the argument are found ('The emergence of the "affluent workers" . . . has lessened the sharpness of the differences between working class and middle class life . . . .' Hurd et al., 1973, p. 151). The tendency for textbooks to give misleading versions of research results has been documented (Hedley and Taveggia, 1977; Spanier and Stump, 1978) and can in part, at least, be attributed to the inherent difficulty of giving adequate elementary summaries of complex work. Are such tendencies absent from sources aimed at more sophisticated audiences?

Every reference (except self-references or those to foreign-language translations) given in the SSCI to selected journals for the sample of years (see above) that was available in the library used was studied.[8] (112 of the 291 references made were excluded by this procedure; those included cannot be taken to be fully representative, but they do cover the mainstream sociology and some of those from outside sociology.) A fair number of definite misrepresentations of the research were found here too. Five writers treat the study as only of car workers (Lansbury, 1974; Cherns, 1969; Blackler and Brown, 1978; Millar, 1978; Rinehart, 1971), and two as of only semi-skilled or mass production workers (Hawthorn and Paddon, 1971; Shepard, 1970). There are also a number of cases where conclusions are treated as applying to all manual workers, most factory workers, or even all capitalist society (Willmott, 1969; Lansbury, 1974; Cotgrove, 1978; Ineichen,

1972; De Fronzo, 1973; Berry, 1979). Finally, there are at least six cases where major conclusions are more or less subtly misrepresented in other ways – for example: 'Equally notable is the assumption of new and often "bourgeois" reference groups by the more affluent workers . . .' (Kavanagh, 1971, p. 358). 'an embourgeoisified worker can continue to feel comfortable in voting for the Labour Party . . .' (Inglehart, 1971, p. 1016).

Clearly some of these misrepresentations are just plain careless, some fail to distinguish between citing a conclusion and drawing an inference from it, and others can at least to some extent be justified by the ambiguities of the original material. (Although on our own terms of reference we demolished the embourgeoisement thesis, there are other terms within which what we did assert to be taking place could be described as sectors of the working class becoming middle class.) The frequent occurrence of car workers as the whole sample may partly be accounted for by the appearance of one article (Goldthorpe, 1966) based only on them before the main reports. (If so, this would be a relatively clear and dramatic example of what I suspect took place on a wider scale – namely, that the books were so well heralded by conference papers and articles that many of those most interested did not give them due weight in forming their impressions of the project.) It is possible, however, that a cultural fascination with the car led to its over-representation here, as in other fields (cf. Glasgow University Media Group, 1976, p. 165).

All this, however, draws attention to the variety of ways in which others can use a work for their own purposes, and this seems worth exploring a little further. The references made were classified in terms of the degree of centrality of the point referred to to the *Affluent Worker*, the degree of centrality to the argument of the article of the *Affluent Worker* reference, and the subject area of the article as a whole. (Obviously, such classification involves an element of judgment, so little weight can be attached to the exact numbers.) It is hardly surprising that most of the references were to central points; more interesting, however, is that 19 per cent were to non-central points, while 12 per cent were even less central, or about it rather than referring to points in it. (Examples of these categories are the use of single findings such as the proportion of workers saying trade unions are too strong, or the use of the work as an example of basic as opposed to applied research.) In less than a fifth of the cases (25) was the use of the *Affluent Worker* central to the argument; most commonly it was just one among other sources referred to for a point fairly central to the argument, while in 32 per cent the use made was trivial or virtually irrelevant. The subject areas of the articles were classified as follows: embourgeoisement (12), class consciousness (26), orientation to work and alienation (38),[9] stratification more generally (16), trade unionism and the labour movement (7), miscellaneous industrial and organisational topics (9), miscellaneous political topics (5), theory (5), and other (27). The first 4 may be taken to be those directly related to the project's own concerns; thus 37 per cent are in areas not closely related. Of the 145 references, only 24 use a point central to the *Affluent Worker* centrally in their argument, and thus show a significant direct influence. The extent to which uses can be peripheral, bizarre or imprecise is best shown by example:

AWCS is cited as one example of the use of manual/non-manual as the principal class division (Vanneman, 1980). Lockwood (1966) is cited, in an article on the Scottish Enlightenment, as a later user of the idea of the privatised worker said to have been used by Ferguson (Swingewood, 1970).

AWCS is cited in support of the point that cultural supremacy gives the upper class control over the means of creating social consciousness. (George and Wilding, 1972; the book makes this point only as part of a summary of the views of certain marxists, which are rejected.)

AWCS is also cited, in an article on the economics of demand for non-work travel, in supplementary support of the contention that locational variables may be used as an indicator of social-structural influence on social trips (Vickerman, 1972).

Well, perhaps number of citations *can* be used as a meaningful indicator of intellectual influence — but instances such as these give one pause.[10] It is at least necessary to distinguish between mere use as part of 'the literature' available to be drawn on for one's own purposes, and serious influence, based on reasonably correct interpretation, on key ideas of the work influenced. Misuse is also, in its way, a tribute. One might speculate that for all widely used works there will be some basic minimum of misuses or trivial uses, while the character of the work and its relation to its social context will lead to variations above that minimum.

The extent to which *Affluent Worker* material has been misrepresented or dragged in in surprising contexts perhaps indicates that it was in the air, and sometimes even perhaps transmitted orally rather than actually read. This impression is increased by the tendency to refer to all three volumes at once, and/or to no specific page or chapter. The fact that it *was* so much in the air could be attributed both to its own characteristics and their relation to the situation, as discussed above, and, in some instances, to the absence of any alternative source usable for the purpose in hand.

The fact that references may have this character could go some way to account for the continuing use of the work despite the passage of time and the existence of powerful criticisms; there are, however, other aspects of this which merit consideration. Those parts of the work which have been heavily referred to and most directly influential are the idea of the instrumental orientation to work, and the typology of situations seen as generating different modes of working-class consciousness. Both of these have been attacked on good empirical grounds. The initial imputation of instrumentalism to the Luton sample rested, not on direct measures designed for that purpose, but on the overall interpretation of a variety of data collected for other purposes — and some of the analysis of that is quite tendentious; it also rested on a comparison with traditional workers, for whom no precisely comparable data were available. (Several critics have suggested that the degree of instrumentalism of the Luton workers was not really unusual.) In so far as the Luton sample are treated as prototypical, many writers have pointed out that it is likely they had very special characteristics which made them unrepresentative (e.g. Grieco); in so far as they are seen as special, the general interest of findings on them is limited. On working-class consciousness, the volume edited by Bulmer showed the extent to which it can be questioned whether 'traditional' workers, with the characteristics imputed to them by the theory, actually exist in the appropriate situations.[11] If the uses made of the work in references are plotted by year, the most noticeable feature is the absence of any clear trend over time. In particular, the theme of embourgeoisement has consistently been a fairly unimportant context of use, while those of orientation to work and class consciousness have always outnumbered it, usually substantially. This suggests that, had the work confined itself strictly to the original theme of the project, it would have been much less widely used; no doubt it would also have been much less criticised, since there it stood on firmer empirical ground. It is notorious that theoretical work tends to be accorded higher status than empirical, and this could be taken as another instance of that point.

Why has its use in fields still of interest not been superseded by that of later work, building on its strengths and improving on its weaknesses? Here one can only speculate. One possible reason is that no other work which combines a high level of generality in its conclusions with rich first-hand empirical data has appeared, although there have been important theoretical works and valuable empirical studies. (This could be taken to show increased sophistication and specialisation, rather than failure to do as well subsequently.) In Britain, too, those empirical studies have often been in one way or another inspired by the *Affluent Worker* ideas, and so have maintained the reference back to it. Another possible reason for its continuing use, especially in teaching, is the convenient way in which it summarises and labels a variety of possible approaches, thus providing mnemonic devices and ways of organising complex bodies of ideas.[12]

Perhaps the most important factor may have been the simple accident of timing. When the work first started British sociology really was a small world, both in its size and in its social organisation. Everyone knew everyone else and met at conferences, and although there were disagreements there was scarcely room for the segmentation that now exists; consequently, knowledge of work in progress was very well diffused.[13] But at just the period when the *Affluent Worker* books were coming out, this world suddenly started to expand enormously. During that flush of expansion, a high proportion of the present sociology faculty were appointed. The generations of sociology students taught then were larger than subsequent ones, and must have provided a fair proportion both of the younger faculty and of those teaching sociology outside higher education. Thus the age structure of British sociology encapsulates a certain moment in time — which happens to have been the moment of the *Affluent Worker*. (The discrepancy between the trends noted in book sales and in references would be simply explained if the later references were made by people who had already bought the book at an earlier period.) There is no reason to believe sociologists immune from the cohort effects found in other fields (Butler and Stokes, 1971; Wilkins, 1970); this could help explain what might otherwise seem a surprising persistence.[14]

Conclusion

In sum, the argument is this. The *Affluent Worker* project was on a topical theme which ensured wide initial interest, and was well publicised within the then small British sociological community. Historical changes external to the project led to the books taking a direction not originally anticipated; this change of direction ensured greater interest in the results, at the same time as it made the conclusions more speculative and open to criticism. Irrespective of the work's particular content, the very wide range of material covered and the richness of both empirical data and theoretical ideas made it open to many uses. Some of the uses it received were casual and imprecise, and others involved definite misrepresentation. Contributory factors in this were probably the wide and staggered diffusion, sometimes oral, of the material; wishful thinking and stretching of the data to serve other writers' purposes; and the relative complexity of the arguments.[15] The accident of timing in relation to the development of British sociology produced a cohort effect which gave it a higher level of institutionalisation than it would otherwise have received. It seems likely that, independently of these factors, its perceived intellectual merits were a necessary but not a sufficient condition for its success; these must be left to others to evaluate. This analysis of the fate of one project may, it is hoped, throw some more general light on the social circumstances of the creation of a standard work, and the meanings that can be attached to the status as such.

Notes

1   Although my colleagues have helped in providing material, and have had the opportunity to comment on a draft, they should not be taken to share responsibility for the paper's approach, views or interpretations.

2   These data come from the *Social Science Citation Index*, which only started in 1969, and from the publishers; it cannot be assumed that the lists thus compiled are complete, though it is reasonable to assume that the majority of reviews are covered. My thanks to Cambridge University Press for providing copies of some material not already in my files.

3   The data necessarily (see above) omit the earliest references, which might be of some interest, and only include those in journals covered by the *SSCI*. This list has expanded over the period but is, broadly, limited to academic periodicals in or related to the social sciences.

4   I am grateful to Richard Stiff and Tom Whiteside for providing me with material on this.

5   This astonishment was not only because of the novelty of mass meetings of students attacking faculty. I thought of the project, in so far as it had a political character, as being rather left-wing, and as quite marxisant in its approach. After all, did *AWCS* not end with suggestions as to how the leadership of the Labour party might act to elicit a more radical response? And was it not a crucial part of the argument that the objective class position of wage-workers was one of essential deprivation unchanged by 'affluence'? It may also be of interest to note here that I was, as far as I know, the only one of the authors with any active political involvement at the time, on what was then the left of the Labour party. I, however, was the one who went through the draft of the final chapter of *AWCS* suggesting deletions of

parts that seemed normative in tone. I no longer remember which, if any, of my suggestions were acted on.

6   It may, however, be of some interest to note that it was only when reading the material for this paper that I realised the extent to which, for other people, the project was not about the embourgeoisement thesis. My early involvement, close contact with the data-collection, and lesser contribution to the more theoretical and speculative aspects of the writing, had given me an atypical perspective on the work.

7   However, John Goldthorpe, in a recent letter, suggests that it was a mistake in *IAB* not to spell out the concept of 'orientation' as it was developed by Parsons in the sense of a resolution of an action dilemma. This was so familiar to David Lockwood and him, as a result of all the seminars and debates on Parsons at LSE in the 1950s, that it did not seem necessary. To have done so might have averted some misunderstandings, especially among those in the industrial field whose background was not in mainstream sociology. This suggests one of the penalties of appealing to a wide audience (on which cf. Davis, 1971, pp. 329-31).

8   The journals selected were all those in British, French and US sociology (broadly defined), and all those (identified as) in management/industrial relations, political science, economics or social work. This selection excludes, apart from sociology of other national origins, journals in psychology, education, history, law and town planning, and those of general interest. The exclusions made were designed to limit the work involved while still including a wide range of sources inside and outside sociology — and to exclude languages I cannot read adequately. The journals not available in the library were the less well-known ones.

9   The heavy emphasis on this owes something to the sample of journals used. Only 13 of the references, however, come from journals in the industrial field, so even if all those were excluded it would still be one of the most popular themes. It seems *prima facie* unlikely that inclusion of the excluded journals would make a significant difference to the overall pattern.

10 It is not the case, as might be suspected, that many of the references are critical ones, so their number cannot be accounted for by the large number of grounds for criticism.

11 Perhaps a transitory effect of the Bulmer volume is shown in the fact that references to Lockwood, 1966, steady at 2-4 a year to 1976, are absent in 1978; but in 1980 there are 7, more than ever before.

12 Note, too, the extent to which the way in which this is done tends to fit the material to the criteria Davis outlines for being found interesting.

13 Halsey's recent article (1982b) about his fellow graduate students at LSE gives some sense of this for the period immediately before this one.

14   Part of the phenomenon could be due to the expansion of the total social-science literature, which could have made a constant or declining *proportion* of the total number of references a constant or even rising absolute number. This hypothesis is in principle testable.

15   It is hoped to pursue the points suggested about the rhetoric of citation, and their implications for the cumulation of sociological knowledge, in detail elsewhere.

Appendix

Main publications associated with the *Affluent Worker* project.

1960	D. Lockwood	'The New Working Class', *European Journal of Sociology*, vol. 1, no. 2.
1962	J.H. Goldthorpe and D. Lockwood	'Not so Bourgeois after all', *New Society*, 18 Oct.
1963	J.H. Goldthorpe and D. Lockwood	'Affluence and the British Class Structure', *Sociological Review*, vol. 11, no. 2.
1966	D. Lockwood	'Sources of Variation in Working-class Images of Society', *Sociological Review*, vol. 14, no. 3.
	J.H. Goldthorpe	'Attitudes and behaviour of car assembly workers: a deviant case and a theoretical critique', *British Journal of Sociology*, vol. 17, no. 3.
1967	J.H. Goldthorpe, D. Lockwood, F. Bechhofer and J. Platt	'The affluent worker and the thesis of embourgeoisement', *Sociology*, vol. 1, no. 1.
1968	J.H. Goldthorpe et al.	*The Affluent Worker: Industrial Attitudes and Behaviour*, Cambridge University Press.

1968 J.H. Goldthorpe et al. *The Affluent Worker: Political Attitudes and Behaviour*, Cambridge University Press.

1969 J.H. Goldthorpe et al. *The Affluent Worker in the Class Structure*, Cambridge University Press.

        J. Platt 'Some problems in measuring the jointness of conjugal role - relationships', *Sociology*, vol. 3, no. 3.

1970 J.H. Goldthorpe 'L'image des classes chez les travailleurs manuels aisés', *Revue Française de Sociologie,* vol. 11, no. 3.

1971 J. Platt 'Variations in answers to different questions on perceptions of class', *Sociological Review*, vol. 19, no. 3.

11
Putting the show on the road:
the dissemination of research findings
Helen Roberts

*This chapter examines an aspect of the research process which,
although vitally important, tends to be given scant attention
in methodology textbooks and courses. This part of the
process concerns not the way in which research is funded or
carried out, as discussed in the earlier chapters, but the end
product of the research, and the way it is packaged, marketed
and disseminated. Spender (1981) and others have documented problems concerning the publication of research in
the academic press and scholarly journals; this chapter is
concerned with the problems of publishing for a wider
readership or audience.*

*Referring to some of the other chapters in this book,
and using as examples three pieces of research on which she
has worked, Helen Roberts discusses the problem of the dissemination of research findings beyond an academic readership. She looks at the politics of the popularisation of research findings, the (sometimes unexpected) media interpretations of research projects, and strategies for getting
research findings through to areas where they might have
some effect (not always the corridors of power). She asks
who we are writing for when we describe our research and
its results. Are we writing for ourselves, our colleagues,*

*policy-makers or the 'subjects' of our research? To whom
does our primary duty as researchers lie, and how can we
maximise the effectiveness of the work we do?*

While methodology and 'how to do it' textbooks, as others
(Graham, this volume; Oakley, 1981) have shown, tend to be
deficient in the advice given on certain key aspects of the
research process, there is one area of social research where
the advice is not only deficient in quality but lacking in
substance. This is the problem of the dissemination of
research findings. To get to the stage in a research project
of *having* findings poses one set of problems, elevating
those findings from the filing-cabinet drawer and into the
consciousness of others poses another. More fortunate
research students or research assistants may be given ad
hoc 'on the job' advice from their supervisors or those in
charge of the research, but since, as Spender (1981) aptly
points out, as academics we 'publish or perish' rather than
'read or perish' this is hardly adequate for what may ultimately be the most important part of the research endeavour.

   Moreover to talk of publication is not to talk just of
getting something into print. 'Publication' also means 'to
make generally known'. 'Publication' in the narrow sense
is only one part of this process, and, one is tempted to say,
may sometimes not be part of it at all. Even if academic
prose passes the boundary between obscurity and understanding, something which appears only as a monograph
or a journal article is unlikely to be 'generally known'. That
degree of dissemination can only occur with either a pheno-
menal bestseller (and there are more *Watership Downs* than
Montaillous) or through the medium of the press, radio,
and television.

   To a greater or lesser degree, dissemination, relationships
with an audience 'out there' and the effective communication
of findings is a problem faced by all the contributors to this
book. Indeed, this sort of book specifically disseminates
some of the sorts of 'backstage' material which might not
otherwise see the light of day. Important to all of us in the

social scientific community is how our work gets funded, by whom and under what constraints. The questions concerning who actually gets the cash to do research and the sorts of control exercised by the paymasters are not normally matters for public discussion. The fact that Bell, in common with his SSRC colleagues, had to sign the Official Secrets Act indicates that by no means all aspects of the research funding process are as open as we might like. Similarly, Hanmer and Leonard bring to our attention concerns which are frequently only disseminated at the level of the small group. The importance of a wider dissemination in these two cases is that they help us, in Scott's terms, 'to be more sociological about our social science' and to understand that the distribution of funding is neither random nor strictly on the basis of merit and that structural as well as individual factors affect the outcome of grant applications. But the audience for the chapters by Bell and Hanmer and Leonard is clearly very well defined. It is the academic social science community. For the other chapters in this book, the audiences are wider. Naturally, there are issues which specifically address the social scientific community, but other communities too have a legitimate interest. Collins himself points to the wide interest in spoon-bending (and the suspicion of the academic community of people like himself, doing the sort of work which attracts the attention of the media). The Lads, the Ordinary Kids and the Citizens with whom Jenkins worked might legitimately have an interest in his findings, as might others with an interest in youth.

Professionals concerned with the care of the dying (to say nothing of the dying themselves and their relatives) could well wish to read James's work. It is not only the SSRC and other agencies concerned with the training or education of postgraduates who will be interested in the work of Scott and her colleagues – postgraduates and supervisors alike will be all agog. Those concerned with the welfare of wives who are 'married to the job', including the wives themselves, have a legitimate interest in Finch's work,[1] as do bodies concerned with the setting up and management of playgroups. Graham's work is not only of interest to mothers, the narrative form which she discusses is readily accessible to them.

Frankenberg's work will not only be of interest to others involved in community studies: one assumes that it will also be of interest to the politicians and producers and consumers of health care in the comune where he is working. Platt specifically refers to the variety of audiences for the *Affluent Worker* studies —ranging from social-science, trade-union and industrial-relations journals to the *Methodist Recorder* and the *Swindon Evening Advertiser*. As she makes clear, the message transmitted is by no means always identical to (or even all that similar to) the one received. This chapter looks at the means by which findings are transmitted, what colours the transmission, and who, if anyone, controls it. What understanding of the findings do the receiving groups gain, and what effect, if any, on what the receiving group does, or tries to do, does all this have?

Drawing on three research projects in which I have been involved, this chapter looks at the dangers (and otherwise) of the popularisation of research findings within a general context of the dissemination of information about research projects and research findings.

There are three principal audiences for research: the subjects of the research; the 'expert community' whether of academic (the 'scientific experts') or policy-makers (the 'practical experts'); and the broad world of public opinion, which includes both the relatively powerful opinions of politicians and journalists, and the normally relatively powerless opinions of the general readership.

The Social Science Research Council (rightly in my opinion) asks questions about proposals for dissemination in grant applications, and likes to know more about this aspect of the project in the final report. Naturally, when most academics think about dissemination (and this would presumably go for the applicants for grants as well as the committees judging them), what they have in mind is the learned journal, the monograph, perhaps the book for the academic publisher. It would hardly be reasonable to expect academics, after all, to consider the dissemination possibilities of the *Express* or the *News of the World*, let alone *Woman* or *Woman's Own* or the Jimmy Young Show. If one had wanted to become a journalist, one would have become one, and not a sociologist. But however much popular publicity might stick in the academic craw, there are presumably things to be said for ensuring that one's work reaches the widest possible audience. And even were there not things to be said in favour of this, for good or for bad, the media have an interest in social science. Although the subject matter of sociology is no less complex (and is probably more so) than nuclear physics, the language in which sociology is written is (usually) more accessible to the journalist than the language of other disciplines, and the subject matter of sociology more susceptible (than, for instance, a molecule) to the human interest story. Were it a matter of simple description of research, or even simple discussion, there would not be a problem, but it is not so straightforward. As Jennifer Platt points out in her chapter, there has been a well-documented tendency for textbooks to give misleading accounts of research results, and if this is the case with some textbooks, the problems with research reporting in the press, and in particular in the non-specialist press, are even more acute. David Morgan (1972) discusses one example of this in an article on press reports of a serious paper he gave to the British Association. Having himself given the paper the rather unspectacular title: 'Women in Industry – The Factory and the Home', newspaper headlines such as 'A Factory Girl's Dream of Romance' in the *Daily Mirror* and 'What a Giggle. When a Man Tells the Secrets of Life Among the Girls' in the *Daily Express* must have provided a rude shock for researcher and researched alike.

For us, similar problems arose when, beginning our first post-doctoral research project, Michele Barrett and I were looking at the relatively high consultation rates of middle-aged women at their GPs' surgeries and considering various explanations for these. When the press officer at the University of Sussex (which was administering the grant) asked us to write a press release, the idea appealed. What glamour after three years of relatively solitary work on our doctorates! The press officer turned our prose (at the time still deeply affected by our recently written academic theses) into something approaching normal English, but the guidance we should have sought (though whether it could have been given is a different question) was not literary but of a rather different order. It is difficult to remember after six years whether we were actively pleased by the telephone calls from journalists which followed the issuing of the press release, but we were by no means irritated (as I was later to become) by the questions which demanded a black and white answer which at that stage in the project (i.e. after receipt of the grant but before the work had begun) we were hardly equipped to answer. On the other hand, our feelings about what was actually published were less ambiguous. The harshest treatment of our research came from the 'popular' medical press, the papers funded by drug companies and sent free to GPs. This tended to be of the 'Social Science Research Council funds another silly piece of research telling us what we already know' variety. Headlines such as 'Why are Middle Aged Women always in the Surgery?', 'Why GPs see so many Middle Aged Women' and 'Those Middle Aged Women never out of the Surgery', while by no means as dramatic as those describing Morgan's research, nevertheless gave a misleading impression of the work we were doing, since as social scientists and feminists, we naturally felt that there was not much to be said for the 'blaming the victim' approach, and felt that 'common-sense' explanations such as the so-called 'emptying of the nest syndrome' left a good deal to be desired. It was probably fortunate for us that the doctors with whom we were working were not, apparently, avid readers of this press, since there was no comeback (as there had been in Morgan's case) from those giving us the access we needed to do our research. More irritating, though possibly less serious than subtle misrepresentations of the research we were doing, were the references to us: 'Two twenty seven year old sociologists ...' 'The two sociologists are committed women's libbers' (not a term we would have used to describe ourselves). It was my sociological peers, rather than the subjects of my research, I was worried about when earnest explanations of our research were transmuted into print as: ' "Stop treating your wives like old cart horses" is tip No. 1 from Dr Roberts' and deeply reflective statements such as 'The greatest problem of all is the housewife's isolation', must have made any fellow sociologist reading the popular press wonder, whether in fact, the SSRC's money was being well spent if these were the only conclusions reached.

Although our experience with the press with this research was not an entirely rosy one, the unexpected side benefits — letters from women about their health and their doctors, and, notwithstanding the (to us) misleading accounts in the popular press, an appreciation from some of the women we worked with that this was indeed serious and sensible research if it was reported nationally, convinced me that there was something to be said for making journalists aware of the work one was doing, so that they in turn could inform the 'subjects'.

It was with this in mind that I sent a copy of a report of a subsequent piece of research to a Woman's Page journalist on the local paper. The Report: *After Sixteen: What Happens to the Girls?* (Roberts and Sharp, 1982) described in some eighty or so pages the aspirations and achievements of a cohort of 16-year-old girls in the Bradford district. The tenor of the report was not particularly optimistic. Many of the girls were not doing very well, but then, neither were their mothers, fathers, brothers or neighbours. They did not have particularly high aspirations, but why should they in a city where they were quite as well aware as everyone else of the high unemployment levels? A large part of the report was taken up with interview data from the girls, admirably illustrating (or so I thought) the difficult situations large numbers of them were in. What I was convinced the report revealed was that in spite of a long history of women working and of working-class radicalism in Bradford, girls were still not getting a proper chance to succeed alongside the boys, and those who found work were still going into traditional women's work with low pay and low promotion prospects. In spite of this, many girls were succeeding in the face of tremendous odds. While helping out with aged grandparents, disabled relatives, or younger brothers and sisters, a good number nevertheless managed to find, and hang on to, jobs of their own. But not surprisingly, some of the girls did not have such a clear vision of their future as did the boys. Given all this, I was dismayed to find a report on the Woman's Page under the headline: "'Bradford Girls Lack Drive" — report reveals'. Minor inaccuracies in the journalist's article (such as the doubling of our grant from the Equal Opportunities Commission) were as nothing compared to the effect which I felt the headline and its implications might have on the girls we had worked with. The main reason for sending the report to the local press was to let the subjects of the research have some feedback on the research. Most of them, after all, were not going to be buying the report or reading accounts of various aspects of the research in sociological or educational journals. They had received bulletins summarising various aspects of the research, but I had hoped that a piece in the local paper would be more interesting to them than a run-off sheet in a buff envelope. As 'subjects' of the research, they had after all given their time freely to be interviewed. They had often spoken at considerable length and with a great degree of insight, and on three occasions, they had filled in questionnaires for a more broadly based study[2] of which our look at girls was only a part. By the time the newspaper piece appeared, the research was complete, we had held a Girls' Night for the girls who had taken part in the survey and their friends, and our contact with them was over — in fact we had specifically said that we would not be in contact with them again, as they had been taking part in the larger project over quite a sustained period of almost two years. We did not, therefore, have the opportunity of going back to the girls, or their parents, and explaining ourselves in the same way that Morgan did. And although the paper subsequently printed a letter from me setting the record straight, I am left with the knowledge that many of the girls who were so generous to us in terms of time and information will think twice before letting themselves be interviewed again.

Both the projects described above were, by and large, unfortunately reported, although there were nevertheless some gains from the reporting of the women and doctors study. A third project in which I was involved (with Alan Graham, a mathematician) was an action research project concerned with devising a numeracy course for women. Our project, which we called *Sums for Mums*[3] was based around a series of lessons to mothers in a Bradford school followed by interviews in the women's homes. Over the ten weeks that the course ran, we got to know the women well, and when the report described above as 'Bradford Girls Lack Drive' appeared in the local paper a week before the same journalist was to interview 'our' mothers, I became alarmed. Would the article I wondered, be titled 'Dull Bradford Mums given another Chance'? In the event, reports in that particular paper, headlined 'Sums for Mums and Daughters' and 'Maths? Child's Play Say Mums' were unexceptional pieces of reporting, though in the six months between the first newspaper report and the second, the project had gone from being presented as Alan's 'brainchild' to being presented as mine. The desire of journalists to attribute a project to a particular named 'expert' has been commented on by others. Since any male (of however low a status) tends to be seen as senior to any female (however elevated) perhaps I was lucky to get any credit at all, particularly in such an 'unwomanly' area as maths. A fuller feature was produced in another local paper. Showing us cosily drinking cups of tea and fiddling with our calculators, the article, under the title 'When Mother Counts' comprised a clear, witty and intelligent account of the problems women and girls have with maths, a description of the project, laced with some quotable quotes from the mothers. The fact that the report (mistakenly) suggested that I maintained that I was 'no good at maths', and that Alan's wife Hilary Graham was referred to not in her capacity as a sociologist and a researcher (see Hilary Graham, this volume) but as a productive (of children not research) wife were relatively minor problems presumably intended to add 'human interest' to the story. A fourth report of the research appeared, somewhat incongruously, in the magazine *Home and Freezer*, a magazine which apparently caters for the housewife with a freezer as well as a family to look after. Although this was a very short (and slightly inaccurate) mention in what was a very perceptive piece on women and maths, this report and the one described immediately above had unexpected results. As a direct result of the *Home and Freezer* article, Alan received over 300 unsolicited queries from mothers asking for more information about the course. Many of these described in some considerable detail their own early experiences with maths (and maths teachers) which had made the subject so difficult for them to learn. These have provided both material for the subsequent *Sums for Mums* book (Graham, in preparation) and more importantly, given insights concerning the sort of course which might most usefully help women who have had unfortunate early experiences with mathematics.

These three brief cameos are intended to give examples of both good and bad outcomes from media attention to research and to raise the ethical question of whom we are writing for when we describe our research. The academics are reached by articles and reports, the general public by the press, and the subjects by — what? In theory each constituency has its own particular mode of communication, but in fact it does not work like that. The subjects are often reached most effectively not by the special efforts of the researchers but by the press, and the same may often be true of the expert community. Yet at precisely the point at which the results may be disseminated with most effect, the researcher has least control.

As Platt points out in her chapter, there is a less than perfect general correlation between intellectual merit and the fame or popularity of sociological work. This is undoubtedly true (though there is no reason why good work should not also be popular), and indeed the scholarly community will tend to view with some suspicion anything which attracts vulgar attention from the press. It is perhaps a fear of being thought un-serious which frequently leads academics to write their more journalistic pieces, or novels, under pseudonyms. Collins points out in his chapter that we depend to a very great extent in our work on support from our colleagues and obtaining their support often means adopting certain norms of 'good academic behaviour'. However good good journalism may be (and however bad bad sociology), if a book review of a sociology text describes it as journalistic, it is rarely meant as a compliment, or as an indication that the piece is clear and easily understood.

One of the values of qualitative sociology or of reflexive work in general is sometimes said to be that respondents can answer back. (In addition, given the dismal numeracy skills of most British sociologists, qualitative work tends to be more accountable within the profession as well as outside it.) But if a value of qualitative research is that the subjects can answer back, perhaps we should be asking how many of them read *Sociology*, the *British Journal of Sociology* or *Sociological Review*? One of the instructive points made by Morgan in his (1972) piece on the press and research was that the subjects of his research did, as it turned out, have strong views on what had been written about them, and these did not always coincide with the sociologist's view. The responsibility of the researcher, as Finch's chapter shows, does not end when the last question is asked. If anything is to happen to the research and its findings, then it must be made known by one means or another to a wider audience than simply the researcher and one or two of her colleagues. In the case of the research on women and their doctors referred to above, the work resulted in a couple of chapters in feminist collections (Barrett and Roberts, 1978; Roberts, 1981b), half a dozen articles in magazines for doctors such as *World Medicine* and *G.P.*, various papers given to audiences of academics, medical staff and patients, and a non-academic book on the doctor-patient relationship based on some of the findings of the research (Roberts, 1984). Our work was relatively well received by feminists working on health and by radical doctors (in a conservative profession such as medicine, you do not have to deviate very far to be radical).

Although the SSRC certainly got their £1903.32 pence worth, the pay-off to and for the women who spent so long talking to us was relatively slight. We thus had the dubious pleasure of writing research thought of as 'right on' by feminist colleagues, which sociologically speaking was sensible, if unspectacular, but which on the whole is unlikely to have a great effect on doctors or the way they treat women. This is partly due to a self-conscious desire to communicate with the patients rather than the doctors and partly due to the knowledge that much of the data we collected — 'subjective' interview data — would not strike those in the medical profession we were trying to influence as very 'scientific'. As one of the doctors said at the beginning of the study: 'the conclusions one draws from such (sociological) data are radically variable depending on your point of view. . . . Speculation is much more fun than specification. . . . However, I'm sure quantification is worth doing.' In the light of my own experience, it would seem that an important and neglected part of any researcher's training — and perhaps an element which should be included in courses even at undergraduate level, is a component on report writing and publishing, both scholarly and popular. Popular because however distasteful the world outside might seem from within the ivory tower (which is becoming distinctly less ivory these days), there is a good deal to be said for using every avenue at our disposal for making sure that the research we believe to be useful reaches those areas where it might have an effect. While recent work on social research and public policy-making (Kallen et al., 1982) suggests that the power of the media is often over-rated, common sense might lead one to suppose that research which has a wide audience is more likely to have an effect than research which languishes in the filing cabinet. There are three reasons for making the results of research known to as wide an audience as possible:

1 *Responsibility to respondents* To want to make the results of one's research known to a wider public than the academic community is not merely a wish to pass the time of readers of the *Sun*, or the *Express*, or to entertain listeners to the Jimmy Young show, but a reflexive responsibility towards the long-suffering general public who act as respondents ('subjects' or 'objects') in social science research. Why should they not have the opportunity to hear more about the research, to find out what was found out, and if they wish to, to comment or criticise?

2 *Credibility of the social sciences* It is not that sociology and the other social sciences have too much publicity which makes the general public suspicious of their worth. It is that they have too little — or too little of the right sort. One game which university researchers rarely know the rules of (though the independent research institutes are rather better) is

publishing for a wider audience — though universities are increasingly courting a good press and expanding the PR side of their work. One need only look at medicine, which has a wide press, a favourable press and a popular press, to see that a discipline need not lose credibility by popularity.

3 Effect on an elite audience Popularisation may also affect an elite audience — sometimes a good deal more forcibly than the carefully argued paper or memorandum. Changes in the management of childbirth, for instance, have undoubtedly come from pressure from 'below' (the consumer (or producer) groups) as well as from those doing serious research in the area.

The consequences of an acceptance of this responsibility are of two principal kinds. In the first place the sociologist must learn how best to reach her various audiences, and what skills there are to enable her to make the message received as close as possible to the message sent. The more she tries to reach the subjects of her research, the more she depends on a medium of communication over which she has little control. But the reporting of the Sums for Mums project, compared with that of the After Sixteen Report, suggests that even if the press cannot be managed, it can at least on occasion be shamed. Moreover, as with the After Sixteen project, the researcher can communicate directly with her respondents, even though this clearly only involves a very specialised public. In the second place, sociologists need to develop the awareness which they already have of the structural constraints on and opportunities for communication through the mass media, into an awareness, both theoretical and practical, of the ways in which their own work is presented to the various publics who consume it.

Malcolm Bradbury has observed that a sociologist is always on duty, but as Sue Scott's chapter shows, sociologists do not always extend their sociology to social relations in the areas considered to be outside their work. Accessibility of data is an important issue for those who under the thin veneer of either other-worldly scholar, or revolutionary, are actually closet social reformers. It is precisely because there is not one dominant view that one has a chance of making change and exercising influence through research — notwithstanding the fact that the direction of change, and its extent, may be extremely difficult to manipulate.

In the case of the three research projects outlined above, there were positive benefits of a wide readership. Women wrote to us about their experiences with their doctors, and, in the case of Sums for Mums, we were contacted by others wanting to run similar courses after press reports of our work. Small gains, perhaps, for those with ambitions to change the world (surely the ambition of any sociologist who was a student in the 1960s), but gains nevertheless, and gains which repay some of the work put in by those most powerless in the research process — the respondents.

Notes

1 As this book was going to press, an example of one of the more unfortunate aspects of dissemination for a popular audience appeared in the *Daily Mail* (Kupferman, 1983). A woman journalist who herself had an academic background interviewed Janet Finch, a contributor to this volume, about her book *Married to the Job* (Finch, 1983a). Unable to get Janet to give her details of her private life, she proceeded to write a bitter half-page attack. 'How' asked Kupferman, 'can she claim to speak in the name of science about marriage to women if she is too coy to make it clear where she herself stands?' (One wonders if Willmott and Young were similarly pressed for details of their family lives and marriages after the publication of *Family and Kinship in East London*.) The journalist concluded her article: 'Barbara Cartland is probably a better sociologist than any of them, largely because she understands sexual chemistry a little better than Marx.' Clearly, attempting to reach a wide audience is not without its pitfalls.

2 The larger *After Sixteen* study was carried out by Ivan Maxted, Research and Information Officer, Directorate of Education, Provincial House, Bradford.

3 *Sums for Mums* was funded by the Equal Opportunities Commission and the full report can be obtained from Sue Sinclair at Bradford and Ilkley Community College, price £2.50.

Bibliography

Abrams, P. (1981), 'Visionaries and Virtuosi: Competence and Purpose in the Education of Sociologists', *Sociology*, vol. 15. no. 4, November, pp. 530-8.

Acker, J., Barry, K. and Esseveld, J. (1982), 'Issues in Feminist Research: An Account of an Effort to Practice What We Preach', unpublished paper, University of Lund, Sweden, Department of Sociology.

Ackroyd, S. and Hughes, J. (1981), *Data Collection in Context*, London, Longman.

Ardener, E. (1978), 'Belief and the Problem of Women', in S. Ardener (ed.), *Perceiving Women*, London, Dent.

Armstrong, K. and Beynon, H. (eds) (1977), *Hello, Are You Working?: Memories of the Thirties in the North East of England*, Whitley Bay, Tyne and Wear, Strong Words Collective.

Armstrong, P. (1982), *The Use of the Life History Method in Social and Educational Research*, Newland Papers No. 7, Department of Adult Education, University of Hull.

Balbo, L. and Siebert-Zahar, R. (eds) (1979), *Interferenze: lo stato, la vita familiare, la vita privata*, Milan, Feltrinelli.

Balbo, L. and Zanuso, L. (eds) (1982), 'Piu facce, molto teste: La condizione della donna', *Inchiesta*, vol. XII, no. 55, pp. 1-87, January-March, Bologna and Bari, Edizione Dedalo.

Baldamus, W. (1972), 'The Role of Discoveries in Social Science', in R. Shanin (ed.), *The Rules of the Game*, London, Tavistock.

Baldamus, W. (1976), *Structure and Proof in Sociological Theory*, Oxford, Martin Robertson.

Banks, J.A. (1967), 'The British Sociological Association: The First Fifteen Years', *Sociology*, vol. 1, no. 1, pp. 1-9.

Barnes, J. (1979), *Who Should Know What?*, Harmondsworth, Penguin.

Barrett, M. and Roberts, H. (1978), 'Doctors and Their Patients: The Social Control of Women in General Practice', in C. and B. Smart (eds), *Women, Sexuality and Social Control*, London, Routledge & Kegan Paul.

213

Barro, G. (1980), *Guida al Distretto Sanitaria*, Rome, Collana NIS, no. 26.

Bates, F. (1981), 'A Plea for the Battered Husband', *Family Law*, vol. 11, no. 3, pp. 90-3.

Becker, H. (1967), 'Whose Side Are We On?', *Social Problems*, vol. 14, pp. 239-47.

Becker, H. (1978), 'The Relevance of Life Histories', in N. Denzin (ed.), *Sociological Methods: A Sourcebook*, New York, McGraw-Hill.

Bell, C. (1969), 'A Note on Participant Observation', *Sociology*, vol. 3, no. 3, pp. 417-18.

Bell, C. (1975), 'Replication and Reality or the Future of Sociology', *Futures*, June, pp. 253-60.

Bell, C. and Encel, S. (eds) (1978), *Inside the Whale*, Sydney, Pergamon.

Bell, C. and Newby, H. (1977), *Doing Sociological Research*, London, Allen & Unwin.

Berlinguer, G. (1982), *Glia anni difficili della riforma Sanitaria*, Bari De Donato, Collana Riforme e Potere no. 40.

Bernabei, P., Cirinei, G., and Zolo, P. (1980), *L'Unita Sanitaria Locale*, Rome, Collana NIS no. 1.

Berry, C.J. (1979), 'Idiotic Politics', *Political Studies*, vol. 27, no. 4, pp. 550-63.

Binney, V., Harkell, G. and Nixon, J. (1981), *Leaving Violent Men: A Study of Refuges and Housing for Battered Women*, London, Women's Aid Federation, England.

Black D. (1980), *Inequalities in Health*, London, DHSS.

Blackburn, R. (1967), 'The Unequal Society', in R. Blackburn and A. Cockburn (eds), *The Incompatibles*, Harmondsworth, Penguin.

Blackburn, R. (1969), 'A Brief Guide to Bourgeois Ideology', in R. Blackburn and A. Cockburn (eds), *Student Power*, Harmondsworth, Penguin.

Blackburn, R.M. and Mann, M. (1979), *The Working Class in the Labour Market*, London, Macmillan.

Blackler, F. and Brown, C.A. (1978), 'Organizational Psychology: Good Intentions and False Promises', *Human Relations*, vol. 31, no. 4, pp. 333-51.

Boissevain, J. and Friedl, J. (eds) (1975), *Beyond the Community*, The Hague, Ministry of Education and Science.

Boserup, E. (1970), *Women in Economic Development*, London, Allen & Unwin.

Bottomore, T.B. (1972), *Sociology*, 2nd edn, London, Allen & Unwin.

Bowen, E.S. (1964), *Return to Laughter*, New York, Doubleday.

Brody, H. (1981), *Maps and Dreams*, London, Jill Norman.

Brown, R. (1973), 'Sources of Objectives in Work and Employment', in J. Child (ed.), *Man and Organisation*, London, Allen & Unwin.

Bruyn, S.T. (1966), *The Human Perspective in Sociology*, Englewood Cliffs, N.J., Prentice Hall.

Bulmer, M. (ed.) (1975), *Working-Class Images of Society*, London, Routledge & Kegan Paul.

Bulmer, M. (ed.) (1982), *Social Research Ethics*, London, Allen & Unwin.

Burton, F. (1978), *The Politics of Legitimacy*, London, Routledge & Kegan Paul.

Butler, D. and Stokes, D. (1971), *Political Change in Britain*, Harmondsworth, Penguin.

Cain, M. and Finch J. (1981), 'Towards a Rehabilitation of Data', in P. Abrams, R. Deem, J. Finch and P. Rock (eds), *Practice and Progress: British Sociology 1950-1980*, London, Allen & Unwin.

Caldwell, L. (1982), 'Discussion of the Family as an Instance of Church-State Relations', BSA typescript, Manchester.

Cherns, A. (1969), 'Social Research and its Diffusion', *Human Relations*, vol. 22, no. 3, pp. 210-18.

Collins, H.M. (1975), 'The Seven Sexes: A Study in the Sociology of a Phenomenon, or the Replication of Experiments in Physics', *Sociology*, vol. 9, no. 2, pp. 205-24.

Collins, H.M. (1979), 'The Investigation of Frames of Meaning in Science: Complementarity and Compromise', *Sociological Review*, vol. 27, no. 4, pp. 703-18.

Collins, H.M. and Cox, G.E. (1976), 'Recovering Relativity: Did Prophecy Fail?', *Social Studies of Science*, vol. 6, pp. 423-44.

Collins, H.M. and Pinch, T.J. (1982), *Frames of Meaning: The Social Construction of Extraordinary Science*, London, Routledge & Kegan Paul.

Cotgrove, S.F. (1978), *The Science of Society*, 4th edn, London, Allen & Unwin.

Crewe, I. (1973), 'The Politics of "Affluent" and "Traditional" Workers in Britain', *British Journal of Political Science*, vol. 3, pp. 29-52.

Cullen, I. (1979), 'Urban Social Policy and the Problems of Family Life: The Use of an Extended Diary Method to Inform Decision Analysis', in C.C. Harris (ed.) (1979), *The Sociology of the Family: New Directions for Britain*, Sociological Review Monograph 28, University of Keele.

Daniel, W. (1969), 'Industrial Behaviour and Orientation to Work: A Critique', *Journal of Management Studies*, vol. 6, pp. 366-75.

Daniels, A. (1967), 'The Low Caste Stranger in Social Research', in Sjoberg, 1967.

Davis, J. (1975), 'Beyond the Hyphen: Some Notes and Documents on Community-State Relations in South Italy', in J. Boissevain and J. Friedl (eds), 1975.

Davis, M.S. (1971), 'That's Interesting! . . .', *Philosophy of Social Science*, vol. 1, pp. 309-44.

De Fronzo, J. (1973), 'Embourgeoisement in Indianapolis?', *Social Problems*, vol. 21, no. 2, pp. 269-83.

De Martin, Stefano (1982), *Famiglia contadina e classe operaia nelle campagna ubanizzata del Chianti*, Tavarnelle V.P. (Florence), Comune di Tavarnelle Val di Pesa.

Denzin, N. (ed.) (1978), *Sociological Methods: A Sourcebook*, New York, McGraw-Hill.

DHSS (1978), *Homelessness and Addictions Research Liaison Group: Meeting of Researchers into Violence in Marriage*, 17 February.

DHSS (1980), *Homelessness and Addictions Research Liaison Group: Strategy for Research on Domestic Violence*, January.

Dingwall, R. (1980), 'Ethics and Ethnography', *Sociological Review*, vol. 28, no. 4, pp. 871-91.

Ditton, J. and Williams, R. (1981), 'The Fundable versus the Doable', background paper, Department of Sociology, University of Glasgow.

Dobash, R., Cavanagh, K. and Wilson, M. (1976), 'Methodological Issues Concerning the Study of Marital Violence: A Case Study', paper presented at the Conference of the American Sociological Association, September.

Dobash, R.E. and Dobash, R. (1979), *Violence Against Wives: A Case Against the Patriarchy*, New York, Free Press; Shepton Mallet, Open Books, 1980.

Elshtain, J.B. (1981), *Public Man, Private Woman: Women in Social and Political Thought*, Oxford, Martin Robertson.

Ennew, J. (1980), *The Western Isles Today*, Cambridge, Cambridge University Press.

Etzioni, A. (1961), *A Comparative Analysis of Complex Organisations*, New York, Free Press.

Falassi, A. (1980), *Folklore of the Fireside*, London, Scolar Press.

Festinger, L., Riecken, H.W. and Schachter, S. (1956), *When Prophecy Fails*, New York, Harper.

Filstead, W.J. (ed.) (1970), *Qualitative Methodology: Firsthand Involvement with the Social World*, Chicago, Markham.

Finch, J. (1980), 'Devising Conventional Performances: The Case of Clergymen's Wives', *Sociological Review*, vol. 28, no. 4, pp. 851-70.

Finch, J. (1981), *Working Class Women and Preschool Playgroups*, Report to the Social Science Research Council.

Finch, J. (1983a), *Married to the Job: Wives' Incorporation in Men's Work*, London, Allen & Unwin.

Finch, J. (1983b), 'Dividing the Rough and the Respectable: Working Class Women and Preschool Playgroups', in E. Gamarnikov et al. (eds), *The Public and the Private*, London, Heinemann.

Finch, J. (1983c), 'A First Class Environment? Working Class Playgroups as Preschool Experience', *British Education Research Journal*, November.

Fleming, S. and Broad, R. (1982), *Nella Last's War - A Mother's Diary - 1939-1945*, London, Falling Wall Press.

Floud, J.E. et al. (1957), *Social Class and Educational Opportunity*, London, Heinemann.

Francis, S. (1982), 'Review of "Nella Last's War" ', *Women's Research and Resources Centre Newsletter*, no. 5, p. 8.

Frankenberg, R. (1972), 'Taking the Blame and Passing the Buck or the Carpet of Agamemnon', in M. Gluckman (ed.), *The Allocation of Responsibility*, Manchester, Manchester University Press.

Frankenberg, R. (1980), 'Medical Anthropology and Development: A Theoretical Perspective', *Social Science and Medicine*, vol. 14B, pp. 197-207.

Frankenberg, R. (ed.) (1982), *Custom and Conflict in British Society*, Manchester, Manchester University Press.

Freeman, M. (1979), *Violence in the Home*, Farnborough, Hants, Saxon House.

Friedrichs, J. and Ludtke, H. (1975), *Participant Observation:Theory and Practice*, New York, Lexington Books.

Frith, S. (1978), *The Sociology of Rock*, London, Constable.

Gallie, D. (1978), *In Search of the New Working Class*, Cambridge, Cambridge University Press.

Galtung, J. (1967), *Theory and Methods of Social Research*, London, Allen & Unwin.

Gellner, E. (1970), 'Concepts and Society', in D. Emmet and A. MacIntrye (eds), *Sociological Theory and Philosophical Analysis*, London, Macmillan.

George, V. and Wilding, P. (1972), 'Social Values, Social Class and Social Policy', *Social and Economic Administration*, vol. 6, no. 3, pp. 236-48.

Glasgow University Media Group (1976), *Bad News*, London, Routledge & Kegan Paul.

Glastonbury, M. (1979), 'The Best Kept Secret — How Working Class Women Live and What They Know', *Women's Studies International Quarterly*, vol. 2, pp. 171-81.

Goldthorpe, J.E. (1968), *An Introduction to Sociology*, Cambridge, Cambridge University Press.

Goldthorpe, J.H. (1966), 'Attitudes and Behaviour of Car Assembly Workers: A Deviant Case and a Theoretical Critique', *British Journal of Sociology*, vol. 17, no. 3, pp. 227-44.

Goldthorpe, J H. (1970), 'L'image des classes chez les travailleurs manuels aisés', *Revue Française de Sociologie*, vol. 11, no. 3, pp. 311-38.

Goldthorpe, J.H. and Lockwood, D. (1962), 'Not So Bourgeois After All', *New Society*, 18 October, no. 3, pp. 18-19.

Goldthorpe, J.H. and Lockwood, D. (1963), 'Affluence and the British Class Structure', *Sociological Review*, vol. 11, no. 2, pp. 133-63.

Goldthorpe, J.H., Lockwood, D., Bechhofer, F. and Platt, J. (1967), 'The Affluent Worker and the Thesis of Embourgeoisement', *Sociology*, vol. 1, no. 1, pp. 11-31.

Goldthorpe, J.H. et al. (1968), *The Affluent Worker: Political Attitudes and Behaviour*, Cambridge, Cambridge University Press.

Goldthorpe, J.H. et al. (1968), *The Affluent Worker: Industrial Attitudes and Behaviour*, Cambridge University Press.

Goldthorpe, J.H. et al. (1969), *The Affluent Worker in the Class Structure*, Cambridge, Cambridge University Press.

Goode, W. and Hatt, P. (1952), *Methods in Social Research*, New York, McGraw-Hill.

Gorz, A. (1970), 'Workers' Control: Some European Experiences', lecture given at Harvard, 12 November (xeroxed).

Gouldner, A. (1973), 'The Sociologist as Partisan', in *For Sociology: Renewal and Critique in Sociology Today*, London, Allen Lane.

Graham, A. (forthcoming), *Sums for Mums*.

Graham, A. and Roberts, H. (1982), *Sums for Mums*, Report produced by Bradford and Ilkley Community College.

Graham, H. (1983) 'Do Her Answers Fit His Questions: Women and the Survey Method', in E. Gamarnikov, D. Morgan, J. Purvis and D. Taylorson, (eds), *The Public and the Private*, London, Heinemann.

Graham, H. and McKee, L. (1980), *The First Months of Motherhood*, Research Monograph No. 3, London, Health Education Council.

Grieco, M. (1981), 'The Shaping of a Work Force: A Critique of the *Affluent Worker* Study', *International Journal of Sociology and Social Policy*, vol. 1, no. 1, pp. 62-88.

Grillo, R.D. (ed.) (1980), *'Nation' and 'State' in Europe: Anthropological Perspectives*, London, Academic Press.

Gruppi Parliamentari, DC (1982), *La Riforma Sanitaria a due anni dalla rua approvazione*, Studi e Documenti 7, Rome, Edizione Cinque Luni.

Hakim, C. (1982), *Secondary Analysis in Social Research*, London, Allen & Unwin.

Halfpenny, P. (1979), 'The Analysis of Qualitative Data', *Sociological Review*, vol. 27, November, pp. 799-825.

Halsey, A.H. (ed.) (1972), *Trends in British Society Since 1900*, London, Macmillan.

Halsey, A.H. (1982a), 'Why Rothschild Spared the Axe', *New Society*, 27 May, p. 336.

Halsey, A.H. (1982b), 'Provincials and Professionals: The British Post-War Sociologists', *Archives Européennes de Sociologie*, vol. 23, no. 1, pp. 150-75.

Hanmer, J. and Saunders, S. (1984), *We Are the Subjects of Our Own Research: A Community Study of Violence to Women*, London, Hutchinson.

Haralambos, M. (1980), *Sociology: Themes and Perspectives*, London, University Tutorial Press.

Hargreaves, D.H. (1967), *Social Relations in a Secondary School*, London, Routledge & Kegan Paul.

Hart, J.T. (1971), 'The Inverse Care Law', *Lancet*, vol. I, pp. 606-12.

Hawthorn, G. and Paddon, M. (1971), 'Work, Family and Fertility', *Human Relations*, vol. 24, no. 6, pp. 611-28.

Hedley, R.A. and Taveggia, T.C. (1977), 'Textbook Sociology: Some Cautionary Remarks', *American Sociologist*, vol. 12, no. 3, pp. 108-16.

Hill, S. (1976), *The Dockers: Class and Tradition in London*, London, Heinemann.

HMSO (1982), 'An Enquiry into the Social Science Research Council' by Lord Rothschild, May, Cmnd 8554.

Hobson, D. (1978), 'Housewives: Isolation as Oppression', in Women's Studies Group, Centre for Contemporary Cultural Studies, *Women Take Issue: Aspects of Women's Subordination*, London, Hutchinson.

Hobson, D. (1980), 'Housewives and the Mass Media', in S. Hall, D. Hobson, A. Lowe and P. Willis (eds), *Culture, Media, Language*, London, Hutchinson.

Hoggart, R. (1957), *The Uses of Literacy*, London, Chatto & Windus.

Holy, L. (1979), 'From Participating Observer to Observing Participant: The Paradox of Participant Observation', paper presented to SSRC conference on participant observation, Birmingham, September.

Hunt, P. (1980), *Gender and Class Consciousness*, London, Macmillan.

Hurd, G. et al. (1973), *Human Societies*, London, Routledge & Kegan Paul.

Illsley, R. (1981), 'Professional or Public Health', *Medical Sociology News*, vol. 8, no. 1.

Imray, L. and Middleton, A. (1983), 'Public and Private: Marking the Boundaries', in E. Gamarnikov et al. (eds), *The Public and the Private*, London, Heinemann.

Ineichen, B. (1972), 'Home Ownership and Manual Workers' Lifestyles', *Sociological Review*, vol. 20, no. 3, pp. 391-412.

Ingham, G.K. (1970), *Size of Industrial Organisation and Worker Behaviour*, Cambridge, Cambridge University Press.

Inglehart, R. (1971), 'The Silent Revolution in Europe: Intergenerational Change in Post-Industrial Societies', *American Political Science Review*, vol. 65, no. 4, pp. 991-1017.

Jenkins, R. (1981), 'Thinking and Doing: Towards a Model of Cognitive Practice', in L. Holy and M. Stuchlik (eds), *The Structure of Folk Models*, London, Academic Press.

Jenkins, R. (1982a), 'Managers, Recruitment Procedures and Black Workers', *Working Papers on Ethnic Relations* No. 18, RUER, Birmingham.

Jenkins, R. (1982b), *Hightown Rules: Coming of Age in a Belfast Housing Estate*, Leicester, National Youth Bureau.

Jenkins, R. (1983a) 'Goals, Constraints and Occupational Choice, *British Journal of Guidance and Counselling*, vol. 11, no. 2.

Jenkins, R. (1983b), *Lads, Citizens and Ordinary Kids: Working Class Youth Life-styles in Belfast*, London, Routledge & Kegan Paul.

Kallen, D.B.P., Kosse, G.B., Wagenaar, H.C., Kloprogge, J.J.J. and Vorbeck, M. (1982), *Social Science Research and Public Policy Making*, London, NFER-Nelson.

Kanter, Moss (1978), *Men and Women of the Corporation*, New York, Harper & Row.

Kavanagh, D. (1971), 'The Deferential English: A Comparative Critique', *Government and Opposition*, vol. 6, no. 3, pp. 333-60.

Kemeny, P.J. (1972), 'The Affluent Worker Project: Some Criticisms and a Derivative Study', *Sociological Review*, vol. 20, pp. 373-89.

Kupferman, J. (1983), 'What a Zany Idea of the *Ideal* Marriage', *Daily Mail*, 20 May, p. 13.

Lambert, R.S. and Beales, H.L. (1934), *Memories of the Unemployed*, London, Victor Gollancz.

Lansbury, R. (1974), 'Careers, Work and Leisure Among the New Professionals', *Sociological Review*, vol. 22, no. 3, pp. 385-400.

Lewis, C. (1982), 'How Families are Facing up to Christmas on the Dole', *Birmingham Mail*, 6 December, p. 9.

Lewis, I.M. (1971), *Ecstatic Religion: An Anthropological Study of Spirit Possession and Shamanism*, Harmondsworth, Penguin Books.

Little, K. (1974), *African Women in Towns*, Cambridge, Cambridge University Press.

Llewelyn Davies, M. (ed.) (1978), *Maternity: Letters from Working Women*, London, Virago (first published by Bell and Sons, 1915).

Lockwood, D. (1960), 'The New Working Class', *European Journal of Sociology*, vol. 1, no. 2, pp. 248-59.

Lockwood, D. (1966), 'Sources of Variation in Working-Class Images of Society', *Sociological Review*, vol. 14, no. 3, pp. 249-63.

London Edinburgh Weekend Return Group (1979), *In and Against the State*, London, London Edinburgh Weekend Return Group.

McCall, G.J. and Simmons, J.L. (eds) (1969), *Issues in Participant Observation: A Text and Reader*, Massachusetts, Addison-Wesley.

McCarthy, M. (1982), 'Epidemiological Targets for District Health Authorities', typescript, University College, London.

McClelland, J. (1982), *A Little Pride and Dignity: The Importance of Child Benefit*, Poverty Pamphlet 54, London, Child Poverty Action Group.

McCrindle, J. and Rowbotham, S. (1977), *Dutiful Daughters: Women Talk About Their Lives*, London, Allen Lane.

MacIntosh, J. (1977), *Communications and Awareness in a Cancer Ward*, London, Croom Helm.

Mackenzie, G. (1974), 'The *Affluent Worker* Study: An Evaluation and Critique', in F. Parkin (ed.), *The Social Analysis of Class Structure*, London, Tavistock.

MacKinnon, M.H. (1980), 'Work Instrumentalism Reconsidered: A Replication of Goldthorpe's Luton Project', *British Journal of Sociology*, vol. 31, no. 1, pp.1-27.

McRobbie, A. (1978), 'Working Class Girls and the Culture of Femininity', in Women's Studies Group, *Women Take Issue*, London, Hutchinson.

McRobbie, A. (1982), 'The Politics of Feminist Research: Between Talks, Text and Action', *Feminist Review*, no. 12, pp. 46-58.

McRobbie, A. and Garber, J. (1976), 'Girls and Subcultures', in S. Hall and T. Jefferson, T. (eds), *Resistance Through Rituals*, London, Hutchinson.

Malinowski, B. (1967), *A Diary in the Strict Sense of the Term*, London, Routledge & Kegan Paul.

Mann, M. (1973), *Workers on the Move*, Cambridge, Cambridge University Press.

Marsh, C. (1982), *The Survey Method*, London, Allen & Unwin.

Marshall, T.H. (1970), Review, *AWCS, Economic Journal*, vol. 80, no. 2, pp. 415-17.

Mead, M. (1977), *Letters from the Field*, 1925-75, New York, Harper & Row.

Mercer, D.E. and Weir, D.T.H. (1972), 'Attitudes to Work and Trade Unionism Among White Collar Workers', *Industrial Relations Journal*, vol. 3, no. 2, summer, pp. 49-60.

Messerschmidt, D.A. (ed.) (1981), *Anthropologists at Home in North America*, Cambridge, Cambridge University Press.

Millar, J.A. (1978), 'Contingency Theory, Values, and Change', *Human Relations*, vol. 31, no. 10, pp. 885-904.

Mills, C.W. (1959), *The Sociological Imagination*, New York, Oxford University Press.

Moore, R. (1978), 'Sociologists not at Work', in G. Littlejohn et al. (eds), *Power and the State*, London, Croom Helm.

Morgan, D.H.J. (1972), 'The British Association Scandal: The Effect of Publicity on a Sociological Investigation', *Sociological Review*, vol. 20, pp. 185-286.

Morgan, D.H.J. (1981), 'Men, Masculinity and Sociological Enquiry', in H. Roberts (ed.), op cit.

Moss-Kanter, R. (1978), *Men, Women and the Corporation*, New York, Harper & Row.

Newby, H., Bell, C., Saunders, P., Rose, D. (1978), *Property Patronage Power: Class and Control in Rural England*, London, Hutchinson.

Nicolaus, M. (1972), 'Sociology Liberation Movement', in T. Pateman, *Counter Course*, Harmondsworth, Penguin.

Noble, T. (1975), *Modern Britain: Structure and Change*, London, Batsford.

NWAF (1976a), *Research Grants or What Do the Poor Have But Their Information?*, Research Group paper to National Conference.

NWAF (1976b), *The Existing Research into Battered Women*, pamphlet prepared by E. Wilson, London, NWAF.

NWAF (1978), Paper Prepared for the Department of Health and Social Security Homelessness and Additions Research Liaison Group Meeting of Researchers into Marital Violence, 17 February.

Oakley, A. (1981), 'Interviewing Women: A Contradiction in Terms', in H. Roberts (ed.), 1981a.

222 *Bibliography*

Paci, M. (1982), *La Struttura Sociale Italiana*, Il Mulino, Bologna, Universale Paperbacks.

Pahl, J. (1978), *A Refuge For Battered Women*, London, HMSO.

Pahl, J. (1981), *A Bridge Over Troubled Waters*, London. DHSS Report.

Parliamentary Select Committee on Violence in Marriage (1975), *Report from the Select Committee on Violence in Marriage together with the Proceeding of the Committee. Vol. 1 Report, Vol. 2 Report, Minutes of Evidence and Appendices*, London, HMSO.

Parsler, R. (1970), 'Some Economic Aspects of Embourgeoisement in Australia', *Sociology*, vol. 4, no. 2, pp. 165-79.

Payne, G., Dingwall, R., Payne, J. and Carter, M. (1980), *Sociology and Social Research*, London, Routledge & Kegan Paul.

Pearsall, M. (1970), 'Participant Observation as Role and Method in Behaviour Research', in Filstead, 1970.

Piepe, A. et al. (1969), 'The Location of the Proletarian and Deferential Worker', *Sociology*, vol. 3, no. 2, pp. 239-44.

Pinch, T.J. (1981), 'The Sun-Set: The Presentation of Certainty in Scientific Life', in H.M. Collins (ed.), *Knowledge and Controversy: Studies in Modern Natural Science. Social Studies of Science*, special issue, vol. 11, no. 1, pp. 131-58.

Pinto, D. (ed.) (1981), *Contemporary Italian Sociology: A Reader*, Cambridge, Cambridge University Press.

Platt, J. (1969), 'Some Problems in Measuring the Jointness of Conjugal Role-Relationships', *Sociology*, vol. 3, no. 3, pp. 287-97.

Platt, J. (1971), 'Variations in Answers to Different Questions on Perceptions of Class', *Sociological Review*, vol. 19, no. 3, pp. 409-19.

Platt, J. (1981), 'Interviewing One's Peers', *Sociology*, vol. 15, no. 2, pp. 75-91.

Pleck, E., Pleck, J., Grossman, M. and Bart. P. (1978), 'The Battered Data Syndrome: A Reply to Steinmetz', *Victimology*, vol. 2, nos 3-4, pp. 680-3.

Pridham, G. (1981), *The Nature of the Italian Party System*, London, Croom Helm.

Rex, J.A. (ed.) (1974), *Approaches to Sociology*, London, Routledge & Kegan Paul.

Rich, A. (1980), *On Lies, Secrets and Silences*, London, Virago.

Rinehart, J.W. (1971), 'Affluence and the Embourgeoisement of the Working Class: A Critical Look', *Social Problems*, vol. 19, no. 2, pp. 149-62.

Roberts, H. (ed.) (1981a), *Doing Feminist Research*, London, Routledge & Kegan Paul.

Roberts, H. (1981b), 'Women and Their Doctors: Power and Powerlessness in the Research Process', in H. Roberts (ed.), 1981a.

Roberts, H. (1974), *Women, The Patient Patients*, London, Pandora.

Roberts, H. and Sharp, M. (1982), *After Sixteen: What Happens to the Girls?*, Bradford Metropolitan Authority.

Rosaldo, M.Z. (1974), 'Woman, Culture and Society – A Theoretical Overview', in M.Z. Rosaldo and L. Lamphere (eds), *Woman, Culture and Society*, Stanford, Stanford University Press.

Rose, H. (1978), 'In Practice Supported, In Theory Denied: An Account of an Invisible Urban Movement', *International Journal of Urban and Regional Research*, vol. 2, no. 3, pp. 521-37.

Rose, H. (1982), 'Making Science Feminist', in E. Whitelegg et al. (eds), *The Changing Experience of Women*, Oxford, Martin Robertson.

Rowbotham, S. (1973), *Women's Consciousness, Man's World*, Harmondsworth, Penguin.

Rowbotham, S., Segal, L. and Wainwright, H. (eds) (1979), *Beyond the Fragments: Feminism and the Making of Socialism*, London, Merlin Press.

Ryder, J. and Silver, H. (1970), *Modern English Society*, London, Methuen.

Salaman, G. (1974), *Community and Occupation*, Cambridge, Cambridge University Press.

Salvianti, C. and Ciappetti, R. (1979), *Lotte politiche e sociale in Val di Pesa dal primo dopoguerra alla Liberazione (1919-1944)*, Amministrazione Comunale di San Casciano, San Casciano V.P. Florence, Nuovo Edizione Enrico Valecchi.

Sartre, J.-P. (1963), *The Problem of Method*, translated by H.E. Barnes, London, Methuen.

Scott, S.J. and Porter, M. (1983), 'On the Bottom Rung', *Women's Studies International Forum*, vol. 6, no. 2, pp. 211-21.

Shaffir, W., Stebbins, R. and Turavetz, A. (eds) (1980), *Fieldwork Experience*, New York, St Martin's Press.

Shepard, J.M. (1970), 'Functional Specialisation, Alienation and Job Satisfaction', *Industrial and Labour Relations Review*, vol. 23, no. 2, pp. 207-19.

Sjoberg, G. (1967), *Ethics, Politics and Social Research*, Cambridge Massachussetts, Schenkman.

Smith, D. (1974), 'Women's Perspective as a Radical Critique of Sociology', *Sociological Inquiry*, vol. 44, no. 1, pp. 7-13.

Smith, D. (1979), 'A Sociology for Women', in J.A. Sherman and E. Torton Beck (eds), *The Prison of Sex: Essays in the Sociology of Knowledge*, Madison, University of Wisconsin Press.

Spanier, G.B. and Stump, C.S. (1978), 'The Use of Research in Applied Marriage and Family Text Books', *Contemporary Sociology*, vol. 7, no. 5, pp. 553-63.

Spedding, J. (1975), 'Wives of the Clergy', Ph.D. thesis, University of Bradford.

Spender, D. (1980), *Man Made Language*, London, Routledge & Kegan Paul.

Spender, D. (1981), 'The Gatekeepers: A Feminist Critique of Academic Publishing' in H. Roberts (ed.), 1981a.

Stacey, M. (1981), 'The Division of Labour Revisited or Overcoming the Two Adams', in P. Abrams, R. Deem, J. Finch and P. Rock (eds),

Practice and Progress: British Sociology 1950-1980, London, Allen & Unwin.

Stacey, M. and Price M. (1980), *Women, Power and Politics*, London, Tavistock.

Stanley, L. (1982), 'Review of Doing Feminist Research', *Women's Studies International Quarterly*, vol. 5, no. 2, pp. 116-18.

Stanley, L. and Wise, S. (1979), 'Feminist Research, Feminist Consciousness and Experiences of Sexism', *Women's Studies International Quarterly*, vol. 2, no. 3, pp. 359-74.

Stark, E. (1982), 'Doctors in spite of Themselves: The Limits of Radical Health Criticism', *International Journal of Health Services*, vol. 12, no. 3, pp. 419-57.

Steinmetz, S. (1978), 'The Battered Husband Syndrome', *Victimology*, vol. 2, nos 3-4, pp. 499-509.

Stimson, G. and Webb, B. (1975), *Going to See the Doctor*, London, Routledge & Kegan Paul.

Susser, I. (1982), *Norman Street: Poverty and Politics in an Urban Neighbourhood*, New York and Oxford, Oxford University Press.

Sutton, J. (1978), 'The Growth of the British Movement for Battered Women', *Victimology*, vol. 2, nos 3-4, pp. 576-84.

Swingewood, A. (1970), 'Origins of Sociology: The Case of the Scottish Enlightenment', *British Journal of Sociology*, vol. 21, no. 2, pp. 164-80.

Thomas, R. (1981), 'Problems in the Collection and Analysis of Individual Histories', *Survey Methodology Bulletin* No. 13, October, pp. 2-13.

Thomas, W.I. and Znaniecki, F. (1918), *The Polish Peasant in Europe and America*, Chicago, University of Chicago Press.

Tonkin, E. (1979), 'Anthropologists in a Cool Web: The Processes of Knowledge-making', paper presented to SSRC Conference on Participant Observation', 24-25 September.

Toomey, D.M. (1969), 'Home-Centred Working-Class Parents' Attitudes Towards Their Sons' Education and Careers', *Sociology*, vol. 3, no. 3, pp. 299-320.

Townsend, P. (1979), *Poverty in the United Kingdom*, Harmondsworth, Penguin.

Townsend, P. and Davidson, N. (eds) (1982), *Inequalities in Health: The Black Report*, Harmondsworth, Penguin.

Transport and General Workers' Union, 9/12 Branch (1981), *Stress at Work: Final Report*, Leeds, Region 9 TGWU.

Turner, V. W. (1969, 1981), *The Drums of Affliction*, London, International African Institute/Hutchinson University Library for Africa.

Vanneman, R.D. (1980), 'US and British Perceptions of Class', *American Journal of Sociology*, vol. 85, no. 4, pp. 869-90.

Vickerman, R. (1972), 'The Demand for Non-Work Travel', *Journal of Transport Economics*, vol. VI, no. 2.

Wakeford, J. (1982), 'Directors Dilemmas', unpublished paper presented to the Ethnography of Education Workshop, Whitelands College, July.

Wax, R. (1971), *Doing Fieldwork*, Chicago, University of Chicago Press.

Webb, D.R. (1972), 'The Employment of 1970 Sociology Graduates', *Sociology*, vol. 6, no. 3, pp. 433-42.

Webb, E.J., Campbell, D.T., Schwartz, R.D. and Sechrest, L. (1972), *Unobtrusive Measures: Nonreactive Research in the Social Sciences*, Chicago, Rand McNally.

Weber, M. (1980), *Economy and Society*, New York, Bedminster Press.

Weir, S. (1981), 'The SSRC and its Family', *New Society*, 26 November, p. 365.

Westcott, M (1979), 'Feminist Criticism of the Social Sciences', *Harvard Educational Review*, vol. 49, no. 4, pp. 422-30.

Westergaard, J.H. (1970), 'The Rediscovery of the Cash Nexus', in R. Miliband and J. Saville (eds), *The Socialist Register 1970*, London, Merlin Press.

Whelan, C.T. (1976), 'Orientations to Work: Some Theoretical and Methodological Problems', *British Journal of Industrial Relations*, vol. XIV, no. 2, pp. 142-58.

Whitehead, A. (1976), 'Sexual Antagonism in Herefordshire', in D.L. Barker and S. Allen (eds), *Dependence and Exploitation of Work and Marriage*, London, Longman.

Whyte, W.F. (1955), *Street Corner Society*, Chicago, University of Chicago Press.

Wilkins, E.J. (1970), *An Introduction to Sociology*, Plymouth, Macdonald & Evans.

Wilkins, L.T. (1960), *Delinquent Generations*, London, HMSO.

Willis, P. (1980), 'Notes on Method', in S. Hall, et al. (eds), *Culture, Media Language*, London, Hutchinson.

Willmott, P. (1969), 'Some Social Trends', *Urban Studies*, vol. 6, no. 3, pp. 286-308.

Woodward, D. and Chisholm, L. (1981), 'The Expert's View?', in H. Roberts (ed.), *Doing Feminist Research*.

Woodward, J. (1968), 'We're All Bourgeois Now', *New Society*, 25 July, vol. 12, pp. 132-3.

Worsley, P.M. (ed.) (1970), *Modern Sociology: Introductory Readings*, Harmondsworth, Penguin.

Wrong, D. (1961), 'The Over-Socialised Conception of Man in Western Sociology', *American Sociological Review*, vol. 26, pp. 183-93.

Young, A. (1976), 'Some Implications of Medical Beliefs and Practices for Anthropology', *American Anthropologist*, vol. 78, pp. 5-24.

Young, A. (1982), 'The Anthropologies of Illness and Sickness', *Yearbook of Anthropology*.

Young, M. and Willmott, P. (1957), *Family and Kinship in East London*, London, Routledge & Kegan Paul.

Zimmerman, D. and Wieder, D. (1977), 'Diary – Interview Method', *Urban Life*, vol. 5, no. 4, January, pp. 479-98.

Index